STILL HUNTING

a memoir

MARTIN HUNTER

ECW PRESS

Published by ECW Press
2120 Queen Street East, Suite 200, Toronto, Ontario, Canada M4E 1E2
416-694-3348 / info@ecwpress.com

LIBRARY AND ARCHIVES CANADA CATALOGUING IN PUBLICATION

Hunter, Martin, 1933–
Still hunting / Martin Hunter.

ISBN 978-1-77041-126-5
ALSO ISSUED AS: 978-1-77090-402-6 (PDF); 978-1-77090-403-3 (EPUB)

1. Hunter, Martin, 1933–. 2. Dramatists, Canadian (English)—
20th century—Biography. 3. Toronto (Ont.)—Biography. I. Title.

PS8565.U58Z477 2013   c812'.54   C2012-907511-6

Editor for the press: Michael Holmes
Text design: Stan Bevington
Cover image: Richard Williams
Printing: Coach House Printing   5   4   3   2   1

The publication of Still Hunting has been generously supported by the Canada Council
for the Arts which last year invested $20.1 million in writing and publishing throughout
Canada, and by the Ontario Arts Council, an agency of the Government of Ontario. We
also acknowledge the financial support of the Government of Canada through the Canada
Book Fund for our publishing activities, and the contribution of the Government of
Ontario through the Ontario Book Publishing Tax Credit. The marketing of this book was
made possible with the support of the Ontario Media Development Corporation.

PRINTED AND BOUND IN CANADA

CONTENTS

This memoir is dedicated to all the actors, child, student, amateur, and professional with whom it has been my privilege and pleasure to work in the past seventy years. To all of you, as the French say, *merde.*

Once again I claim the licence of a storyteller who has told most of these tales many times. This is the way I remember it.

ACKNOWLEDGEMENTS

The cover drawing was done many years ago by my lifelong friend Richard Williams. It is the way I looked during the period covered by this book.

I am grateful for the advice and encouragement of several early readers of parts of this manuscript: Jim Bartley, Stan Bevington, Ramsay Derry, Susan Walker, and especially my editor Michael Holmes.

Pictures of many of the stage productions mentioned in this memoir can be viewed at martinhunter.org.

Nel mezzo del cammin di nostra vita mi ritrovai per una selva oscura che la diritta via era smarrita.

— Dante, *Inferno*

DANCING IN THE DARK

It was our first trip anywhere since we were married. I thought of London and Paris but Judy said she wanted sun, the hotter the better. She asked a friend who had grown up in Trinidad where we should go and her friend, who considered herself something of an authority on exotic holiday destinations, suggested a small island we had never heard of, an island visited by a few discerning travellers for its coral reefs, deserted palm-fringed beaches, and the opportunity to eat fresh mangoes and papaya, which in those days were not available in North American supermarkets. It sounded perfect. Judy called a tourist agent to book a flight and make a hotel reservation. With her friend's only-too-willing participation, she chose two bright new bathing suits and a backless dancing dress, and we took off.

We changed planes in Barbados, then landed at an airport so tiny, we didn't see it till we were on the ground. A gangling black man who seemed to know our names and destination scooped up our bags and sauntered towards a dilapidated taxi. We got in and he tied the door to the frame with a piece of rope. He drove along the bumpy road at a dizzying speed, steering with one elbow and honking at every curve.

On our right was the sea, great waves rolling up across the white sand. Palm trees towered above, just as Judy's friend had promised. The scarlet disc of the sun went down behind them at an alarming rate. In mere minutes, the sky changed from blood to ink. It was completely dark by the time we reached the hotel. A small parade of grinning black boys took our bags and led us to a grass-thatched hut on the beach. We fell on the bed and lay together holding hands, breathing in the moist tropical air and listening to the churring of tree frogs.

Four months earlier, Judy had produced our third child in three and a half years. Our domestic life was dominated by feeding times, diapers, and visits to the pediatrician, who scolded me for not helping my wife. "Listen," I said, "I do everything for those kids except suckle them at my own breast."

I was working as a junior in my father's office. I was only home eight or nine hours out of the twenty-four. My weight dipped below one hundred and fifty for the first time since I was fifteen. Judy was so thin she had to give up nursing young Guy. Her doctor told her she should either spend a month in a convalescent hospital or run away to a desert island. I had a large overdraft, and the idea of leaving the chondroplastic dwarf who currently served as our mother's helper in charge of the kids was unthinkable. (She had been hired by my father-in-law to help out over Christmas, the only caregiver the agency had available. They told us we were lucky to get her.) Suddenly a friend's miscarriage freed up a Scottish housekeeper, who agreed to come to us for three weeks. My father had made a bundle on a mining stock and gave us a thousand dollars. This combination of circumstances obviously meant we were intended to have a holiday. And here we were.

We showered and changed. Still holding hands, we walked through scented darkness towards the glimmering lights of the hotel terrace. Men in white jackets and women in floating, flowery prints clustered around the bar, sipping drinks and exchanging rippling laughs provoked by what I imagined to be witty repartee. I expected Noel Coward to put in an appearance at any moment.

A languid, deeply tanned man with thinning blond hair greeted us without taking his hands from the keys of a white piano on which he was tinkling "I've Got You Under My Skin." He smiled confidently and drawled, "Hi, I'm Andy Graham. Glad you could join us. You're going to have a great time here. You're going to learn how to spree."

"Spree?"

"Native lingo for partying."

He nodded and a huge black man in a brilliant red jacket ambled towards us with two pinkish-coloured drinks in tall, sweating glasses. "Welcome, sir, I be call Steadroy. I gonna look after you." His smile stretched beyond the bounds of probability. "How you are this evenin', sir?"

"Fine, Steadroy, how are you?"

"I be any better, sir, I think I have to go see de doctor." Steadroy retired, still grinning. It occurred to me that the repartee practiced on the island might not quite be up to Noel Coward's standards.

A short, handsome man with a splendid moustache and a cultivated British accent came over and introduced himself as Tony Smith. He informed us he was here on his honeymoon. "My third, as a matter of fact. Best so far. Brought along my mother-in-law. She and Melissa go shopping together so I can get in some tennis. Do you play?"

"My game's pretty rusty."

"Bridge?"

"Not really."

"Ah well." He shrugged his shapely eyebrows in gallant resignation. "Can I get you the other half? What about a decent drink? Whisky? They don't really know how to do martinis here."

"You know the island pretty well?"

"I know the Caribbean. My mother's husband has a place in Barbados. Unfortunately, his son wants it. Anyway, there are too many goddamned English in Barbados."

"You don't care for your countrymen?"

"I'm a New Yorker."

"I thought from your accent —"

"You think all New Yorkers talk like Harry the Horse, I suppose. I went to Groton." I was used to being put in my place by Englishmen, but upper-class American snobbery was new to me. "Frankly, this trip is an experiment. If we find enough entertaining people, we might consider buying a piece of land here. We'd have to train our own servants, but in the long run that's an advantage. Ah, here's Melissa."

Melissa had huge green eyes, heavy, serene brows and thick, dark hair in a plait that reached below her waist. It was no surprise to learn she was a model and had been photographed by Avedon. She let Tony kiss her and light her cigarette. He nibbled on her ear. She turned and blew smoke in his face.

Melissa's mother turned out to be a rather fierce Montreal matron, whom Tony addressed as "Mrs. D." She immediately began to quiz us about our acquaintance in Toronto. She was somewhat appeased to learn Judy had gone to school with the sister of her daughter's husband.

"Jenny seems to like Toronto. And I go there to visit her and a few old friends, Connie Matthews and Polly Armstrong. I sometimes feel really I've been rather unfair to the place. Then I walk along Bloor Street and I think: this just isn't a real city and that's all about it."

Tony asked us to join them and we all sat at a round table decorated with hibiscus blossoms. There was fish served with rice and fried plantain. "In Barbados they call this coolie food," said Tony.

"I prefer it now that they've sent their European chef home for the summer. All those failed French sauces were getting me down."

"What do you think, Mel? You happy with a diet of rice and peas?" Melissa had taken one bite, then lit a cigarette. After two puffs, she ground her butt into the mound of rice on her plate and let out a long sigh. A small band of shy-looking blacks dressed in country clothes had started to play island music: calypso with a slightly accentuated beat. Melissa started to move her shoulders languorously. She narrowed her eyes at Tony.

"Just let me finish my fish, do you mind?" Melissa's shoulders continued to move. Tony put his fork down and said, "Oh, very well." They stood facing each other on the dance floor, Melissa half a head taller than her husband. He closed in to take her in his arms and they began to move together smoothly, economically, but with no hint of passionate commitment.

"They are pretty, aren't they?" said Mrs. D. "I wonder how long they've got?" She put a cigarette in a tortoise-shell holder and turned to me for a light. "I don't know why they got married. Everyone knows marriage is passé. In another five years it'll be completely gone. You'll never hear the word again."

On a sudden whim I asked her to dance. "My dear boy, aren't you gall*ant*? Well, I can't imagine when I'll have another opportunity like this."

She took up a position in my outstretched arms and followed my lead with unexpected grace, anticipating my every move intuitively, daring me to be inventive, to surprise her. What I had expected to be a perfunctory courtesy turned into a challenge. I slid into a sort of modified tango step and she quickly picked up the clues, alternating between long, gliding steps and sudden hesitations. At the end of the song, two or three people applauded. Mrs. D. smiled in acknowledgement, her lips turned down at the corners like a female Somerset Maugham.

"I think we'd better call it quits while we're ahead, don't you?"

I led her back to the table where Judy was waiting alone. "Your husband's really not bad. Most young men don't know how to dance at all."

"You inspired me. You must have been fabulous in the '30s."

"Try the '20s. I used to love it." She put another cigarette in her holder, turned to me for a light, and then exhaled slowly, as if looking back across the years through a screen of nicotine smoke. "The year I came out, I wore out six pairs of slippers before the end of the season." She gave a deprecating grimace. "Tony and Melissa seem to have vanished into the night. Do you suppose you could stand to order me a double brandy?"

I signalled to Steadroy, who stood smiling vacantly into the darkness. A skinny black kid with a shock of hair that seemed to come to a point above his face had begun to dance alone in the middle of the floor. He had a serious expression as if he were concentrating on some complex inner problem. The movements of his body were spontaneous, fluid to the point of being improbable. His articulation was like a snake's rather than a human's, not limited by joints like knees, ankles, and elbows. He established a pattern of sliding sidesteps, then varied the pace, slowing down, speeding up, his extended arms making circles in the air. I thought I'd never seen anyone dance like this. It owed nothing to Astaire or Bolger; the kid was an original. He danced for maybe ten minutes. There was applause from the audience, most of whom had obviously seen him do this before. He bobbed his head at them and disappeared into the kitchen.

I signalled and finally managed to catch Steadroy's attention. He ambled over to the table. "Who's that?"

"That Sylvester."

"He's pretty good."

"Yes, sir. We call that Sylvester our dancin' fool."

"Where does he come from?"

"Him work in de kitchen. I get you somethin', sir?" I ordered three brandies and he went off smiling. The band had started to play "Yellow Bird." I asked Judy to dance.

We stepped self-consciously across the floor, realizing we hadn't danced together for nearly two years. That wasn't what our relationship was about, though I remembered I had been Judy's date at her first formal (mine too). I had worn my father's tails and bought her a gardenia corsage. There were sherry parties and dinner parties beforehand and coffee parties afterwards and I didn't remember much about the dancing part of the evening, except for some Scottish novelty called the Gay Gordons, which Judy knew how to do and I didn't.

Before that I had once or twice gone to tea dances at high school and got up the nerve to ask some girl to let me steer her in a one-way circle, my left hand spread out against the base of her spine, our other hands clammily clasped while a scratchy rendition of "Perfidia" or "A String of Pearls" filled the stale air of the gym. To cover the fact I didn't really know how to do the foxtrot or whatever it was we were supposed to be performing, I desperately made conversation. I was always relieved when the music finished, and I was sure the girl was too.

Later on when I was at university, the Charleston experienced a brief revival and I teamed up with an actress friend to do a series of frantic antics that usually cleared the floor and garnered a round of applause. We added a showy tango routine to our repertoire and gained a reputation as party animals. This nourished my ego at the time. Now, as I scrupulously propelled Judy through a limited series of patterns that seemed to have little to do with the light, easy beat of the band, I felt disjointed, awkward, cut off from the brief virtuoso moment I'd shared with Mrs. D. or the easy exuberance of Sylvester dancing solo. Judy smiled at me when the number finished. I'd fulfilled my social obligation and she seemed satisfied. "Darling, I'm tired. Why don't we finish our brandy and go to bed?" We did.

In the next few days we established a routine. I got up early and swam, then walked along the empty beach watching fishermen come out of the sea with their wriggling pink and silver catches loaded in baskets on their heads. We had breakfast on the terrace where birds landed on our table to peck at the sugar bowl. Judy tried to get the waiters to identify them, but they were not ornithologists. "We call he yellow bird," Steadroy volunteered, smiling broadly as ever.

We ate mango and papaya and pineapple, so sweet and juicy it was unrecognizable as the same sour, woody fruit my mother used to dice up for dessert in the middle of Toronto winters. We lingered over coffee. Then I went to the beach with my writing pad and pencil. I had a play in my head that I'd wanted to write for the past two years. I set myself an agenda of one act each week. I worked till lunchtime, spent an hour in the water, and revised the morning's work till the sun hung low over the sea. Judy and I walked together along the beach and watched the fast-paced splendour of the sunset, then went back to our hut for a snuggle before dinner. For the first time since we were married we had time just to lie in bed together. The warm, humid air, the salt still caked on my skin, the sweet, lingering taste of rum punch in my mouth, the memory of the almost-naked bodies on the beach, the sinuous Melissa, and the lean black boys combined in a sensual blur that stimulated my erotic imagination. Judy became more relaxed, more receptive, as we got physically reacquainted.

Then we dressed up for dinner. We ate under the stars, sometimes just the two of us, sometimes sharing a table with Mrs. D. Tony and Melissa had hopped over to Barbados but she stayed on, hoping to avoid the heel of the Canadian winter, slushy thaws, and quick, vengeful freezes. "Mr. Eliot's right.

April is indeed the cruelest month, not because it breeds lilacs out of the dead land but because in Canada, our lilacs never get going until the middle of May at the earliest." Usually I didn't ask Judy or Mrs. D. to dance, but every night we watched Sylvester perform.

One night after we'd retired to our hut, I went back to the terrace alone to look for Judy's purse, which she thought she'd left at our table. She said nobody would want to steal it; there wasn't any money in it, just her lipstick and a handkerchief. Two people were still sitting at the bar. Behind it Steadroy was polishing glasses and talking to Sylvester, who was still wearing his high white chef's hat. I asked if they'd seen Judy's purse. Steadroy said yes, he'd put it inside the office; Sylvester would go and get it. Steadroy poured me a brandy and sighed. "I real tired now. I ready go home to my Granny."

"You live with your Granny?"

"Yes, sir. Her carin' me real good. Her all I got now. My daddy gone to New York. Some day soon him gonna send for me. Then I gonna work at de Waldorf-Astoria." He grinned broadly. I grinned back, not sure if this was supposed to be a joke. The other drinkers headed off to bed. Steadroy stopped polishing glasses. "You wantin' something mo', sir?"

"No, you go ahead and close up." Steadroy slowly closed the bar and disappeared into the night. I sat sipping my brandy. Sylvester came back.

"Everything all lock up, sir. You don' worry. You' missus' purse be safe."

"Sure. How'd you get started dancing, Sylvester?"

"I always done it. Used to dance with me sister market days. We get fifteen, maybe twenty, twenty-five pennies."

"People ever give you money when you dance here?"

"Sometimes. If I dance real good. Or maybe if —"

"If what?"

"Nothin'. I see you dance with that old lady. Her really like to dance."

"Maybe you should dance with her."

"I don' think so. Her too proper. She son' wife now mighta dance with me. But they's took off. Isn' nobody here now likes to dance. 'Cep' maybe you."

"Me?"

"You dance good. Only you scared."

"Why scared?"

"Maybe you worry what people gonna think of you' dancin'."

"Well — I don't like to make a fool of myself."

"You wanna dance, you jus' go dance."

"Where I come from, you're supposed to know how to dance. There are steps you have to learn —"

"You make up you' steps, man. Look, I show you." Sylvester clicked his fingers and started to move his hips, then his feet. He smiled shyly. "Hey, you wan' dance with me, man?"

"I — I don't know."

"Sure, you do. Come on. You follow me feet." I moved my feet tentatively, minimally. "No, don' look, man. Hey, you all tie up in knots." Sylvester took my hands in his and started to swing his arms lightly. "Close you' eyes and let me lead. You don' worry 'bout you' feet or nothin'."

I let Sylvester swing me. He made clicking noises with his tongue. He moved in close and held me and we moved together, swaying slowly. I could smell him, sweat overlaid with musky perfume. I could feel Sylvester's belly flex against my own. Then Sylvester began to move. His hips and shoulders rotated in time to a beat he established with clicks of his tongue, his fingers, the beat of his bare heels on the floor. I tried to match what he did.

"Don' copy me, man. Jus' do what you gonna do."

He backed off and I started to do some exploratory moves. Sylvester modified his clicking rhythm to follow me. He smiled a wide, encouraging smile. "That's right, man. You gettin' it."

I smiled back. "Keep goin', man, you gotta keep goin'." I did keep going. New moves began to come to me. I had no idea where from. "That's good, man. That's real good. Now don' stop. You no allow to stop."

I shut my eyes and kept moving. I had been pushing myself, but slowly I began to feel good about what I was doing. Began to enjoy the feeling that I was moving for myself, not for anybody else, just because I felt like it. I opened my eyes and saw Sylvester still smiling across at me from under his high, white hat. "Tha's great, man. You made de start. Every night now you gonna dance. Time you go home, you gonna be real good dancer." He disappeared, his smile and his hat the last things to vanish into the darkness. I turned and headed back to my straw hut where Judy lay sleeping. I snuggled up against her, but I was still thinking of Sylvester.

For the next ten days I danced every night with Judy, but now I scarcely touched her. I set my own rhythms, worked my own space. Every morning I went to the beach with my notepad and pencil and worked away on my play.

I started to hear the voices of my characters and they began to take charge of their own stories. It was as if my morning writing and my nighttime dancing paralleled each other, as though my feet had freed up my pencil, my body liberated my head.

I finished the first act and headed into the second. Judy, whose pale skin couldn't take very much sun, lingered on the terrace and gossiped with Mrs. D. They soon found they shared an interest in early child development. Mrs. D. had been involved in setting up a Montessori kindergarten in Montreal. She arranged for them to visit a local school. Judy reported at dinner, "This island is a total matriarchy. You should meet the principal of the local elementary school, sort of a cross between Pearl Bailey and Joseph Stalin. She has one man on her staff, the gym teacher. When she claps her hands he jumps. Literally."

Mrs. D. chuckled. "The women run everything here, including the church. I met a woman who told me she's a Pentecostal Baptist Bishop. She weighs over three hundred pounds, which does suggest a certain authority."

"Sounds as if that might be a good line of work for you, Mrs. D."

"If I weren't such an old crock I'd be tempted. No, it's too late for my generation, but Judy should have a crack at a career. Get your children into nursery school and go back to work instead of fiddling about on women's committees. You're adaptable. Look at how the two of you've learned to dance in the last week. Almost like a couple of natives." Her tone was sardonic but also, I realized, tinged with envy. But it was true; Judy was slowly beginning to move to the calypso rhythms. She and I began passing little improvisations back and forth, moving in sync, in sympathy.

I sometimes asked Mrs. D. to dance, but she always declined. She had hooked up with an old acquaintance, a Major Heighington. He had a finely groomed moustache and a wooden leg, so of course he didn't dance. Mrs. D. called him Zulu and encouraged him to tell stories about his time in East Africa. This was entertaining for a few evenings, but before long he began to repeat himself and I started to wish someone new would check into the hotel.

One day, Judy and I were walking along the beach before sunset and saw four people waist-deep in the water, two couples bobbing up and down, all talking simultaneously. They were not young: I remarked that they were in damn good shape for people in their fifties. That evening we saw the two women on the terrace. One wore an emerald green dress and a string of real pearls that reached almost to her waist. The other wore black lace and a diamond on her hand, if not as big as the Ritz, definitely the largest I had ever seen that was not behind glass. The one in emerald green turned her head immediately and said to Judy, "What a divine figure you have, my dear. What exercises do you do?"

"I run up and down stairs all day boiling bottles and changing diapers."

"I have a little Pucci dress I brought back from Florence last summer that would look marvellous on you. You know the one, Naomi. I bought it to wear with my sapphires but it's too purply. You must try it on, my dear. If you like it you can have it."

"I couldn't possibly —"

"Of course you could. I say you should have it and I'm used to getting my way, aren't I, Naomi? Now come and sit with us, the two of you. I'm Ruth and this is Naomi, so of course we stick together. What are your names?"

We introduced ourselves and Ruth said, "I like your names. That's a good sign. I know we're going to get on. I knew the moment I saw you walking along the beach. Ah, here's Max with the martinis." Two men in bright Madras jackets appeared. One of them carried a large silver cocktail shaker. "You can't trust anyone in the Caribbean to make a decent martini or even to have dry vermouth. So we bring our own with us."

Max called for glasses from the bar and poured us each a drink. The martinis were sharp, smooth, and icy cold. "My marinated martinis. I made them after lunch and put them in the freezer in the kitchen. Saul, what about your nuts?"

"'Nuts,' said the duchess. 'If I had them I'd be duke.'" Saul produced a pretty little painted box and passed it around. "Macadamia nuts. We used to have to fly them in from Hawaii ourselves in order to get them fresh, but now there's a little shop at Madison and Sixty-fourth that does it for us."

"We don't have them at home, but then Toronto's a bit backward."

"Ah, Toronto. I sometimes fly there and spend the whole weekend in the Chinese gallery at your museum. It's the best in North America."

"Saul collects T'ang pottery. Largest collection in New York," said Ruth.

"The best, but not necessarily the largest. I have half a dozen really first-rate pieces."

"I should hope so. He paid six thousand dollars the other day for what looks like a plain white saucer with a few cracks in it."

"Wonderful glaze. Absolutely unique. Ruth poses as a philistine but actually she owns a fabulous collection of pre-Columbian pottery."

"My pots have personality. The Incas had a sense of humour."

"Ruth can't resist a good laugh."

"Fortunately for you, Max. You think we'd still be together after forty-eight years if we couldn't laugh at each other?"

"Forty-eight years? I don't believe it."

"Fact."

"I put you guys in your mid-fifties. What's your secret?"

"We just concentrate on having a good time. Isn't that right, Max?"

Max gave a snort of acknowledgement and poured another round of martinis. Mrs. D. joined us at dinner and afterwards we played bridge. Andy Graham and his wife agreed to make up the second table. I was used to the bridge etiquette imposed by my father: intense concentration and virtual silence, except between hands. But these players talked incessantly, occasionally trumping their partners' high cards and saying, "Oh, I didn't mean to do that. I'll take that back." Judy and I didn't care about these misdemeanours, but I could tell Mrs. D. was becoming testy. In spite of her ironic view of life there were some things she felt should be taken seriously, and bridge was definitely one of them. I suspected she was about to give everybody present a piece of her mind when Max stood up. "That's it for tonight. Got to get up early and study my Greek."

"Your Greek?"

"Ruth and I are going on an Aegean cruise in another month. I've got my work cut out for me. But I'm getting there. I can sort of read Plato now. Well, goodnight all."

Next morning at breakfast Mrs. D. announced, "I'm leaving first thing tomorrow. You've been very good company, but I don't want to overstay my welcome."

"What are you talking about, Mrs. D.?"

"Time to get to work on my garden. One has to be serious about something, after all."

"We'll have a proper game of bridge tonight. Just us and Major Heighington."

"You young people shouldn't be stuck with back numbers like Zulu and me. You should be kicking up your heels. Go to that club in town Sylvester told us about."

"I don't remember."

"You weren't here. Sylvester was talking to Judy and me. Apparently he has a girlfriend. He's saving up so they can get married. He's bought her a ring and he has to make payments on it every week. This week he was a bit short, so we each gave him twenty dollars. He offered to take us to his club in town as a way of saying thank you."

"We'll all go tonight. Your last night on the island."

"I have to get up early to catch my plane. I need my beauty sleep. Take your Jewish friends. I'm sure they'll love it." So that was it. Mrs. D. was jealous of the New Yorkers; their enthusiasm, their lack of restraint rubbed her the wrong way. Of course she wouldn't admit this, let alone discuss it. She changed the subject to the outrageous cost of Canadian cigarettes and moved on to the iniquity of Canadian taxes generally. Complaining about taxes was always a safe upper-middle-class topic.

As it turned out we all went into town that night, guided by Steadroy. He had protested, saying he was a good boy and his Granny wouldn't like the idea of him going to any club, but Max appealed to his vanity, claiming we needed him to protect the ladies. Mrs. D. and the major drove with Naomi and Saul, Judy and I with Ruth and Max. The two cars whipped around curving roads through the churring country darkness and into St. John's, where a few isolated streetlights threw a starkly garish light on small, rundown houses shut up for the night. After a couple of tries we found the club down a narrow, almost unlit street.

Inside a smallish hall, decorated as if for Christmas with ropes of tinsel and twisted streamers and red, pleated tissue-paper bells, a steel band was playing. A few people sat at little tables; it was obviously too early by local standards for serious "spreeing." Our group was seated and offered some rum-based concoction. Max's attempt to order whisky for the major drew grinning apologies from the waiter.

Max offered to dance with Mrs. D. and steered her around the floor with limber grace; her eyes signalled me imploringly over his shoulder. I rescued her but this time we failed to click; she seemed somehow careful, formal, remote, following my lead but sending no impulse back. At the end of the song she smiled ruefully, "I'm afraid my dancing days are over."

"Oh, come on now —"

"At my age, one has to be sensible. It's all very well for you young things to go native, as Zulu would say."

"I'm sure he would."

"Zulu's not a complete fool, you know. You have all these liberal ideas. Well, I don't want to stick my nose in where it doesn't belong, but don't forget you have children at home. A marriage to maintain."

"You said the other day marriage was obsolete."

"For people like Melissa and Tony. You and Judy are a different breed of cat. You still have some moral background."

"We never go near a church, if that's what you mean."

"That's not my point. You're having a little holiday, a little escape. Fine. Indulge yourselves. But don't let your fantasies run away with you. I've been watching you. And Judy —"

"Judy?"

"She's given Sylvester quite a bit of money. I know she means well but a black man is apt to misinterpret her generosity."

"Sorry. I don't get you."

"You know Judy rests every afternoon while you're down on the beach. Sylvester's taken to bringing her a glass of milk in her hut. He just might try something. He'd probably think she expects it. Black men look at these things differently. Ask Zulu."

"Really, Mrs. D., I think it's you who's letting your fantasies run away with you."

"I don't want to upset you but I thought a word to the wise . . . I think perhaps I should go back now. I do have an early plane to catch. I'll get a cab. Zulu will come with me. Do ring me when you're in Montreal, won't you?"

Mrs. D. made her exit with Zulu. Ruth said when she was barely out of earshot, "Wonderful type. The aging flapper. I can just see her as she must have been in the '20s. A wild one."

"She's just read me a lecture about the dangers of going native."

"Isn't that darling? Well, I think you should go native while you can. I'm with you all the way, kid."

"Does that mean you'd like to dance?"

"Aren't you sweet? Best offer I've had this week. Max, what do you think?"

"Don't mind me."

Ruth stood up just as the steel band suddenly escalated their sound level and played a sort of triumphant crescendo. There was Sylvester in the middle of the floor, grinning confidently as his friends shouted their greetings. He strutted and pranced and leaped high in the air. Two smiling girls appeared

with a limbo pole and he bent backwards with his body parallel to the ground
while the limbo pole was gradually lowered. One of the girls was something
like seven months pregnant. She looked about fourteen. Sylvester never
deigned to look at her. He was in his element here, no longer the shy little
country boy he pretended to be when he was dancing at the hotel, but jubi-
lant, cocky, deliberately outrageous.

After the dance, Sylvester came over to our table and we introduced him
to our new friends. He accepted Max's offer of a drink and complimented
Ruth on her pearls. Judy asked him to bring his girlfriend over to the table. He
ignored this request for a few minutes, then finally agreed. The girl was introduced as Eulalee. She sat silent and serious, watching Sylvester with upturned
eyes. Judy suggested Sylvester should dance with her. Sylvester grinned.

"Her don' dance. Her shy."

"I'll bet she would if you asked her."

"Anyways, I don' usually dance with no girls. Just solo. You wait. I gonna do
a big number for you, jus' soon as I finish this drink."

Sylvester downed his rum punch in one gulp and took the floor again.
This time he worked a lot of fancy gymnastics into his act: handstands and
cartwheels and the splits. It was an impressive performance but I missed the
in-turned concentration of the dance Sylvester had done the first night at the
hotel. It had been like private poetry, not a swaggering show-off turn.

Afterwards, Sylvester joined us for more drinks. A couple of his friends
came over and the evening ended in a babble of talk blurred by booze and
the ringing echo of the steel band, which seemed prepared to play till dawn.
Judy and I were driven home and stumbled along the dark path to our grass
hut. I wanted to talk about Sylvester but Judy was already asleep, sprawled on
her back and snoring lightly.

The next morning, Judy joined me in my morning walk along the beach. I
wanted to ask her about Sylvester, whether he had ever stepped out of line, as
Mrs. D. might have put it. I couldn't seem to lead into the question as casually
as I had intended. Was it perhaps that I didn't really want to know? That I
wasn't sure of my own feelings about Sylvester?

We had breakfast as usual on the terrace. Ruth joined us; she had left Max
to get on with his Greek. They were leaving the next day and going home by
way of Bermuda. Max wanted to get a lightweight jacket and he hadn't seen
anything he liked in St. John's.

"Of course Max could get a much wider selection at home, but he loves to bring back little treasures that he can show off to his friends. This island's charming, but I'm afraid it's been a dead loss in the shopping department. There's nothing worth buying."

"I've been thinking we might take Sylvester home with us," I blurted out.

"Now that's what I call enterprising," grinned Ruth.

"I thought he could cook for us and drive maybe. Meanwhile he could go to cooking school. It was his idea."

"He's cute, but don't you think he might be rather a handful?"

"I don't think it would work," said Judy suddenly.

"Why?"

"I hate to say it, but I don't think we could trust him."

"You mean you don't think he knows his place?"

"That girl he introduced us to last night. Eulalee. She's not the same girl he had with him the other day."

"Maybe he enjoys playing the field. He's still pretty young."

"They're both pregnant. That girl last night is only thirteen years old. I asked her."

"Yes, well —"

"I can't accept that. I'm sorry. I think it's wrong."

Ruth smiled. "Don't take it to heart, kiddo. These people have their own ways of doing things. We all do, you know, whether we like to admit it or not. And who's to say what's right or not right? It depends on your perspective. Personally, I usually opine it's all good for a laugh. Saves wear and tear on the old heartstrings."

I excused myself and went to the beach. I was now well into my third act. I felt certain I'd have a completed draft by the time we went home on Friday. I was also reassured by what Judy had said. If Sylvester had tried anything on her, I was sure she would have told me. At the same time, I realized I was disappointed. There was no hope of taking Sylvester home with us. He'd have to stay here on the island and face up to his responsibilities, just as I would have to go home and shoulder mine. Put my playscript in a drawer and go back to peddling paper.

I went up to the terrace at lunch and asked for Sylvester, but it was apparently his day off. In fact, he didn't appear for the next two days. Judy retired to our hut with a headache that lasted more than twenty-four hours. I spent all day at the beach and finished my third act. I read the whole thing through and decided it wasn't too bad. It would need some polishing but maybe somehow I could find time to do that when I got home.

On my final afternoon at the beach I lay flat on my back, my eyes closed as I soaked up the sun. I was surprised by the feel of a set of toes planted on my stomach. I looked up and saw long brown legs and a skimpy yellow bathing suit topped by Sylvester's simian face. "Sylvester, where've you been?"

"I been spreein'. Now I ready go to Canada with you."

"I don't think so, Sylvester."

"Why not, boss?"

"Judy thinks you should stay here and look after your girlfriend. Or is it girlfriends? How many have you got on the string anyway?"

"You mean how many girl make the baby for me? Two, as I know of."

"You're a rascal, Sylvester."

"Me bad boy." He grinned. "You wanna be bad boy too, boss?"

"I don't think I know what you mean, Sylvester."

"Oh, you knows, man. You *knows*."

We gave each other a long look, then I closed my eyes. When I opened them, Sylvester had started away down the beach. I watched him walk away slowly. He turned once and grinned and then he was gone. I watched the sun drop rapidly towards the horizon, then disappear. The tree frogs started their nocturnal serenade.

I went up to the hut. Judy was feeling better. We dressed and went to dinner. I asked Steadroy if Sylvester was in the kitchen.

"Yessir, I believe that boy done spreein' for now."

I asked Judy to dance but she said she didn't feel like it. She was already anticipating broken sleep and morning feedings. She headed back to the hut to finish her packing. I sat on the terrace with a brandy and waited for Sylvester to come out of the kitchen. The tables were cleared and the buzz of conversation died down. From the kitchen came the clatter of plates and an occasional loud laugh as somebody made a joke in the impenetrable argot the islanders used among themselves.

Gradually the other guests turned in. Steadroy slipped me an extra drink and shut up the bar for the night. I looked out at the ocean, finally stood up, ready to head back to the hut. It was then I sensed there was someone else on the terrace. I turned back to see Sylvester dancing in his bare feet, a dance like he'd danced that first night, slow and concentrated. I watched for a few minutes, then took a step towards him. Sylvester turned and scampered into the darkness as I stood looking after him.

TALES OF THE PAPER TRADE

I haven't always believed in making decisions. Until I was in my mid-twenties, I just kind of let things happen to me. That seemed to work well enough and quite a few interesting possibilities opened up. Then I made a choice. I decided to get married and in the '50s that meant "settling down." A married man was expected to be a "good provider." I bowed to conventional expectations and went to work for my father at the Buntin Reid Paper Company, fully aware that this was not just a job but carried with it a formidable burden of expectations and responsibilities. I would be exchanging comparative freedom for security, self-expression for conformity. But also it was a chance to make some "real money" that might not come again.

For six weeks before our wedding, I went back to live with my parents after an absence of seven years. The restrictions, the need to follow a set routine seemed unbearable. I considered bolting. But this was a temporary arrangement and I could put up with anything for six weeks. Then Judy and I would have our own little nest and I told myself I would only have to conform for about fifty hours a week.

The Buntin Reid Paper Company was central to my father's life. It sometimes seemed as if it were virtually his whole life. After graduating from high school at the age of sixteen he had worked on his father's farm, ploughing, seeding, haying, threshing, milking the cows, slopping the pigs with the help of his younger brother. At night he took a team of his father's horses and worked on the roads, saving his meagre earnings. At eighteen he set out for Toronto with a hundred dollars in his pocket and began articling for a firm of chartered accountants. He got a room in a boarding house and began dressing like a city slicker, discarding his baggy britches for a pinstriped suit and his flat cloth cap for a bowler.

In his last year of articling, one of his firm's clients, Buntin Reid, offered him a job as their "financial man." He approached one of the accounting partners and asked what he should do. The partner said, "It's your decision, Ken, but of course if you take the job, you won't pass your final exams." Father took the job and did pass his final exams, becoming the youngest C.A. in the province.

The paper company had recently been bought out from the Buntin family. The new principals were T.J. Macabe and George Allen. Macabe was a horseman who hunted with Lady Eaton and sported fine hand-tailored tweed suits that bespoke his status as a country gentleman. He had married an American heiress whose father bought him the controlling interest in the paper company to provide him with a suitable income. George Allen was an irascible Irishman who knew the paper trade and had wide business contacts. They made a workable team because they stayed out of each other's way. T.J. took the upscale customers to lunch at his club; Allen traveled around the city in his shiny black sedan calling on customers and making deals with them.

Neither had anything much in common with my father but they appreciated his ability with numbers (he could add up six columns of figures simultaneously), his capacity for hard work, and his sense of discretion. George Allen ran a tight ship. A Protestant by upbringing, he hired only Scots and Irishmen; no Catholics and, for that matter, no Englishmen. Although there were women who worked in the office, they were secretaries or switchboard operators or filing clerks and were unfailingly addressed as Miss and certainly never considered for management positions. The salesmen called each other by their first names, but no one called Mr. Allen "George" or Mr. Macabe "Tom," though this privilege was accorded my father after about twenty years working for the company.

George Allen expected loyalty and blind obedience and got it. When one of the office clerks drove him downtown for lunch and said, "Nice day, sir," Allen retorted, "You're being paid to drive, not talk." Allen also expected one of his young warehousemen to drive him up to his cottage in Gravenhurst on a Saturday and hang around to take him back to Toronto the next day. The boy got no extra pay for this, merely the price of a meal and coffee, but during the Depression he didn't dare risk losing his job by refusing. Although my father's ethical sense was grounded in a greater belief in fairness than his early employers, his sense of propriety was coloured by his experience of this era; even in the '70s, none of his employees ever called him by his first name. He considered respect his due and got it.

Although my father's job was initially to keep the books, do the banking, and process the payroll, he quickly learned about the various grades of paper and mastered the complicated pricing structure. But his great talent proved to be assessing prospective new customers and deciding who was credit-worthy. In the '30s, he was approached by a penniless young Greek, Art Ginou, who wanted to start a business printing placemats and menus for the burgeoning group of Greek restaurants in Toronto. He and Father came to an agreement and Art Printing became a hugely successful operation. Father's favourable assessment of many applicants from the young Alberta farmboy Stan Bevington, who started Coach House Press, to the O'Born Brothers, who embraced the new Xerox technology and built up The Printing House into a highly profitable chain. He thus developed a greatly increased range of customers. Many years later I had lunch with Father and Roy Thomson at the National Club where Thomson, who had started as a small job printer in New Liskeard said, "I don't know why you decided to give me credit back then, Ken, but if you hadn't, I wouldn't be where I am today."

Macabe and Allen obviously appreciated Father's contribution in building the company, because they signed a document that he would have first refusal to buy up their shares if anything happened to either of them. When they died within slightly more than a year of each other, Father acted on this agreement. In spite of the protest of one of the widows, he went to the bank and borrowed the money and acquired a controlling interest in the company.

When I went to work for him, Father was firmly in control. He had a vice-president, a genial, dapper little man called Arthur Hobson, and two aggressive and ambitious lieutenants: Llew Anderson as his financial manager, and Alex Smith as his sales manager. Both men were products of the Depression. When young Alex was peddling brushes door to door, young Llew was delivering groceries; while Alex was getting books from the local library, Llew was doing correspondence courses; while Alex was spending his Saturdays being a Big Brother, Llew taught swimming at the Y. Llew had joined the army during the war and risen to the rank of major; Alex was ineligible because of poor eyesight and worked for INCO in Sudbury. The two were friendly competitors and their styles complemented each other: they were both sharp and snappy, but Llew was abrasive and confrontational where Alex was dry, ironic, and mockingly complimentary. My father held them in balance: he had a strong belief, what he would have thought of as a moral belief, in fairness. Alex and Llew each owned the same number of shares in the company and received the same salary. Yet I could not help noticing that my father's even-handedness was slightly tilted in favour of Alex. He respected Llew's industry and financial ability, but he could do that work himself, whereas Alex's easygoing facility with customers was something my father couldn't quite manage.

On joining the company I spent a few weeks in the warehouse, but as I had worked there for four summers, there wasn't much more to be learned. I proceeded to the order office, a bear pit of five of us answering phones and a clerk who continuously updated our inventory by hand. The phones rang from eight in the morning till five at night. Our customers expected same-day delivery and got it from our fleet of six trucks. Sometimes they would ask for delivery within an hour. We clerks had to know the price-book backwards, provide quick and accurate answers to queries, be cheerful and jocular or sympathetic and concerned, depending on the moods of our customers. In my six months in the order office, I learned to think fast, be decisive, tactful, and accommodating. It would prove valuable training that could be adapted to many different situations in the future.

In the '50s and '60s the printing and graphic arts industries were an important part of the business community of Toronto. When the city celebrated the centenary of its founding, there were about a dozen companies that had been in existence for a hundred years or more. Two thirds of them were related to the graphic arts and Buntin Reid was one of them. In the '50s, most of these companies were in the downtown area between King and Dundas, Sherbourne and Spadina. The only industry of comparable density was the rag trade. The two mingled at a Zuchter's, a deli on Adelaide Street, where we often had lunch surrounded by colourfully dressed Jewish women who cracked wise and bawdy over their knishes and cabbage rolls. There was much banter about boobs and big dicks. The proprietor, a Greek, assured his Jewish customers, "Mine's the same as yours, only it ain't cut." This was not the sort of repartee that was heard at the National Club, where my father customarily ate his lunch.

After my time in the order office, I was sent out to try my luck as a salesman and assigned several minor accounts. Bright-eyed and bushy-tailed, as the saying was, I would set out early in the morning with an agenda of calls. My customers included a down-at-heel stationery company, whose owner received me in his office, first taking his false teeth out of a desk drawer and putting them in his mouth, and then producing a bottle of whisky and pouring out two glasses at ten o'clock in the morning. Then there was a small job printer on Beverley Street who had a hand press in his living room that he and his wife worked with a treadle, like a sewing machine. He pedalled while his wife fed paper into the press. There was a rather grandiose Englishman who operated out of an office filled with sporting prints. He puffed on cigars and spoke of the wonderful deals he had in the works, none of which ever seemed to materialize. There was a small Italian shop on College Street that seemed to do nothing but fancy announcements of weddings, christenings, and funerals, all printed on lacy, doily-like cards that were one of our specialty items. As he worked he sang "O sole mio" and "La donna è mobile" with gusto.

I learned the fundamentals of selling: first, you must have something of quality to sell; second, you must figure out who has a use for it (you need to know something about the nature of your customer's business); third, you must connect with your customer on a personal basis. A good salesman will know intuitively whom he connects with. If, for whatever reason, the customer doesn't take to you, you will waste your time courting him. Finally, you must learn not to pester your customers; too many calls on him can be more annoying than too few. Consequently, many days I completed my calls in half a day. I would then retire to a coffee shop and work on whatever piece I was writing at the moment. I felt a twinge of guilt about this but decided to keep it to myself.

During this period, my mentor was Alex Smith. He would discuss my various successes and failures in a manner that was sometimes sympathetic, sometimes caustic. He would sometimes take me for a drink after work. We developed a number of ongoing jokes and routines, shared as between friends. Alex was fond of repeating jokes he had learned in grade school.

"What happened when the butcher backed into the meat slicer?
He got a little behind in his orders."

"Confucius say, 'Woman who fly upside down have crack-up.'"

He also enjoyed singing bits of George Formby–like ditties. One I remember was about a young man who worked in a hardware store alongside his boss's pretty daughter, which ended with the refrain:

> "'Rubber,' they said
> And rub her I did
> And I don't work there anymore."

The variations on this were virtually endless.

He had a joke about various men who were asked their trade:

"I'm a sock-tucker,
dock-trucker,
rock-picker,
muck-ducker,
crock-licker,
puck-kicker,
smock-tucker."

Until the last guy says, "I'm the real McCoy."

There were a good many other japes, most of them politically incorrect by today's standards, making fun of Englishmen, Jews, Asians, and natives. One last Smith joke:

Three men, a rabbi, a minister, and a priest, took a boatload of boys on an outing. In the middle of the lake, the boat started to sink.

"Oy vey," said the rabbi, "Vot about the boys?"

"Fuck the boys," said the minister.

"Do you think there's time?" asked the priest.

As well as his arsenal of stories, Alex generously shared with me his considerable knowledge of the paper and printing trades and a good many other things: the quality of single malt whisky and Cuban cigars, the appropriate way to behave at a business lunch and, above all, the difference between a "business friend" and a real friend.

I realized Alex was aware of my position as the potential heir to the business. He once or twice said that Father had been very good to him and he was merely repaying a debt. I thought then and still believe this was sincere. Alex was capable of being scheming and devious but he also had the deeply instilled morality of a good Presbyterian. Though born in Canada, he was a Scot through and through: canny, hard-headed, sharp-witted, and critical. His eye was on the main chance, but he could be very generous to those he liked. (And tough on those he didn't.)

After several months on the road, I asked him if I could have some larger accounts. He replied that he had asked Father to make me assistant sales manager. I now had a small office of my own, but I spent a good deal of time in Alex's office and observed as he seemingly effortlessly switched from easy-going jocularity to good-ol'-boy nostalgia to mock put-downs to suit the style of the range of customers he handled. Alex made a specialty of the tough guys in the printing business. Hugh Ashton at Ashton Potter, Jim Grand of Grand and Toy, Bill Adams at Arthurs-Jones. "If you can sell those guys, you can sell anybody. And nobody else can get to them. They're scared to even try."

This was a transitional period in the printing industry. The centuries-old method of letterpress printing was giving way to the comparatively new technology of lithography. In Toronto, the change was spearheaded by Rolph-Clark-Stone, who specialized in can labels and road maps run in large quanti-ties on enormous presses at high speeds. Although they had their own special arrangements with the paper mills, they were beginning to be challenged by other jobbing lithographers who bought large presses and competed for big jobs at competitive prices: Hugh Ashton, Lorne and Bill Sandiford, and Bud Walters. Alex was one of the first to seize on this development and aggres-sively pursue these printers. Llew collaborated by arranging favourable credit terms. (My father decreed there was to be no price-cutting, but credit con-cessions provided a formidable sales tool.) While Alex was out calling on his key customers, I was in the office as a back-up, a sort of super order clerk, and eventually as I got to know some of them, something of a confidant. Speed was of the essence in our business. Customers wanted someone they could talk to right away. They also wanted instant delivery. I had the idea of keeping one truck ready for emergency deliveries. I also initiated the idea of ordering from the United States by telephone instead of sending in our orders by mail, thus expediting specialty orders.

Alex encouraged me to chart my own territory. I soon found that I could talk easily with many of the prestige printers, most of whom had designers or commercial artists on their staff. It was easy for me to get on their wave-length and I began to develop close contacts with Rous and Mann, Brigdens, R.G. Maclean, Southam Press, and Cooper and Beatty. Rous and Mann was par-ticularly easy for me to deal with partly because Fred Mann had been an actor before going into the family business, so that provided a bond. But the art director Les Trevor had a greater influence on me. He was a bon vivant with a taste for fine art, whisky, and women. Once we went to Montreal together by train. After a few martinis he began to ogle the various women in our car and sidled over to one of them, who seemed responsive to his advances. When he rejoined me, I asked, "What do you say to them?"

"Hi, babe, you wanna fuck?"

"Don't you get your face slapped?"

"Oh, sure. But I get a lot of fucking."

He proceeded to introduce me to his favourite brothel in Montreal, where he was warmly welcomed by the madam. Les advised me to develop some key accounts in Montreal, but father said this was outside our territory and would only lead to retaliation from the Montreal merchants. The next time I was in Montreal, I discovered the madam had closed down her shop and retired.

At that time there was a revolution underway in graphic design and typography. Les put me up for membership in a newly formed association of graphic designers where I hung out with Allan Fleming, Sam Smart, Frank Newfeld, and Clair Stewart, the cutting-edge designers of the day. These men specified the paper used for the various projects they were working on, and this put me on the inside track in supplying the upscale printers they worked with. We had the largest selection of specialty papers, which gave us a decided advantage.

Buntin Reid was already the leading paper merchant of the time. The paper merchants of Toronto had begun by importing paper from Britain and then the United States back in the nineteenth century. When Canadian mills started producing paper, they naturally came to the merchants who controlled the market. By the time I entered the business the vast majority of our paper was manufactured in Canada, but we still imported some grades from Britain, the United States, and even Italy on an exclusive basis. These were highly specialized items that it was not feasible for the domestic mills to produce, but for the importer they were highly profitable. Our argument was you could get anything you might need from us, so why not come to us for all your paper, especially as there were quantity discounts. Even if they didn't give us all their business, all the major printing houses had an active account with us.

The typographers also provided me with an entrée into another arena, the publishing industry. In the '50s, Toronto was one of the major publishing centres of the English-speaking world. Many of the publishers were British-owned such as Longman's, MacMillan, Oxford, and Pitman but there were also sizable

Canadian publishers: the University of Toronto Press, Ryerson Press, Copp Clark, and McClelland & Stewart. The backbone of the industry was the publishing of authorized textbooks, which was profitable; the established companies occasionally brought out a book of Canadian fiction or poetry as a kind of sop to colonial vanity. The industry as a whole was conducted in a very gentlemanly manner and my Trinity-acquired patina of gentility served me well in this milieu. There were a limited number of large letterpress printers who specialized in book production. I had friends at two of these shops, Hunter Rose and Bryant Press. I soon became something of an expert on book papers and was able to add to my customer list T.H. Best and McCorquodale and Blades.

In the '60s, there was an explosion of new small publishers following in the path-breaking footsteps of Jack McClelland: Anansi, Coach House, Key Porter, New Press, and Stoddart. And seemingly miraculously, there sprang into being a generation of exciting new writers: Margaret Atwood, Margaret Laurence, Denis Lee, Alice Munro, and Michael Ondaatje were the most prominent, but there were many others. Around these literary newcomers and their visual counterparts among the members of Painters Eleven, a new bohemia blossomed, with such venues as the Pilot Tavern, the Bohemian Embassy, and the Purple Onion providing a hangout for poets, painters, musicians, and actors. Very quickly I found myself a frequent denizen of these watering holes and they provided a welcome change from my staid lunches at the University and National clubs, which required proper business dress of a suit and tie and a certain understated and decorous mode of behaviour. I also gave a number of parties in my house for a mixed group of printers, designers, and freelance artists and their wives. These were popular and a novelty as most business entertaining was done in restaurants or private clubs.

There were, of course, other social events. Every year the Craftsmen, an organization of printers, gave an annual dinner at which salesmen table-hopped, buying drinks and trading jokes with their best customers. Corny speeches were made and at the height of the festivities the members stood and sang to their wives, "Let Me Call You Sweetheart." Less mawkish and more fun was an annual outing where one of the paper mills entertained its customers with dinner and dancing girls. The first time I attended one of these events, an extremely attractive and almost naked dancer made a bee-line for me and sat on my knee. Rather than blushing, I gave her a big smile and said, "Hi, Mimi, how you doing?" We had dated briefly at university. My standing as a man about town rose considerably.

My father looked on all these diversions with a certain ambiguity. He believed in keeping business and family life separate. He distrusted publishers, who were notoriously slow to pay their bills, but was pleased with the volume of new business I was able to bring in. He also had a notion that most artists were irresponsible, but had to admit they were having a significant impact on the industry as the skylines of Montreal and Toronto featured logos designed by Allan Fleming; CN and Scotiabank in brilliant neon blazing against the night sky.

Father presided in his baronial office. His door was open to anyone, the smallest customer with a complaint, the humblest warehouseman asking for a favour or a small loan, the most obnoxious salesman peddling his wares. Whoever called on him could expect a hearing. He never offered his visitors a cup of coffee. No food or drink were ever consumed in the office; the lunch room was the proper place for this activity.

My father's attitude was paternalistic but not patronizing, fair and judicious, good-humoured but stern, as befitted a man of his principles. One of his precepts was that if you hired a man who was not efficient or responsible, you must get rid of him within a year or else you were stuck with him. Another was that if you handled an account and failed to show a significant increase within two years, it would be given to someone else. He was adamant against price-cutting, believing that there was no sense being in business unless you could turn a decent profit, and such was his influence in the trade, that although there was a little marginal cheating, prices were amazingly stable, even among our hungriest competitors. He was opposed to unions, but every year that the company made a profit (and it always did), every employee received a generous Christmas bonus, which was usually the equivalent of a month's salary. He was confident of his knowledge of the industry and his place in it. He was the man who worked out the extremely complex pricing schedule for the whole trade and for his skills and his ethics he was widely acknowledged as one of its leaders.

Although my own view of human nature and conduct did not exactly square with my father's (he believed he knew what was right and everyone who didn't agree with him was wrong), his moral influence remains with me and the current belief that in business anything goes, as long as you don't get caught, is as alien to me as it would have been to him.

My father's fondest wish was that my brother, Bill, should come into the company. He saw our talents, I think accurately, as complementary. Though superficially we had little in common, Bill and I had always gotten on well, united as teenagers in our battle against our parents' somewhat repressive strictures. When Bill returned from Oxford he made it clear that he was not interested in the business. He wanted to teach and I was able to help him get a position at Ryerson, where my old Trinity friend David Sutherland was the dean of residence. Bill joined a group of young academic Turks which included David Crombie, Graeme Gibson, Bob Rogers, Michael Tait, and Eric Wright, most of whom eventually became writers. We hung out together at various pubs and restaurants, notably Barberian's Steak House and George's Spaghetti House, which featured some of the best jazz musicians who came to town. My father no doubt thought my motivation was to convince Bill to join the company. In fact, I enjoyed the camaraderie of the group, most of whom have remained friends over the years.

I would have been happy to have Bill join us in the company, but it was clear to me that he was unlikely to change his mind. He quickly took to teaching, for which he had a natural talent. He also distrusted Alex and Llew, whom he saw as a pair of scheming sharpies. He was not entirely wrong. They were aggressive and ambitious and they shared each other's confidence. In the early mornings before the phones started ringing and Father made his appearance, they often put their heads together and discussed customers and strategies. I soon found myself included in some of these sessions. Although Alex and Llew were appreciative of Father's generosity, it was easy to see they were restive, impatient as Father showed no sign of letting go. When Arthur Hobson, our vice-president, retired, Father offered his shares to Llew and Alex, in equal amounts of course.

I had already obtained fifty shares in the company from Father, not as a gift, but to be financed by a bank loan, which he would guarantee. I would pay off the loan out of my salary. Now Alex persuaded him to let me have another fifty shares under the same arrangement. It was a shrewd move on Alex's part, which won my gratitude and gave me a meaningful if minor stake in the company. I had only a nine percent interest in comparison with Alex and Llew at eighteen percent each and Father at fifty-five percent, but when

I managed to pay off the bank, I would receive attractive dividends. I was also given the title of general sales manager, reporting to Alex as vice-president of sales.

I now ruled over a "bull pen" of ten salesmen. They were mostly middle-aged guys who had been recruited when they were young, attractive, and personable. They had pleasant but bland personalities, dressed well, spoke carefully. Their conversation was considerably less salty than Alex or Llew's (at least around the office) and they avoided expressing controversial opinions. They concentrated on the latest hockey or ball game, or perhaps some popular television show, but avoided politics and religion. They were more like *Death of a Salesman*'s Willy Loman than David Mamet's sharks in *Glengarry Glen Ross*. My job was to try to put some fire in their bellies, but this was difficult because over the years most of them had become somewhat stale. They received decent salaries and the prospect of a good pension that they were loathe to give up. Alex advocated putting them on commission, but Father was having none of this. We were the industry flagship; why rock the boat?

One of our salesmen was quite unlike the others. Doug Brown had graduated in classics from university before joining Buntin Reid. When I asked him why he made this choice he told me that every ambitious young man wanted to be a salesman in the '20s. I was not convinced by this answer, but I think the fact was that the job gave him a great deal of freedom. He lived on a farm near Alliston where he and his wife had some cattle and a horse; unlike the other salesmen, he didn't come into the office every day at noon but travelled rural Ontario visiting printers in small towns. Unlike the other salesmen, he was up for an intelligent discussion of any topic: philosophy, religion, politics, or international affairs and he was knowledgeable about all of them; opinionated but not didactic, humorous but not easily swayed. He understood the mentality of small-town Ontario; conservative but sharp. Although he wore a suit and tie, he looked like a farmer in his Sunday go-to-meeting clothes and his country customers welcomed him as one of their own.

Once a year I would make a week-long trip with Doug in his three-year-old Pontiac. He was a terrible driver, but in the days before super highways it didn't matter so much. He maintained a steady pace of about forty-five miles an hour, pumping the accelerator constantly so that we literally bumped along. A typical junket might take us to Kapuskasing, New Liskeard, Timmins, Kirkland Lake, Sudbury, and Sault Ste. Marie. On the long drive north, we might discuss immigration policy, Gibbon's *Decline and Fall*, the Canadian contribution to the Second World War, and the poetry of Catullus.

We made calls on the two or three printers in each town, most of whom were noticeably more eccentric than most of our Toronto customers. Many were family businesses and often the printers' wives did the bookkeeping and placed the orders. Doug treated them with rural courtesy and they usually produced homemade butter tarts or date squares and coffee. He rarely left without an order. The formal calls over, we repaired to our hotel room where Doug produced a bottle of rye and asked, "Do you play poker?"

"Not really."

"We usually have a game after supper. You don't have to join in."

"I'm game if you give me a preliminary lesson."

The next half hour was devoted to instruction in the rudiments of the game. We ate in a downtown restaurant: steak and mashed potatoes with gravy. One or two of our customers joined us and the game began.

"Anything wild?"

"Deuces and one-eyed jacks."

"Give me two."

"Okay, ante up."

"Pair of queens."

"I fold."

"I'll see you."

"Would I lie to you?'

"Two queens don't beat an inside straight."

Doug raked in the kitty and our glasses were refilled. These guys were serious drinkers but after three-martini lunches in Toronto, I figured I could hold my own. On the way back to the hotel I felt distinctly woozy and I was down twenty-seven bucks. "You could be a pretty good poker player, only you take too many chances."

The next night I was more cautious and only lost twelve dollars. Our final night in Sudbury I walked away with thirty-three.

"Holy Balda, that's some city slicker cardsharp you brung with you. You better take him back to the city before he cleans us out entirely."

On our way back south, Doug suddenly turned to me. "You in the paper business for the long haul?"

"Why do you ask?"

"Just a hunch. None of my business, really. You may not be the most aggressive salesman I ever met, but you wear well." This was a genuine compliment and I pondered it in the next few years as I began to weigh my options.

As our business expanded my father decided we needed a new, larger building. He had acquired a property on King Street West and asked various architects to draw up plans and submit tenders. He was prepared to spend a million dollars, a sizeable sum at the time. The tenders came in and all of them were considerably over a million. My father put the idea of the new building on hold. The building we were in on Peter Street was rented. One day the owner, Leon Yolles, paid a call on my father. Our lease was up in three months and he did not want to renew; he was working on a deal with the Bank of Nova Scotia who had a piece of downtown property he wanted and they were willing to let him have it if they could move their stationery department into our building. He asked to see the plans for the projected King Street building. He went over them briefly and said. "I'll build your building for a million and it will be ready April 1st." And it was.

I supervised the move, which was complicated as we used only our own trucks and meanwhile carried on doing business as usual. It involved many sixteen-hour days and we worked on weekends as well. This was popular with the men, who made a lot of overtime pay. I had wondered if they would accept my supervision, but they did. When the operation was completed, Father said, "I suppose you know everyone's singing your praises." It was his only comment but I suspect he was more pleased by this performance than anything else I did for the company.

Alex and Llew and I all had brand new offices, roomy and bright. But with typical Presbyterian frugality the office furniture from the old building had been kept. There were no Persian carpets or oil paintings, just a few silkscreen prints from Sampson-Matthews. Most of the office "girls" from the Macabe-Allen years were now retired and had been replaced by younger models. Llew kept a sharp eye on them to see that they were not engaging in any extra-curricular activity with the salesmen, but they were now addressed by their first names. Slowly we were moving into the second half of the twentieth century.

We gave a big housewarming party to show off our new quarters. It was heavily attended, in spite of the fact that we offered no booze. We had a number of customers who were teetotalers, among them the Salvation Army, a major customer. The affair was in effect a tribute to my father and a major recognition of his contribution to the industry. He thoroughly enjoyed it, but it was not in his nature to give any outward indication of his pleasure. He had achieved all his ambitions, save one. My brother, Bill, had by this time married and accepted an offer to teach at Trent University in Peterborough. He had always wanted to be a farmer and now bought a hundred acres a few miles south of the campus. It was clear to me that he was not going to reconsider his options, and I said as much to Father. He stared at me glumly and said nothing.

The business continued to grow as the economy continued to expand. Our salaries increased modestly each year and we paid off our bank loans. The book value of our stock remained stable but we realized that the market value was rapidly growing. This meant that the possibility of any one of us or even all of us buying Father out was becoming more and more remote. Father was nearing sixty-five but gave no inclination of a desire to retire. He was in good health and had few outside interests. Llew and Alex continued in their loyalty to him, but I could not be unaware that they were increasingly restless. They were approaching fifty and as long as Father remained president there was nowhere for them to go within the company. They may have had outside offers, but the fact that they each had a substantial stake of the company weighed against them making a move.

As for me, I had learned a lot in the business, but I had ambitions that lay elsewhere. And the prospect of thirty or forty more years selling paper, comfortable as it might be financially, did not exactly excite me. So the air at Buntin Reid was filled with tension as we watched each other warily and waited with diminishing patience for someone to make a move.

LITTLE BIRDS IN THEIR NESTS AGREE

I had proposed to Judy in the log cabin built by her great-uncle Charlie on the family property at Marshall's Bay. I did not get down on my knees; we were cuddling together on a very narrow daybed. However, the next day I took the traditional step of asking her father for her hand in marriage. Frank Cunningham paused for a moment. "If that's what she wants . . ." he shrugged and poured himself another shot of whisky. Then he went down to the dock, got into his boat and spent the rest of the day alone out in the middle of the lake, fishing.

Judy's mother was more positive. She collapsed on the kitchen floor in surprise and as I helped her up, she said, "I've always liked you, Martin." Jamie, Judy's brother, said, "Thank goodness. He's the only one of your suitors I could bear for you to marry." Her sister Alison gave me a kiss. Our old friend Powell Jones, who was staying at the cottage, congratulated us with a rather strained smile. I thought it was because he had hoped for Judy himself.

Plans began immediately for the wedding, which was to be small but elegant. It took place in Judy's family church, Rosedale United. I had wanted my old friend Jimmy Armour to marry us, and as the resident minister was on vacation, this was permitted. Jimmy got himself ordained just in time. Judy's sister was her bridesmaid. My brother, Bill, was my best man with Jamie and my friend Alastair Grant serving as ushers. The organ was played by our friend George Black, a sometimes suitor of Judy's. About a hundred people attended; family, our parents' closest friends, our music teachers, Mrs. Goulding, Herbert Whittaker, and a few other theatrical mentors. Many of our contemporaries were overseas.

The service was followed by a reception at St. Hilda's College. Speeches were made and the wedding cake, which Judy had made herself, was cut and distributed while Judy and I went upstairs to change from our wedding finery. We asked for a piece of wedding cake and were told it had all been demolished by the guests. We made our departure and drove to the Guild Inn, where we spent our wedding night. Frank Cunningham paid for dinner for the bridal party at the fashionable restaurant at the Benvenuto. They refused to give Jamie a drink, because he looked underage. My brother took a swipe at the waiter and they were thrown out. Meanwhile, Frank and his sister had a row because she didn't think their mother had been properly acknowledged in the speeches.

This was in some ways a harbinger of what lay ahead in terms of family life, but meanwhile Judy and I had gone to the cottage at Marshall's Bay for our honeymoon. We were greeted at the gate by the mother of the farmer whose road we drove through, a rather witchy-looking woman who offered us two pint baskets of her strawberries. "May your future be as rosy as these berries," she said with quite uncharacteristic sentimentality. I can't recall that she ever again made such a flowery speech to us or anyone else.

Marshall's Bay was a community of about twenty cottages that had been built mostly by families with some connection to the local town of Arnprior, around the beginning of the twentieth century. Most of the cottages were still owned by the descendants of the people who had built them. Everyone knew everyone else but there was not a lot of partying. Strung out along the Ontario shore of the Ottawa River at a place where it was about three miles wide, the cottages were surrounded by woodland featuring tall pines and white birches. Judy's great-uncle, a naturalist, had the site declared a game preserve with the name No-piming, part of an Ojibway saying "Ja-wen-imid no-piming endad," which translates roughly as "the dweller in the woods is always happy."

At the cottage we had nothing to do but eat, swim, paddle in a canoe (Judy was a considerably more accomplished paddler than I), and make love. The weather was fine for the most part and the insects not too numerous. The other cottagers tactfully stayed away from us, apart from the Cranston twins, Guy and Goldie (towheaded ten-year-olds so identical that only their mother could tell them apart) who came to fish off our dock every morning.

At the end of our ten-day stay, the neighbouring cottagers gave us a bonfire. They were friendly and jokey and sang several old chestnuts, including, "Can She Bake a Cherry Pie, Billy Boy?" It was my first acquaintance with people I would get to know well over the years. Marshall's Bay would be an important element in our ongoing life. Judy had spent summers there since she was born, and for the next fifty years we would spend time there every year. Although I am essentially a city boy, I came to understand the importance of spending some time away from the hustle, the noise, and the tensions of the workaday world in a space where one could walk in the woods, read, and dream.

Apart from my two-week vacations, I usually drove the two hundred and fifty miles to the cottage every weekend with Frank, my father-in-law. He drove at high speeds but with great accuracy. He was highly critical of my efforts, but he taught me to be a skilled highway driver and we had many lively discussions about politics and art on the way. I learned to challenge his more outrageous pronouncements, which amused rather than annoyed him.

At the bay in the morning, there would be chores supervised by Frank: chopping and piling wood, spraying the poison ivy, and thinning the brush. This would be followed by a swim and a Pimm's before lunch. In the afternoon, we might canoe down the Mississippi or waterski, with Frank manning the outboard motor full speed ahead. After dinner, we all washed dishes and sang: "How could you believe me when I said I loved you, when you know I've been a liar all my life," or "My girl's a corker, she's a New Yorker. That's where all my money goes, keeping her in style." We also sang "Anything you can do, I can do better," intermingled with some hit tunes from the '30s: "Begin the Beguine," "Night and Day," "There's a Small Hotel," "Somebody Loves Me," and "You Are My Lucky Star." Frank supervised and sang along with us in a high scratchy voice. He loved music but couldn't carry a tune, as he himself said, "if you put it in a box."

Frank was stylish and witty, a bon vivant who clued me into the idea that it was important to have a good time, an attitude not shared by my father. Frank was never sentimental and rarely complimentary, and yet I came to understand that I was in some sense the sort of son that he had not found in Jamie. I think more or less unconsciously he became a role model for me, not only aping his sense of fun but also occasionally his vicious outbursts of temper. He encouraged me to spar with him verbally and taught me a good deal about Scotch whisky.

We settled into a duplex after our honeymoon. Judy went back to teaching kindergarten. We gave small dinner parties, often bringing together unlikely groups of people. On one occasion, Jamie commented after our other guests had left, "They look sensitive, but their conversation isn't up to the mark." He was nothing if not critical in those days, a legacy from his father, although he fancied himself much more liberal and open-minded.

Many Saturday evenings, Frank and Jean would ask us to go with them to the supper dance at the King Edward with their close friends Sheila and Jack Amys. Both Frank and Jack were tall and elegant; their wives were small and smart and pretty. All four of them were accomplished dancers. We ate oysters and drank champagne and revelled in our sophistication. My parents entertained us at the National Club; the food was excellent but the atmosphere much more subdued. Although we called Judy's parents Frank and Jean, my parents expected to be called Mr. and Mrs. Hunter.

On several occasions, we had both sets of parents for dinner. They were polite to each other, but it was obvious they did not have a great deal in common, although my mother rather enjoyed Frank's extravagant pronouncements and Jean appreciated my father's commonsensical practicality. In order to avoid a long, boring evening we set up a bridge table immediately after dinner. Both of our fathers were skilled players and their wives had learned how to play up to the strengths of their partners. We were relieved when they went home promptly at nine-thirty.

Shortly before we were married, we discovered that Judy's maternal grandmother and my paternal grandmother had been best friends as young girls and even sat in the same double desk in grade school. My grandmother was dead, but Judy's grandmother was still alive and in her eyes I could do no wrong. In fact, I was readily accepted by Judy's whole family and I hoped the same would apply in my family, but it was not to be. My mother tried to be nice to Judy, but in fact took an instant dislike to her. It was partly a clash of personalities, but mainly that my mother did not want to see me in the clutches of another female. Had Judy been more inclined to be submissive and self-effacing, mother might have accepted her more readily, but this was not Judy's style and a certain degree of antagonism would continue to characterize their relationship over the years.

I realized that Mother loved me in her own possessive way, but I did not want to be the object of her ongoing criticism and endless put-downs, even if I knew this was just a mask to cover her real feelings. Judy, on the other hand, loved me for what I was and I found this reassuring. Not that she was utterly uncritical of me, but her essentially positive support allowed me to feel better about myself and this gave a great boost to my self-confidence. Judy was accepted by my friends and I by hers. Not only did we enjoy each other's company, we had a good sex life, and we had common interests and pleasures: music and theatre, good food, the society of the interesting people we knew and continued to meet.

Yes, we scrapped a certain amount; this was inevitable given the conduct we had observed in our parents. Much as we might consciously try to avoid their example, unconsciously we picked up on the ingrained pattern of barbed skirmishes and surprise tactics we had learned as children. On the surface, our personalities were complementary and easygoing; underneath, our jagged psyches fitted together to produce a fair amount of ongoing conflict. My mother was ever ready to exploit these differences when they surfaced. Sharp and observant, she lost no opportunity to put the pin in. I remember her saying, "After watching you and Judy, I don't suppose Bill will ever want to get married."

We had never had much conversation about children, but we were agreed that we wanted to have a family. When Judy became pregnant about eleven months after our wedding she finished her term of teaching, in spite of severe morning sickness, which often seemed to extend into the afternoon and evening. She took a leave of absence and in January of 1960, Sarah was born. She was a healthy baby, nursed happily at her mother's breast, and usually slept through the night. Judy stayed home and was greatly helped by her mother who gave her practical advice, shopped, and drove her to doctors' appointments. We both learned to burp the baby, warm bottles, and change her diapers.

Six months later, Judy discovered she was pregnant again. We decided we would need more space and bought a house, using as down payment five thousand dollars my father had given us as a wedding present and Judy's salary from her last year of teaching, which I had persuaded her to save and bank. We settled into a pleasant little house in Bennington Heights, north of Rosedale. In August 1961, Ben was born, and fourteen months later Guy arrived. Unlike their sister, the boys were not easy or amenable. They were cranky and demanding and it required all the time and energy both of us could give them.

The folly of having three children in three years was denounced by our families. Certainly it made for sleepless nights and long, trying days. I don't know how we coped, but we didn't have time to think about it. Certainly the help Jean gave Judy was invaluable. It was grim when all three were in diapers, but a few years later they were all good friends and did everything together. We hadn't planned it; like so many things in our lives, it just happened.

We did have occasional help from Miss Blackley, a diminutive sharp-eyed nurse. A sort of Scottish Mary Poppins, she rose at six to bake brown bread flavoured with molasses and oatmeal porridge, which she insisted on spooning down "the little red lane" before the first sip of juice or coffee. She sang Scottish songs in a quavery baritone and even once gave us a demonstration of the highland fling that nearly landed her on her backside. Then there was a plump, squidgy woman who must have had a name, but insisted she be called Nursie; she never learned the children's names, but called all of them Baby. The second time she came to us she had no recollection of her earlier visit; she lived completely in the present moment. Strangest of all was Miss Roe, a tiny creature with no neck and webbed fingers, who broke so many glasses that on her day off she went to the Five and Dime and bought us some replacements. It was winter and she slipped on the ice coming home so that she arrived at our doorstep with a parcel of shattered glass fragments. Miss Roe needed extra time off because she was taking hormone treatments so she would be able to menstruate. The reason she wanted to achieve this was unclear, unless she was hoping to find another chondroplastic dwarf to marry.

There were the usual childhood crises to contend with. All the kids fell down stairs or toppled off swings. Sarah cut her head open when she inadvertently crashed into a glass door. She was rushed to hospital, where they shaved one side of her head before giving her stitches. As Ben had already cut off most of her hair to make her look like a boy, this didn't upset her unduly. Ben was also rushed to hospital after he was thought to have swallowed a whole bottle of aspirin. He was stoic when they pumped his stomach but refused to take off his red baseball cap. Afterwards all he said was, "That nurse lady wanted my hat."

Guy presented a more serious problem: he had chronic asthma. After his tenth trip to Sick Kids to get supplementary oxygen, the doctors suggested he spend some time at the MacMillan Centre at Sunnybrook. He spent six months there, coming home on weekends. The staff devised a routine of exercise and treatment, so that he was able to lead a normal life when he was discharged and even play high school football. I was keen that these various incidents be treated as part of normal life; as a child, my mother had tried to turn me into a little invalid and I didn't want our kids to be subjected to similar histrionics and scenes of hysteria.

Heathbridge Park was a very pleasant little community, isolated from traffic. A nearby playground had swings and slides for the kids to play on. We quickly made friends of our next-door neighbours, Hugh and Bernice

Smythe. He was the son of Conn Smythe, the sporting owner of the Maple Leafs and a string of racehorses. Hugh was a specialist in the field of arthritis; Bernice was an artist, whose special interest was photography. They had three children close in age to our three, and all the kids were in and out of both houses. Bernice was an active volunteer at the Art Gallery of Ontario and she and Judy attended cooking lessons there under the guidance of an accomplished French chef, Dionne Lucas, which led to a friendly rivalry as each tried to outdo the other in a series of gourmet dinner parties.

Across the street were Betty and Sanford Jackson, a middle-aged couple both of whom were paraplegics. They were fond of gossip and equally fond of the bottle. They gave frequent cocktail parties at which we met most of our other neighbours and learned about their various foibles and eccentricities. To Betty's disappointment, these were mostly mild peculiarities rather than flagrant misdeeds or outrageous scandals. This was, after all, suburbia in the '50s.

The least sociable were the neighbours who lived on the other side of us, a middle-aged couple with no children but a small yappy dog. Eldred, the wife, explained over the back fence, "We bought it for Mother and then she up and died." We were delighted to discover that her husband called her "Eldorado"; she invariably referred to her husband as "Himself." Rather to our surprise, they invited us one night after dinner to see slides of their recent trip to Europe. Each slide was similar and was accompanied by the explanation, "This is Eldorado in front of . . ."

"Notre Dame," I ventured.

"That's right. And here's Eldorado in front of . . ."

"The Colosseum."

And so on. At the end of the evening, Himself said to me, "Say, this is great. You really know your stuff. I wonder if you could come over Saturday afternoon and help me label these things."

Some months later, I got a late-evening call from Eldred. "I hate to bother you, but I wonder if you could come over. He's in a bad way." I discovered her husband lying in the front hall suffering from severe back pain that had completely immobilized him. I don't know why Eldred thought I could help, unless she felt my knowledge of the sights of Europe meant I could solve any problem. Then I realized why she called. There was a chiropractor in attendance who, was trying to get Himself to turn over; as he weighed well over two hundred and fifty pounds, he needed my assistance. Afraid that turning him over might only do more damage, I insisted we call Hugh Smythe, who soon arrived on the scene. He took one look at the chiropractor and said, "If I'm staying, you're going." Such was the prestige of medical doctors at the time that the chiropractor simply turned around and vanished into the night. Hugh examined the patient, sent for an ambulance, and a few weeks later, Himself was back at work.

One evening, Alison, Judy's sister, arrived for dinner and announced she was sailing for England in a few days. She would join her brother Jamie and perhaps try her success in the theatre. She then revealed that she was pregnant. David, the father of her child, wanted to marry her, but she was not ready to settle for bourgeois domesticity. She would give up her child for adoption in England and try to make her way there. We were both shocked by her ruthless determination but also admiring of her bravery. We wouldn't see her again for nearly five years, when she returned to Canada having married David, who pursued her to England. Before long they produced a son, Ben, but they had no idea of the whereabouts of their first child.

As soon as Sarah was three, she started at the nursery school of the Institute of Child Study. This was the creation of the notorious Dr. Blatz, who still presided over the school on a daily basis, although by then he had become something of a celebrity on television. When I was young, I remember hearing that Dr. Blatz was crazy; he believed children should be allowed to do whatever they wanted. You had only to look at his own sons to see the disastrous results of his theories. In fact, he had no sons, but only a daughter who taught at the school. Jean Cunningham had worked as a graduate student with Blatz at the Institute before she was married. Her three children had gone to his nursery school, and as Blatz and his acolytes were embarked on a longitudinal study of certain tendencies in families, they readily accepted our children.

We went to evening lectures given by D. Blatz. The theories he propounded to us about childrearing were some of the most commonsensical I had ever heard. He believed in established routines and consequences when children disobeyed clearly defined rules but forbade physical punishment. In his view, discipline should be "immediate, appropriate, and inevitable." He thought that parents should encourage children to follow their natural bent and interests. In his eyes, one of the most important attributes for a parent was consistency. I told him that I found this was impossible and he replied, "Then perhaps you can be consistently inconsistent."

At the school, Blatz was surrounded by a bevy of adoring females, most of them middle-aged. Some were married; many were not. This made no difference to their devotion to the man and his ideas. This loyalty to a system whose values they all shared gave the Institute an ambience of good-humoured cohesiveness. There seemed to be no competition among the various teachers, who approached each child as an individual.

As the children began at the age of three there were many problems to be dealt with: temper tantrums, pants-wetting "accidents," finicky food preferences. The children went to school from nine to three. They were fed a hot lunch every day, after which they had a nap. They had the same peers every year, and consequently they got to know each other very well. The teachers assessed not only their intellectual progress but also their social development. Troublemakers were isolated until they were ready to play in a cooperative way, sharing their toys with others. All our children had hearty appetites; they were placed next to children who wouldn't eat, in hopes that they would set a good example. Years later, they would still remember some of the dishes: shepherd's pie and floating island.

Above all, the children were encouraged to be individuals. This was inculcated from the very beginning by Margaret Fletcher. She seemed to be able to accept everyone, child or adult, for what they were and make then feel good about themselves. Her kindergarten had small chairs and tables, small scissors and blocks, even small toilets, which encouraged the sense that small people were important. They were in a world that was configured for them, not little people trying to cope with a big, adult world.

There were play centres of various kinds indoors, but also regular time spent outdoors involving both free play and organized games. Our boys were keen on hockey, which they played at school and at home in our backyard. Sarah often joined them at home and campaigned to be allowed to play hockey at school. Typically the teachers soon approved the idea and before long other girls joined in. However, when asked about their memories of the school our kids mention not hockey games but kissing tag. Obviously Blatz's concentration on social development was fostering some rather more intimate encounters than he had envisaged. Or maybe not; Blatz was a highly sophisticated and savvy character.

The Institute had two particularly gifted teachers: Dotty Medhurst, who taught art, recognized very early on that Sarah had a strong visual bent and encouraged her to experiment with various media from paint to clay to *papier mâché;* and Margaret Galloway, who taught music, using a variety of simple pentatonic instruments she invented that the children could play. She also devised a game, a bit like musical chairs, which involved her beating out ever more elaborate rhythms which the kids had to replicate, dropping out when they couldn't master it until only one was left. Ben took a particular interest in this game and was almost always the winner. Today, Sarah is a visual artist and Ben is a musician.

Sarah remembers with particular fondness the many field trips that the Institute organized. Dotty Medhurst went on most of them. She was a highly knowledgeable field naturalist, a hiker and skier who seemed to know the name of every plant she encountered. These trips were organized by the various teachers, often around their particular interests. Parents were encouraged to be part of this experience. I went on a winter trip, which involved snowshoeing. The other parent was a woman named Joyce, who turned out to be a psychiatrist specializing in scream therapy. After supper she led us all in a session of screaming, which turned out to be very popular with the kids. The problem was getting them calmed down when the therapy was supposed to be over. The two teachers had disappeared and it was up to Joyce and me to restore order. I improvised a story about some children who were befriended by a friendly walrus and rode on his back until they came to the land of the Terrible Tickler, who tickled children to death. In the end they were saved by a good witch, named Crony Baloney. Eventually most of the kids stopped screaming and went to sleep.

"What happened to the teachers?"

"They're having a fling. The kids all know."

"Really?'

"Absolutely. We might as well follow their example."

I had already realized that children are very much themselves right from the beginning. A parent is foolish to think he can turn them into something other than who they are. Having experienced my father's efforts to remake me in the image of what he wished I were, I determined not to follow in his path. Thus Sarah was a sensitive, determined, and somewhat solitary child, satisfied with one or two friends; Ben was outgoing and gregarious to the point where I would sometimes take him with me to adult parties, where he would enjoy charming the entire company. Guy was curious and open to experience, but cooler and more rational than his brother. They all shared a keen sense of humour, which Ben would later characterize as "terminal silliness." Even today whenever the three get together, the air rings with peals of laughter.

The emphasis on individual development promoted by Blatz and the Institute consolidated my views to the point where sometimes even Judy protested, as when I argued that Ben should be allowed to go to Sunday school dressed as Superman if he wanted. Needless to say, he was a big success with his peers, and we were not thrown out of the church, but only eyed suspiciously.

From the beginning, I drove children to the Institute every morning; mothers who could drive picked them up in the afternoon and returned them to their homes. Perhaps partly because Blatz had married Ann Harris of the meat-packing and banking family, his school attracted the attention of a number of prominent Torontonians: the Burtons, the Jackmans, the Laidlaws, and the McCutcheons, among others. Some of their kids were among my passengers. One of the brightest was young Stephen Sutherland, aged four, who at the end of our journey the first morning I drove him said, "I know a better way, Mr. Hunter." "Fine, Stephen," I replied. "Tomorrow we'll take your route." And in fact it was a better route. There were some very bright kids at the Institute.

The fees for the Institute were low; several hundred dollars per child per year. This was because it was heavily subsidized by the university. About every three years we parents would be summoned to a meeting and some senior official from Simcoe Hall would announce that they were planning to close the Institute. After politely listening, the scions of the wealthy families, many of whom were on the university senate and were major donors would reply, "We don't think so," and the subject would be dropped for the next several years.

Once all our children were at the Institute, Judy began working there as a supply teacher. My parents disapproved of this, but I encouraged her. Before long she would go back to full-time teaching. I had watched my mother's boredom once my brother and I were at school all day, and I thought it would be better for all of us if Judy could return to her career, especially as she loved her work and was recognized as being very good at it.

My father told us she was making a big mistake. "You have three lovely children and you're ruining them," he said to me on one occasion. Frank was also critical of our parenting. Eventually I had to tell both of them that if they wanted to keep seeing their grandchildren, they had better stop giving us unwanted advice and interference. This was reasonably effective. In fact, both sets of parents competed to give the children elaborate presents. Our living room on Christmas Eve rivalled Eaton's Toyland. If anyone could be accused of spoiling our kids, it was their grandparents.

Although we had full schedules we still found time to play, mainly with the kids. Our closest friends were John and Judy Saxton. John was a master at Ridley College and we often spent part of the Christmas holidays with them in St. Catharine's. The Ridley residences were empty, so the kids could run through the halls playing tag and hide and seek. The swimming pool was available for a primitive form of water polo. We would spend New Year's Eve at the Oban Inn, which had been bought and refurbished by Edna Burroughs, Jackie's mother, who sat at the piano with her friend Judy Finch and led the assembled company in singing songs, many of them bawdy music hall songs like "Knees Up, Mother Brown" or "My Old Man Said Follow the Van." A particular favourite was a Second World War ditty sung to the tune of "Colonel Bogey":

"Hitler, he only had one ball.
Goering had two, but they were small
Himmler had something sim'lar
But poor old Goebbels had no balls at all."

In later years it would sometimes prove useful when we were asked to New Year's Eve parties we didn't want to attend. "We always spend New Year's Eve with the Saxtons," when in fact the tradition had lapsed long since. In the summers, Judy Saxton and her son Christopher would join my Judy at Marshall's Bay, sometimes with Martha Southgate and her children Barnaby and Rebecca. Much of their time was spent cooking and doing laundry, which involved taking over a laundromat in Arnprior for a whole afternoon twice a week.

The women were much aided by Granny Mac, Jean's mother who spent most of the summer at the cottage. Although in her eighties and suffering from arthritis, she was constantly busy, a reminder of the hard life of farm women in an earlier day. She baked pies, chopped kindling, picked wild raspberries, and gathered pinecones to burn in the wood stove and the fireplace. She had been widowed at an early age and taught school all her working life. She was informed about politics and Canadian history, quoted Shakespeare, Tennyson, and Swinburne and could name all the wildflowers in woods and fields, the capital of every country on the map and almost all the stars in the sky. Three months before Guy was born, she broke her usual reticence and presented Judy with a bonnet she had knitted "for the little one who's coming." Judy was surprised she hadn't waited till the baby was born. "I won't be here, dear," she replied. A month later, she died of a stroke at the age of eighty-seven.

As the boys got older, they joined in all-day games with the kids from other Bay families: Tony and Max Christie, Tim and Chris August, and Stephen Mulkins. Some days they ranged through the woods pretending to be Indians; other days they played a war game using improvised rifles that were rigged to fire elastics. In their canoes, they fought naval battles. Some of the older boys, led by Bobby Morgan and Mark Christie, organized a "snipe hunt," the object of which was to try to sight this mysterious (and mythical) bird in the forest at night. The kids set out without flashlights so as not to scare their prey and were properly terrified by the weird noises produced by Bobby and Mark. They returned home to be comforted by hot chocolate and toasted marshmallows. Sarah had fewer playmates but bonded with the Finnie girls Susan and Diane, who, being somewhat older, drove her into town to savour the more grown-up pleasures of shopping for cosmetics and eating ice cream sundaes.

We husbands would appear on weekends and cook up English-style breakfasts of bacon and bangers, organize swimming races at the beach, and carouse in the evening around a campfire with beer and roasted wieners. John, who had a good voice, would lead us in English folk songs like "The Foggy, Foggy Dew" and "Green Grow the Rushes O." Judy would add sea shanties like "Shenandoah" and "Billy's Gone Down to Hilo." Consequently, the kids developed a taste for the kind of music that would be made popular in the '60s sung by Peter, Paul, and Mary, Gordon Lightfoot, Ian and Sylvia Tyson, and Simon and Garfunkel.

Martha Southgate was a particularly tireless and indomitable worker. Once I was driving her home with her two kids in the back seat when I realized that something had gone wrong with the car. Intuitively, I knew that if I stopped we would not be able to get going again. I kept driving for another forty miles till we reached Kingston. Many women would have been beside themselves, but Martha calmly phoned her friend Fred Euringer, who agreed to put us up for the night, kids and all. Martha settled Barnaby and Rebecca in bed and then returned to the living room where we all had several shots of whisky. At two o'clock, I went to bed. When I awoke, I discovered Martha had called a garage and had the car towed and installed with a new alternator. By noon, we were on our way back to the city with Martha keeping up a steady flow of conversation in the seat beside me.

One day when I was driving to work, I passed a house in south Rosedale with a "for sale" sign. I thought, this is exactly where I want to live. I inspected it that evening with Judy, who was charmed by it. Our house on Heathbridge was a bit small for our needs with three children. It was rather poorly built and consequently cold in the winter. I had doubts about renovating it, whereas the house I saw on Sherbourne Street had just been renovated. We had been told by the agent that if we wanted the house, we should move fast. The couple who owned it were on the point of getting a divorce, but they had changed their minds more than once before. I put in an offer and it was accepted. My father said, "You're paying forty thousand dollars for a house? Are you out of your mind? You'll never get your money out of it." My father was a shrewd businessman but he was wrong that time, as we discovered when we sold the house forty-five years later for a million and a half.

The children were somewhat uneasy in the bigger house at first, but before long they settled in. The backyard was bricked and surrounded by a high wooden fence. The children rode their tricycles around on the bricks. Before long, the yard became the neighbourhood ball-hockey court. The yard and the house were full of children who came and went. Their parents were relieved to learn they were not playing in the street. By the time the kids were teenagers the fence had been rebuilt twice and many of the local boys were playing serious hockey in the midget major leagues.

It was a bit of a surprise to find that all of my children were quite athletic, whereas neither Judy nor I had the slightest ability or inclination in that area. I was a reasonably proficient swimmer, and so teaching the kids to swim at the cottage was fairly easy. However, I decided that the best strategy was to pretend a competence I didn't have and so I batted balls at them on the tennis court and took them to skating rinks in the winter. Before long they were returning serves and gliding over the ice much more expertly than I, whereupon I happily retired to the sidelines and watched. However, my efforts to interest them in skiing and sailing didn't catch on. I think these activities need a longer and greater commitment on the part of parents than we were willing to put in.

South Rosedale had gone steadily downhill during and since the Second World War. Many of its stately Edwardian mansions had been turned into rooming houses and were poorly maintained. This was one reason my father objected to me buying the house on Sherbourne Street. Typical was the somewhat larger house to the immediate south of us. It was owned by Mr. Machevsky, a Polish immigrant who had worked in Russian mines during the war. Coming to Canada in the late '40s, he had somehow scraped together the money to make a down payment on a fine old red-brick house which he converted into three flats, mainly with his own hands. He lived in the basement with an assortment of treasures he had accumulated.

Mr. Machevsky was fascinated by our children. He would often spend half an hour watching them play in the garden. It was a while before I realized his feet were not touching the ground; such was his strength that he appeared to be casually leaning on the top of the fence. He gave them regular handouts of candy. Our first Christmas on Sherbourne Street, he made an evening appearance, braying a loud ho, ho, ho like Santa Claus. The children ran to the door. "It's Mr. Machevsky wearing a false beard," they said but welcomed him in to receive his presents: a doll, a toy car, and a toy gun. He also brought a large bag of candy. His presents were much more appreciated than some of the more elaborate gifts from their grandparents.

At the time, we had a Polish cleaning woman called Mrs. Gallus. She came on Saturdays and would sometimes eat lunch with us. She would sit in silence until somebody opened the conversation and then she would launch into tales of the horrors of war. "Everybody blow up. Arms, legs, blood. Kerbang, no more head." We thought Mr. Machevsky might cheer her up but she was having none of it. "Silly old man. No good. You watch out this man," she said, eyeing him suspiciously through the window. Sometime later Mr. Machevsky said, "That woman. Be careful. Is witch." We never discovered what lay behind these allegations, but they continued to regard each other with deep suspicion until Mrs. Gallus defected because of her arthritis.

After two or three years, Mr. Machevsky appeared one day to announce that his furnace had blown up. He was putting the house up for sale and moving out right away to live with a friend. Could he store a few things in our house till he found somewhere permanent to live? I agreed, saying that we were going to the cottage the next day and giving him a key. When we returned home, the front hall and living room were full of racks of clothing:

twenty-three overcoats, forty-two suits, sixty-eight shirts and seventy-five pairs of shoes. He had been collecting used clothing to send back to friends and relatives in Poland. He paid a visit shortly after and helped me move his collection into our basement. During the next few months he would appear at the door occasionally. He was still looking for a suitable place to live. He had a plan. He would ride around on his bicycle and jot down the addresses of houses with a "Room to Let" sign. He would then wait a week or two and check the place out again. If the sign was still there, he knew the room was no good; if the sign was gone, the room was probably all right, but it was no longer available. Gradually his visits stopped. Eventually I shipped his clothing collection to the Crippled Civilians, who were pleased to get it.

More through luck than good management I had bought the house at just the right time. Within a few years, people began buying up houses in south Rosedale and renovating them. If I had waited five years longer, I wouldn't have been able to afford our house. A number of our friends moved into the neighbourhood: Wendy Blair, Lisa and Walter Bowen, Mary Ann and Roddy Brinckman, Adrienne and Stephen Clarkson, Coco and Jamie Cran, Honor and Michael de Pencier, Jane and Bill Glassco, Virginia and Jamie Mainprize. We entertained each other at dinner parties and larger evening parties.

The Glasscos gave a party to which we were asked to wear "groovy formal attire." I well remember the somewhat shocked look of their parents, the Glasscos and the Gordons, at the bare legs and midriffs and plunging necklines of both sexes. Adrienne and Stephen Clarkson gave a party involving a treasure hunt. The clues required a knowledge of who lived where, smart shops, and a few cultural monuments. I was paired with Dodie Robb, a wonderfully outspoken television producer who looked like a female pirate. We managed to solve all the clues but arrived back at home base four minutes after the winning pair.

Our own most memorable party was designed to celebrate the upcoming weddings of Michael Tait to Anne Weldon and Jo Armstrong to Laurier LaPierre (two couplings that were not destined to last). Miss Blackley was staying with us and in the late morning, she came upstairs and announced to Judy, "They've shot him."

"Shot who?"

"President Kennedy."

Judy phoned me at the office and we decided we couldn't possibly get in touch with all of the fifty or so guests we had invited. Almost all the guests, stunned by the news, arrived early and seemed grateful to have other people to talk to. Not for the first (or last) time there were people at the party we didn't recognize, who had come with friends or maybe just wandered in off the street. The party went on into the small hours. It was after four o'clock when we finally got to bed. I don't recall whether I had to get up the next morning and go to work, but I do remember that I often turned up at the office in a distinctly groggy state.

It will be evident that by the mid '60s we had found a place in the bourgeois society of Toronto. We were managing well financially and emotionally. I had paid off the bank loans that had been guaranteed against my shares in the paper company and also my mortgage. The children seemed to be off to a good start; they enjoyed their school and seemed to have lots of friends. Most of the pressures from our parents had eased up. Judy and I had more or less accepted the life we had made for ourselves and for the most part thoroughly enjoyed it.

At Christmas in 1968 we took our first holiday with the children. In my brief time with External Affairs, I had become friendly with Dwight and Barbara Fulford. I had known Dwight at Trinity; we had a number of friends in common and were both interested in the arts. At this time, Dwight was posted as second secretary at the embassy in Mexico and they invited us to spend the holidays with them.

They lived in a large house on the outskirts of Mexico City with their six children. Barbara was busy with the numerous activities involved in motherhood but she had already begun one of her crusades, which involved setting up playrooms for children in hospitals. The house was run by the cook Angelina, a fiery Mexican woman with two children of her own: Juan, a teenager, and a five-year-old daughter Manuela. During our stay, Angelina produced three meals a day for sixteen people, beginning with hand-squeezed orange juice at breakfast. (She bought oranges at the market by the gross.) She and Barbara quarrelled regularly over the treatment of the children and various other matters. On one occasion, Barbara kicked her. On another, when we were away on an expedition for the day, we returned to find that Angelina had set a formal table with a white cloth and the best china and glasses. Barbara scolded her for going to such extra and unnecessary trouble, whereupon Angelina seized the table cloth, pulling it and all the dishes to the floor and stamped off to her room in a fit of pique.

Dwight, in contrast, was implacably calm, though he teased Barbara continuously, ruffling her feathers and challenging her serious psychological views, which were based in a deep commitment to the theories of Freud. Dwight was delighted with the many colourful handicrafts of Mexico and bought paintings, hangings, carvings, and sculptures at every opportunity. Every other day some Mexican artisan would arrive at the front door with some work Dwight had commissioned: a huge clay tree of life, a gilded mirror, a wrought iron and copper chandelier. Barbara protested against the extravagance of these objects, but in vain.

Dwight was determined that we should see as much of Mexico as possible. Every second day we would set out in the family's van, Dwight at the wheel driving in his bare feet, which he claimed gave him better control on the treacherous roads; usually I sat beside him, Barbara and Judy sat behind us, and in the back of the van the ten children, singing, playing games, and squabbling among themselves. We visited the city of Tasco, with its churches whose altars were made of solid silver worked into extravagant baroque arabesques and gargoyles; Patzcuaro, where we bought primitive wooden masks and watched a child's funeral on an island across the lake, the mourners with candles proceeding up a path to the church at the top of the hill; and Teotihuacan and Tulum, where the children enthusiastically climbed up the pyramids, but the younger ones were afraid of climbing down and had to be rescued by the adults.

One evening on the way home, we passed a small factory famous for making liqueurs. Dwight suggested that he and I should sample their wares, leaving Barbara, Judy, and the kids in the van. By the time Barbara came to get us we were on our fifteenth sampling. Barbara gave us both a dressing-down in front of the astonished proprietor, who was not accustomed to women scolding their husbands in public, and then drove us home in a silence as deafening as thunder.

Dwight was also keen that we should see the sights of Mexico City: the fabulous collection of pre-Colombian sculptures at the museum, the mariachi bands who played in squares of the old city, the murals of Rivera, Orozco, and Sequieros, the floating flower gardens at Xochimilco, the changing of the guard in the Zocalo, the native dance company at the Teatro de Bellas Artes. We ate various Mexican foods bought from street vendors; Barbara seemed to know instinctively which foods were safe to eat without inducing Montezuma's revenge.

One of our most memorable shopping expeditions occurred when I told Dwight I was interested in buying blankets. Dwight insisted we must go to a town only two hundred kilometres away which was famous for its blankets. This time the women and children were left at home. No sooner had we arrived than we were approached by vendors selling pulque, the fermented cactus milk, which is the beer of the local farmers. We each had a couple of shots and realized it was much more powerful than beer. Thus fortified, we proceeded to haggle over the price of blankets. This is a Mexican tradition and Dwight was quite skilled in the art, something that the Mexicans appreciated as they dragged out the process to an interminable length. The word quickly spread that there were two gringos buying blankets, and a crowd began to gather around us, including a man peddling an almost life-size straw donkey. After considerable bargaining, we each bought several blankets and had another smash of pulque. The donkey man approached us and made his pitch, which although I could not understand it, appealed to me with its histrionic grimaces and gestures. At the finish Dwight said, "After all that performance, you can't refuse him. The pitch alone was worth the price." So I dutifully paid the man the modest price he was asking. He smiled broadly, shoved the donkey between my legs and said, "Now, gringo, ride home." The crowd cheered as we clambered back into the van with our treasures and drove off.

Although Dwight went to the office every working day, he did not seem to be very busy. It was after all the Christmas holidays, which Mexicans extend to Twelfth Night when there is a big celebration of the Night of the Three Kings. One crisis did occur, however, when a middle-aged Toronto couple arrived looking for their son John, who had eloped from his boarding school Ridley College with Scott Symons. "We insist you find him and send him home immediately," the outraged father stated.

"Mexico is a big country."

"We're going to the police."

"I hope you can afford to give them a substantial bribe."

"What kind of a country is this?"

"A Latin-American one. The people are very poor, including government officials. They make money whichever way they can."

The federales agreed to conduct a search, so their palms must have been suitably greased. Scott and his paramour were flushed out of their hiding place in San Miguel de Allende. Barbara invited them to tea, which was a rather comical affair. Scott accosted Dwight on the feebleness of Canadian diplomatic policy, while John sat silent beside him, a pout on his pretty face. Scott positively boasted about his powers of seduction, but after he'd gone, Barbara opined that young John was eminently seducible. The couple returned to Canada on embassy funds but John did not return to Ridley, and indeed stayed with Scott for several years.

On our final night in Mexico, we were invited to the embassy for a New Year's Eve party hosted by the ambassador Saul Rae, father of Bob. Rae was a charming and gracious host. He loved to play the piano and beat out a variety of Gershwin and Cole Porter tunes. Judy and I knew the words to most of them and belted them out lustily, which seemed to please the ambassador. Among his guests were Mike and Marion Pearson on their way to a conference in Buenos Aires. My former boss came over to me and asked genially, "So, Martin, how's the paper business?" I realized that he couldn't possibly have remembered, but the fact that he had taken the trouble to inquire about my present profession and get it right was impressive. He was, of course, not just a diplomat but a politician.

We left the next morning and arrived in Toronto laden with blankets, pottery, carvings, and glassware. Each of us was wearing a sombrero. The customs official took one look at us and said, "Just keep on going." Our first family holiday had been a huge success, largely because of Dwight's enthusiasm and generosity. While I did not envy his position and wish I had chosen to stay in the diplomatic service, it did make me question the conventionality of my own life. The zest and imagination that the Fulfords had displayed was catching and I determined to find a way to introduce more of these elements into our own lives.

THE MUSE BECKONS

I had not been involved in any theatrical activity since leaving university. Then my brother-in-law Jamie called one night. He was directing a production of T.S. Eliot's *Murder in the Cathedral* in the newly constructed Trinity College chapel, a building with soaring Gothic arches and splendid ecclesiastical trappings. He was midway through the rehearsals when one of his actors dropped out. Would I be willing to step in and take his place in a small role, as one of the Tempters?

I willingly agreed, especially as several friends were already involved. John Saxton was playing Thomàs Becket, a role for which he was admirably suited with his imposing stature, sonorous voice, and natural air of superiority. His wife, Judy, was the leader of the women's chorus which also included a vividly pretty girl, Sheila Macdonald, who would go on to make her mark as a producer with the National Film Board, and a striking redhead of obvious talent named Jackie Burroughs. Jackie and I had to spend twenty minutes alone together before the show in the tiny vestry from which we made our entrances, there being no way we could get into it without being seen by the incoming audience. We exchanged a number of salty stories, most of them in my case somewhat exaggerated, but in Jackie's probably not, and formed a friendship which would last for fifty years.

The provost of Trinity was delighted with the production as it drew attention to his splendid new building, but the chaplain was outraged that such scurrilous goings-on were being perpetrated in the hallowed precincts over which he presided or perhaps I should say reigned. "It's like trying to celebrate mass in the wings of the Met," he declared on one occasion, tossing his tonsured head and rolling his eyes. The public and the critics considered the production a great success and Jamie was hailed as an up-and-coming director while the designer, Martha Mann, also received accolades, which started her upon what would be a highly successful career.

My tiny contribution was not particularly noteworthy, but it brought me to the attention of several members of the foremost amateur theatre ensemble of the day, the University Women's Alumnae. This was a formidable group of Thespian ladies who produced a series of plays every year in a variety of different venues. Their choice of plays was highbrow, as befitted their educational and social status; they were all university graduates operating in the bluestocking tradition of such forbears as Aphra Behn, Fanny Burney, and Jane Austen, all of whose works they staged. They resolutely resisted the temptation to admit male members but recruited some of the most promising young actors of the day including John Colicos and Richard Easton, who would go on to have distinguished professional careers, in addition to some lesser lights. I already knew several Alum members: Judy Saxton, Molly Golby, a former Toronto Children Player, and Francess Halpenny, a senior editor at the University of Toronto Press.

Francess, though not always the president, was the acknowledged leader of the group. She had served as a sergeant major in the RCAF during the Second World War, so the habit of command came easily to her. She was a natural feminist before any such label was current, and she trained many young female editors who would make an important contribution to the burgeoning Canadian publishing industry before becoming the founding editor of the *Dictionary of Canadian Biography* and dean of the Library School. But the Alum was an ongoing passion that claimed her loyal support over several decades.

Other members included a number of the Old Guard, who had founded the club: Agatha Leonard, Christina Templeton, Peggy Tytler, and Eleanor Woodstock, many of whom attended rehearsals properly accoutred in hats and gloves and carrying purses. There were also younger members who were professional women: Eleanor Beecroft, Diane Buchan, Helen Dunlop, Betty Grey, Anne Tait, Pamela Terry, Jackie White, and Eileen Williams, who provided the club with various kinds of expertise as well as being competent and sometimes highly accomplished actresses.

My wife Judy, though not a university graduate, was made an honorary member of the club, largely because she was an extremely capable stage manager and props mistress and our house was a convenient location for club meetings. I recall one when Francess arrived slightly late and took up an unobtrusive position on the stairs. Before long I heard her voice from my study. "What we need to do is get rid of this motion and replace it with a more sensible one." She of course had a more sensible motion ready for discussion and deftly took charge of the meeting.

As a director, Francess always knew what she wanted and was determined to get it. On one occasion, she told an actress she must project more.

"I'm sorry, Francess, I can't give you one more decibel," the actress whined. "Nonsense, dear, you must simply try harder." She would frequently say to her cast at one in the morning, "We will just run through the whole thing one more time." As most of her actors had to get up and go to work in the morning, this would be greeted with groans. But Francess was implacable in her efforts to get from her actors nothing less than their all.

My first Alum show was *The Beaux' Stratagem*, directed by Molly Golby, who had had a great success with *The Way of the World* the previous season and now set out to do all the major Restoration plays. I was cast as a drunken, loutish country squire, a role for which I had no affinity. The production had several pretty women and handsome young men and my friend Powell Jones gave a highly comic performance as an Irish priest, but my performance was pretty abysmal.

Nevertheless I was cast soon after as a sullen, loutish Spanish peasant in García Lorca's *Yerma*. The play is poetic and full of passion, but none of us had the remotest connection with the frustrations and torments of its characters. My friend Powell, who was also cast in it, referred to it as *Yessir, Yerma Baby* and we amused ourselves by doing mock-Spanish numbers backstage, but we were well aware that the evening was a dreary event for the audience. I came to the conclusion that the piece was unplayable, until some years later I saw it performed in Barcelona by a troupe of ballsy Spanish women jumping up and down on a trampoline; they possessed what we insipid Anglos sorely lacked: *duende.*

We were not surprised when the adjudicator of the drama festival in which the show was entered ripped it to shreds. My mother said to one of my friends, "Please try to persuade Martin to stop making a fool of himself," and I knew her comment was justified. This would have been the end of my career with the Alum had I not formed a strong rapport with Betty Mascall, a handsome dark-haired woman with a beautiful contralto voice, who played the title role in *Yerma*. Judy was pregnant with our first child at the time and Betty was particularly nice to her, giving her advice and lending her baby clothes and diapers. She and her husband David had us to dinner and we met their three children, with whom we would have an ongoing connection.

Some months later, Betty phoned me. I had apparently expressed an interest in directing. The next Alumnae show was to be Durrenmatt's *The Deadly Game*. The director had cast the show and then dropped out. Would I be interested in taking it over? My cast included several actors with whom I had a nodding acquaintance: Marshall Bruce Evoy, Ivor Jackson, Michael Ney, and Garnett Truax, a highly eccentric and rather spooky character who would have a long career as a Toronto actor playing eccentric and spooky characters, a sort of local cross between Peter Lorre and Boris Karloff. The play took place in an improvised courtroom and I deliberately set it up in the tiny theatre with two of the principal characters in chairs facing away from the audience. This gained me points for originality. The actors were cooperative and the production was a modest success.

Consequently, I was accepted as one of their regular directors and allotted a yearly show. Although the members liked to act, very few of them felt qualified to direct, other than Molly and Francess. They had a stable of male guest directors that now included me, Gordon Johnson, and their headliner, Herbert Whittaker, who usually directed a show that they entered in the competitive Central Ontario Drama Festival.

In the next few years I had a chance to learn my craft working on several very different shows: *The Wings of the Dove,* an adaptation of Henry James' novel in a muted, low-key adaptation by Canadian writer Christopher Taylor, with a lovely performance by American actress Barbara Jean Friend and a bombastic one as a dowager by Cicely Thomson (mother of R.H.); *Mister, Mister*, a highly expressionistic drama by Gunter Grass that featured a rare performance by the future Shelagh Kareda; and *The Eccentricities of a Nightingale*, a rewrite by Tennessee Williams of his *Summer and Smoke*, which I considered superior to the original although Nathan Cohen considered both versions sentimental to the point of banality.

This production was the best work I did for the Alum, thanks in large measure to the luminous performance of Maureen Fox in the role of Alma. She combined a vivid personality, eccentric indeed, with great sensitivity, bringing both humour and pathos to the role. She was ably supported by a young Geza Kovacs as the object of her youthful infatuation, with stalwarts Marshal Bruce Evoy, Francess Halpenny, and Eileen Williams in the supporting cast. This production reawakened my interest in Williams, who would resurface at several points in my future. Not always easily pleased with my own work, I was proud of this production, which strengthened not only my own belief in my abilities as a director but also that of others in the amateur theatrical community.

During this period, the Alum produced two truly remarkable shows. The first Canadian production of Beckett's *Waiting for Godot*, directed by Pamela Terry, had an almost perfect cast of Fred Euringer, Ivor Jackson, Powell Jones, and Kenneth Wickes. A second and almost equally influential production was Ionesco's *The Lesson* with Francess Halpenny, Powell Jones, and Astrid Weyman. These two shows introduced Toronto to the Theatre of the Absurd and established the group as a serious player in Canadian theatre, lighting the way for the alternate theatres that were about to spring to life in the city.

In writing of the Alum I must not neglect the annual garden party, which took place each year in the spacious grounds of Cicely Thomson's house in Richmond Hill. The ladies convened in the early afternoon bearing vessels of potato salad, tomato aspic, and macaroni and cheese. They retired to the house for their annual meeting and we drones were bid to arrive at five o'clock for food and skits. Besides me and Herbert, there were a number of regular Alum male adherents; John Beckwith (the composer), Harold Burke, Michael Polley (father of Sarah), Rex Southgate, Michael Spence, Michael Tait, and Kenneth Wickes, as well as the actors already mentioned. All of these men were either the husbands of Alum members or "perennial bachelors." Beer and wine were in plentiful supply and skits were enacted. One I recall involved the following couplet:

> "Four shows this season
> How loyal can you get?
> Here's to Harold Burke,
> Honorary Alumnette."

The spirit of Gilbert and Sullivan lived on. Budding actors strove to connect with directors and much well-intentioned advice was dished out. I recall Herbert telling Gino Empry he was not really an actor and should perhaps consider being a publicist. Herbert also advised me to try my hand at playwriting, something I had already started. A little uncertainly I gave him a recent script, a bold action which would eventually bear interesting fruit.

Ten years after graduating from Trinity, I decided to go back to school. I enrolled in an M.A. program, and chose courses which I could attend over the lunch hour or in the late afternoon, so that they did not seriously interfere with my working life. Determined to take my studies a little more seriously than I had as an undergraduate, I called on my future professors to inquire what texts we would be reading. The reply: "I have no idea. I'm off to Rome. I'll be drawing up a list in September." However, I drew up my own lists and read over the summer, so that when classes began I was prepared.

One course was taught by Robertson Davies and covered English drama in the nineteenth century, one of his many enthusiasms. He conducted the seminars in his study, which was adorned with many prints of actors and antique playbills. As was his custom he performed rather than taught, giving his impressions of Kean and Irving, extolling the entertainment value of melodrama and farce in contrast to the overly subtle or high-flown dramas of Henry James or Tennyson. The class was lively, with a number of bright students including future film producer Joe Medchuk and historian Peter Briggs, but I was surprised to see that Davies singled out a whipping boy, or rather girl, whom he pilloried verbally. We wrote essays, which he gathered and presumably read and marked. At the last seminar, at which he served sherry and homemade shortbread, courtesy of his wife Brenda, he announced, "The race has been run and prizes have been awarded to all. Those who wish to recover their essays may do so. I shall not treasure them always." Altogether a very civilized and civilizing experience.

My other course was in Jacobean comedy, taught by Brian Parker, then a bright-eyed and enthusiastic young scholar with a quick wit and an encyclopedic knowledge of sixteenth- and seventeenth-century drama, poetry, and thought. His lectures were delivered at a rapid pace, full of often-obscure quotations and fine distinctions as he led us through the complex plots and bizarre characters devised by Beaumont and Fletcher, Ben Jonson, Marston, Middleton, and Webster. Here my summer reading stood me in good stead and allowed me to keep up with some very bright fellow students including Allan Thomas and a long-legged beauty named Elspeth Cameron, who was rumoured to be having an affair with one of the professors. In a way I couldn't have predicted, my choice of professors was extremely fortunate and not just because I managed to score firsts in both courses. It seemed that if you read the texts and attended the classes, acing the courses was a cinch.

The next year I took two more courses. The first was with Miller McClure, who communicated his love of Elizabethan poetry to us with great good humour. He was more of a conventional lecturer, questioning and drawing out his students, and again I was prepared. I already knew about Marlowe and Shakespeare and Spenser, but under his guidance I discovered Sidney and particularly Raleigh, a fascinating character about whom someone should write a play or novel, now that Anthony Burgess is no longer around to do it.

My other course was with Clifford Leech, a famous jet-setting scholar who lectured all over the world. He was confident and sometimes overbearing, but witty and perceptive. His subject was the work of Christopher Marlowe and his comments ranged not only the whole gamut of dramatic literature but also film, which was one of his great interests. I wrote an essay comparing Marlowe's *Edward II* to Bertolt Brecht's treatment of the same subject, which pleased him. We would become friends and I attended his fascinating seminar on film a year or two later.

In my second year, I received a first and a second and was poised to write a thesis on the dramatic works of Thornton Wilder under the direction of Robertson Davies when the English department changed the rules: the requirement for an M.A. was the completion of four courses; no thesis was needed. "Just as well," said Davies, "It might have proved a wedge between us." I was encouraged to enrol at once in the Ph.D. program but decided to take a break. I had enjoyed my studies and my return to academe but I had quite enough on my plate for the moment.

One Friday afternoon, Judy came home from school with two aboriginal children; John, aged five, and his older sister Lavina, aged six-and-a-half. Their mother had disappeared and they had no friends or relatives to take them in. They were fairly readily accepted by our kids, who were much the same age. As my daughter Sarah said later, "We were used to a lot of people coming and going." After a week or so, the kids' mother, Mrs. Nepinak, reappeared. She wanted John back but she didn't want Lavina. The girl asked an unanswerable question: "How come my Mum don' wants me?" We asked the Catholic Children's Aid if she could stay with us for a while and they somewhat grudgingly agreed, because of our religion, or lack of it.

Lavina was a rather pretty little girl with big eyes, almost black, and long black hair. She loved pretty things and for months trailed around the house in Judy's wedding gown and veil. She had cerebral palsy, which left her with a distinct limp; after two operations, this was corrected to some extent, though not entirely. She also had a very low IQ. Judy realized that this was at least partly because no one had spent any time with her teaching her the most obvious things; she did not, for instance, know the difference between a spoon and a fork; nor did she have names for any articles of clothing other than shoe and dress. Her mother was a prostitute who had borne seven children to different men; she had used her daughters as an attraction and they had no doubt been sexually abused. Consequently, Lavina was used to and craved physical attention.

Because she was still so young, it was possible to satisfy her emotional needs simply by cuddling. Our kids were fairly physical anyway as they all played sports like ground hockey and baseball, and they included Lavina in their games in spite of her obvious lack of ability. Neither Judy nor I had been good at sports and we pointed out to the kids that we had both experienced what it felt like to be excluded.

But our main effort was to try to make up for Lavina's lack of experience of what we considered to be normal life. We taught her the names of things, took her to movies and the zoo and the cottage, where she learned to swim and paddle a canoe. She went to school; not the Institute, but the school where Judy taught and could be in close touch with her teacher. Within two years, her IQ had risen from forty-one to eighty-five and she could read simple stories. We came to understand that however disadvantaged Lavina might be, she was very determined and this would stand her in good stead in years to come.

About this time, we began to have live-in housekeepers who prepared meals, did laundry, cleaned, and supervised the children until Judy came home from school. Many of these were unmarried mothers. Several of them spent a good deal of time with Lavina, showing her things and adding to her vocabulary. Our house was often full of kids in the afternoon. Mostly they accepted Lavina. They were a varied crew; some came from broken homes, others came from families who had maids whose children lived as part of the family. Rosedale in that era was not exactly the snotty, uptight WASP enclave that was painted by the popular press.

This is not to suggest that there were no problems: fights, tears, and sulks were fairly prevalent. Lavina demanded and received a great deal of attention and undoubtedly to some extent our other children resented this. But Judy and I both felt that it was good for them to experience something other than middle-class life and in retrospect, they would agree.

In Brian Parker's class I had met a handsome twenty-one-year-old Jewish boy from Boston. He was bright, perceptive, sensitive, and quick-witted. We began having coffee together and then sometimes lunch. We talked not only about English literature and art and theatre but also politics. (The Americans were at the beginning of the Vietnam War.) Dan was not a draft dodger. He had come to Toronto because of the eminent professors. Like me, he was interested in the Elizabethan and Jacobean period, but he was a serious and extremely hard-working scholar. He completed his M.A. in one year and his Ph.D. in two.

Some months after we met, we would occasionally have dinner together. Dan provided a welcome change from the demands of domesticity. One night, we got rather drunk in a dark and largely deserted restaurant. I had a strong feeling of attraction to Dan, which I felt sure was reciprocated. I leaned across the table and kissed him. He did not flinch, but after a moment said, "I'm a virgin."

"Not a problem. Off with your pants."

"Here?"

"I'll meet you in the washroom."

We both enjoyed this first encounter. It was only partly accidental. At least semiconsciously, I knew what I was doing. And I didn't feel even a twinge of guilt. My teenage Presbyterian angst had somehow evaporated. Over the next several months, Dan and I met regularly and happily explored each other's bodies. He had smooth dark skin and smelled of patchouli. We had sex in an abandoned classroom, in a parking garage, in the library stacks. Before long he had found a single room where we could meet at almost any hour of the day or night. When Judy and the kids were at the cottage, we would sometimes spend the night together.

One day I was amused to find that Dan had mounted a large reproduction of El Greco's *St. Martin and the Beggar* on the wall over his bed. It may be remembered that St. Martin offered *half* his cloak to a beggar. A rather meagre recommendation for sainthood, but typical of Dan's sense of humour. As he approached his doctoral exams Dan became more and more preoccupied, but we continued to meet. He seemed strained, no doubt because of his work. The exams were passed *summa cum laude*, but he seemed more troubled, even desperate. I thought about this and decided to tackle it head on. I told him that I felt he wanted more from me than I could give. I had grown very fond of him but I was not going to leave my wife and family for him. He had a right to something better. I thought we should stop seeing each other. His beautiful face was contorted with pain. Tears ran down his cheeks. He got up without a word and walked away. I never saw him again.

It was at about this time Jamie came back from England to take up a job as movement coach for the Stratford Festival. He brought with him his current boyfriend Richard, an aspiring actor who had grown up in Brooklyn, the pampered son of adoring Jewish parents. They spent a stormy summer at Stratford, where Richard was openly contemptuous of most of the work and Jamie's innovations were not universally accepted, especially by some of the older actors.

After the Stratford season ended, they came to Toronto expecting to settle into Jamie's parents' house but after a brief experience of Richard's erratic behaviour, Frank put them out. They took up residence at Donald Himes' house on Washington Avenue, along with David Earle and his new lover Peter Randazzo. In spite of a common interest in modern dance, black female jazz singers, and beautiful young men, this *ménage à cinq* also proved unworkable and so Jamie and Richard moved in with us on Sherbourne Street. Rather like Sheridan Whiteside, they came for the weekend and stayed for six months.

Richard had the highly distinctive look of a sexy, young goat but great charm when he chose to exercise it. He also loved kids and joined in as our gang chased each other round and round the main floor of the house, sometimes hiding in a cupboard and suddenly jumping out to scare them. He introduced us to Bob Dylan and the Beatles and we all learned to dance in the freeform style of the '60s and '70s. Our housekeeper at the time was Sheila, a Trinidadian of Indian descent who had a merry disposition and a love of games. She and Richard and one or two of the kids often played cards until two in the morning and peals of laughter would ring through the house.

Richard also had a violent temper and on more than one occasion, Judy and I would arrive home from a dinner party at eleven o'clock at night to find clothes and books being hurled out the window of the second floor room where Jamie and Richard slept, accompanied by screams and groans. Then Richard would disappear for two or three days and return looking gaunt and dishevelled. He had a love of exotic clothing: silver chains and bracelets, coloured scarves, and sashes and high-heeled boots, which he proudly flaunted. The kids picked up on this and started to develop their own styles, particularly Sarah, who wouldn't wear a dress again for a good many years.

Jamie and Richard had some strange guests: an actress who weighed over three hundred pounds, a black drummer who performed constantly through a period of several days, and a South American dancer who wore a costume inspired by Carmen Miranda and told fortunes. Our house had become Liberty Hall and the neighbourhood kids came by in large numbers to enjoy the show. None of the parents ever called the police, though sometimes one of them would call at ten in the morning and ask if young Nick or Charlie had slept over. Judy and I would inspect the kids' rooms and reply in the negative. As often as not, the boy would come downstairs an hour later looking for breakfast.

I remember one Christmas Eve we went to midnight mass at St. Mary Magdelene. After the service, Polly Armstrong came down the aisle on the arm of Vincent Massey. "Of course you know Martin Hunter," she said. They surveyed Jamie, wrapped in a scarf like Aristide Bruant, Richard wearing a pirate's scarlet headscarf, Sheila, hugely pregnant in a spangled Indian dress, and Lavina with her wedding veil. Massey drew himself up to his full five feet and seven inches, looked down his long aristocratic nose, nodded incredulously, and passed imperiously on. Obviously his early infatuation with bohemia did not extend to our raggedy crew.

Not long after, Sheila had her baby. The baby's father had offered to marry her, but Sheila was not about to tie herself down to a demanding Indian husband. Instead she gave the boy over for adoption by her married brother and his wife in Montreal. Judy and I took the baby on the plane. We wondered how we would be recognized by her family, but Sheila laughed and said, "I don't think there will be many white women disembarking with an Indian baby in her arms." Her son grew up thinking her brother and his wife were his natural parents and Sheila was his aunt. When he learned the truth as a young adult he showed little interest, but by that time Sheila had became a school principal and found a compatible Caucasian partner.

Jamie was restless with nothing to do in Toronto, and so just before Christmas we conceived of the idea of a children's show, based on Hans Christian Andersen's *The Snow Queen*. I had absorbed a fair amount from Dorf Goulding, who had written plays for us when we acted for the Toronto Children Players. I treated Andersen's characters with respect, gave them funny lines whenever possible, and wrote some simple lyrics. I knew I was no poet, but thought I might be able to compose some doggerel that would pass with children. The opening song went like this:

"There was a little boy,
Had a sharp eye
He was fast and tricky,
Quicker than a fly.
He could whistle like a thrush
And eat a whole apple pie,
Run like a rabbit
And that's no lie,
Add up figures
Subtract and multiply:
Seven plus eight times nine minus sixteen
Divided by five, plus thirty-eight minus seventeen plus two,
divided by six minus eight equals zero.
His name is Kay."

Donald Himes composed original music, which he played live while Jamie staged a series of dance numbers with a cast that included Richard as the boy Kay and the old witch, David Earle as a comic robber and a reindeer, and a very pretty and determined young dancer named Kevin McGarrigle as the heroine Gerda. The production was simple; we gathered, borrowed, and made the costumes and staged it at the old Central Library Theatre at College and St. George streets. At the opening performance the young actress playing the Snow Queen failed to show up, so Jamie and I pressed Judy, who was in the audience with our kids, to take on the role. We quickly dressed her in a white cheesecloth costume, set a crown on her head and sent her onstage. Fortunately, she had virtually no lines. The other actors guided her around the stage as she viewed them all with a regal mien and somehow got through the first performance.

Herbert Whittaker wrote a somewhat snide review of the first performance, calling attention to Judy's remarkable feat. As a result, the production did well with several sold-out performances. We didn't really make any money but didn't lose any. And the show helped to set up Jamie and me as director and playwright respectively. The script was done several more times by companies playing for young actors, and in the long term did make me a few thousand dollars.

Richard felt we had used his talents without giving his brilliance proper recognition, either financial or critical, and before long decamped to New York. Jamie soon followed him and after a short and tempestuous time together, they parted company. Jamie said, "I thought my life was over, but after a month or so I came to my senses and thought, thank God." Jamie and I would continue to work together in the future, but Richard disappeared. We would hear rumours that he was living with a matador in Mexico, that he had become a Buddhist monk, that he was in jail in Quebec for joining a band of separatist anarchists. He was a wild one, but he lived life utterly on his own terms and that could not help but have an effect on all of us.

OUT FLEW THE WEB

For several years I kept tinkering with the play I had written on holiday in Antigua. It was centred on a dysfunctional family, a less hackneyed subject at the time than it is now. It owed more to Kaufman and Hart's *You Can't Take It With You* than to Ibsen and Strindberg. The central character was the family matriarch, a character loosely based on Judy's grandmother, an amiable and ample woman, who was vain of both her Edwardian figure and her tiny ankles. Grandma had a good heart but a sharp tongue. She was full of country expressions and like many country people quick with a put-down. On seeing her granddaughter dressed up for a formal dance she commented, "All you need is a ring in your nose." She was also known for malapropisms and spoonerisms, one of her most famous being that she would not be caught dead reading *Lady Loverley's Chatter.*

Hoping to move towards a production, I gave copies of my script to both Robert Gill and Herbert Whittaker. Gill had a favourable response but felt it was unsuitable for a university production as it contained some bad language and sexual hijinks. Herbert was even more enthusiastic and I believe suggested it to the University Women's Alumnae, who at the time mainly did established repertoire. At about this time, I met Nathan Cohen at a party; he said he had heard of my play and could undoubtedly do more to arrange for a production than Herbert. I sent him a copy but heard no more.

Then in 1967 for Canada's centennial, it was decided that all the entries in the Dominion Drama Festival were to be original Canadian plays. This was Whittaker's brainchild and he managed to sell it to the festival's authorities. It was decided that four plays would be chosen to compete in the Central Ontario region. Both Gill and Whittaker were on the selection committee and my play was selected as one of the four. Obviously, my earlier promotion had paid off.

The four plays were assigned to four producers who were to choose directors and hold open castings. My producer was Cicely Thomson. We had already established a rapport when she had acted for me at the Alum, so this was a plus. Whittaker, in his usual oblique style, let it be known that he might be interested in directing. I was determined that my brother-in-law Jamie should direct. I met with Whittaker, who expected to be wooed. Rather than jump at the chance I expressed some reservations, I thought quite subtly. Herbert withdrew and I thought I had cleared the path for Jamie. However, Cicely said she must consult with some of her peers, a group that included Whittaker. Whether he saw through my little ploy and decided to block it I never knew; shrewd and quick to take offence, he was quite capable of this kind of intrigue. In any event, I was informed by Cicely that Jamie was considered too inexperienced and they had decided to hire Ron Hartmann, an experienced actor who had recently begun to direct. I had outfoxed myself. Whether Whittaker would have given me a better production I will never know, but he would almost certainly have been more sensitive to the play's milieu than Hartmann.

I had thought of the characters in my play as a middle-class family much like my own; Ron thought I was portraying Toronto aristocrats. This idea would be picked up by the press and used as a publicity gimmick: "Insider reveals the sleazy side of Rosedale." However, the actors who came out to casting calls were an assortment of middle-class types, so in fact I achieved pretty much what I had been shooting for.

Ron and I collaborated with Cicely in choosing the actors. Cicely had close connections with both the Alum and the Richmond Hill Players and most of the hopefuls who turned out to audition came from these sources. In those days there was not a host of would-be amateur actors and we had to scrounge to find people to play some of the roles, in particular the homosexual younger son. I had hoped for a sort of ensemble à la Stanislavsky, but this was clearly impossible with these players, many of whom were meeting for the first time. In the end three actors would carry the show: Muriel Cuttle, an established Alum actress; Terry Tweed, daughter of actor Tommy Tweed and a young protégé of Ron; and Cicely's son Robert, who would later become well known as R.H. Thomson.

We assembled the cast and they read the script through. On the whole I was pleased with them, and happily answered their many questions about the characters, their background, motivation, and intentions: the sort of questions all actors ask when beginning to work on their characters. At the end of the session Ron asked me to stay on and then announced that I was not to attend any more rehearsals until he invited me. In the meantime, he would go to work on the text.

I was more than somewhat annoyed, but fortunately swallowed my pride and agreed. Some weeks later I was presented with a revised script by Ron, who had worked with the cast, trimming and sharpening my dialogue. Once again my vanity was stung, but I accepted their version. I now realize that my original text was overwritten; influenced by Shakespeare, Brecht, Fry, and Eliot, I had striven for a poetic or at least lyrical effect that was not only inflated but pretentious. What I had written was basically a realistic comedy and it was a credit to Ron's good sense that he saw this.

Since then I have myself directed scripts by beginning dramatists, most of whom resist attempts to cut and tighten their texts, a process that often occurs in the workshops which are now almost universally obligatory in professional theatres. While it may be the right of experienced and highly gifted playwrights from Ayckbourn to Albee to insist that not a word of their texts be tampered with, most beginning writers are wise to listen and learn what they can from the experience of working with established actors and directors.

The rehearsal process continued over many months. The cast, most of whom could only meet on weekends because they either had full-time jobs or were attending school, were slow to learn their lines, as most amateur actors are. But they accepted Ron's direction and strove to do what he asked them, whereas many professional actors resist a director's ideas, either because they are confident they know what works for them or feel that they are not being treated with the respect which is their due.

Finally I was allowed to come and see a runthrough, which took place in a space in Thornhill. I was pleasantly surprised by what they had achieved and realized that the show was well on the way to a satisfying if not ideal performance. I said this and praised the cast and Ron, avoiding giving detailed notes. It was a Sunday evening and the cast dispersed to their homes; most of them had school or work the next day. Cicely asked me to go back to her house for a drink.

As we sat in her living room with our glasses of whisky, I suddenly experienced a feeling of great warmth for Cicely. She was often bossy and abrupt, but it was she who was pulling this whole enterprise together, driving around in her Jaguar, gathering props and costumes, giving actors a lift home, spending hours on the phone arranging details, finding a replacement when one of the actresses discovered she was pregnant and dropped out. And what was her reward? A solitary, consoling glass of rye before she tumbled into bed.

"Now — what did you really think?" she asked.

"I think it's coming along nicely, but we have to get it in front of an audience."

"Impossible. It's against the rules."

"You'll think of something if you want us to win."

And she did. A week later Cicely had arranged that we would give a performance at an old people's home in Richmond Hill. She had persuaded the committee that this was a charitable offering for these deprived shut-ins. It was an inspired choice of venue. Within minutes the old ladies in the audience identified with Grandma. They laughed along with her and cheered her every move. Their applause at the final curtain was vigorous and sincere. I went backstage and the actors were astonished. "Did you think your play was that funny?"

"As a matter of fact I did. It's a comedy."

"Oh."

There were only two more rehearsals and Ron put them to good use. He had been working to achieve some reality in the characters and in that he had been largely successful. A comic actor himself, Ron now worked to sharpen the comic delivery of lines and added some clever bits of business. The show took a big leap forward as we marched inexorably towards the opening.

There were three other shows in the competition, and of course I went to see all of them. The first was an experimental piece strongly influenced by the then-fashionable theatre of the absurd and directed by Pamela Terry. The next was a Jewish family drama written by Aviva Ravel. Then came my play. There was a third play which was historical and rather heavy going. On the final night I entered Hart House Theatre five minutes before curtain to discover that the audience contained almost every person I had ever known in my life, from my music teacher to my family dentist: my family, my friends and my friends' parents and my parents' friends.

The performance began with a round for the set, which featured a sort of Edwardian living room with large open spaces showing projections of Rosedale streets with snow on the ground and the bare branches of towering trees. This had been devised by Richard Silver, who was still living with us at the time, and his work proved highly effective. Muriel as Grandma, confident from the old people's applause, set the pace in the first scenes. The audience began to laugh early on and continued to do so, even during the love scenes, which were meant to have a comic tone.

I had learned about two weeks before that the adjudicator was to be Robertson Davies, about whom I felt somewhat ambivalent. He had treated me well as a student, but would he go out of his way not to seem unduly partial? In his remarks following the play, he was positive and indeed scolded the audience for laughing at scenes they should have taken more seriously. "Canadian theatre will never mature unless its audiences mature," he pronounced.

We went afterwards to a party at the apartment of Terry's mother Jean Tweed, a series of large, almost empty rooms over a bookstore across from the Central Library on College Street. The actors danced and drank together almost for the first time and there was a general feeling of release and satisfaction. Even Ron, who had made no secret, at least to me, of his reservations about the play seemed pleased and relaxed. For some reason I was the last to leave. I think I had probably fallen asleep on the sofa. I awoke to see Terry sitting across from me with a mischievous look in her eye. She leaped up and said, "Catch me if you can," and bounded away into the darkness. We played a game of hide and seek in the dark rooms until Terry allowed me to find her hiding in a big, old wardrobe.

"So which of your characters is you? Teddy, right?"

The older brother in the play was a handsome young womanizer. "Only in my wildest fantasies."

"At least you admit it." She came over and gave me a kiss. I responded. "You're a good kisser. I had to teach Robert how to kiss." She grinned at the thought of it.

"You're obviously a good teacher.'

"He was a willing pupil. You could be too."

"As a married man, I think I'd better take a rain check on the next lesson."

On the final night of the festival, Davies, resplendent in white tie and tails, handed out the prizes. Our play did very well. He gave Muriel the award for best supporting actress, Terry the award for best actress, and Robert Thomson was named best actor. I was acclaimed "the playwright who showed the most promise" and handed the Lieutenant-Governor's Medal by Pauline McGibbon. It was a gunmetal disc with the words on the reverse side "Presented To." I took it to Birks' and had my name engraved at my own expense. The only award I would ever receive, I think I still have it in my handkerchief drawer.

The reception that followed was decidedly more decorous than Terry's party the night before. No dancing and only wine and beer served. We were all duly congratulated. I was astonished to hear Davies remark to Muriel, "I couldn't help realizing you had based your characterization on Mother." I would later learn that Muriel had at one time been married to Davies' older brother Fred. "I don't believe the marriage was ever consummated," Davies later confided to me with a wicked chortle.

I could not help but be aware that both Pamela Terry and Aviva Ravel had strong feelings of resentment. Aviva's play had been condemned by Davies for exploiting the worst stereotypes of Jewish behaviour. Pamela, who had gained a deserved reputation as an experimental director with her excellent productions of *Waiting for Godot* and James Reaney's *The Kildeer*, was annoyed that her production was pronounced to be superficial. Both women harboured ill feelings towards Davies for years afterwards.

I wondered then and I wonder still about the real value of competitions in the arts. Like Bottom the Weaver, I find that "comparisons are odorous." Nevertheless they have become omnipresent in the cultural sphere, and there can be no doubt of their importance to an artist seeking to build a reputation. This was certainly borne out by my own experience. I was interviewed on radio and television, profiled in the Toronto newspapers and in *Toronto Life* and received many letters of congratulation, including one from a former high school teacher now living in South Africa. Did it go to my head? At least a little bit. The most positive effect of all this attention was that it convinced me I had some talent as an artist and that I should continue to work to develop it rather than devoting my leisure hours to bridge or sky-diving.

Having won the Central Ontario laurels, we were invited to compete in the finals for the Dominion Drama Festival, which was to be held in St. John's, Newfoundland, in a brand new theatre that had been built as a centennial project. We gave two extra performances to raise funds for the trip. Jeannie Hersenhoren, the prime organizer, complained that the title wouldn't be an easy sell. I had picked up on the then-fashion of choosing a title that was a quote from a well-known classic (*Blithe Spirit, Awake and Sing, Present Laughter, O Mistress Mine,* among many others). Professor Clifford Leech said to me one day after class, "Mr. Hunter, I hear you've written a play. What is it called?"

"*Out Flew the Web.* I won't have to tell you the source."

"I'm afraid you do."

"Tennyson. *The Lady of Shalott.*"

"Not my field," he replied without the slightest trace of irony. The two nights sold out, thanks to all the publicity, and we boarded a plane for St. John's.

We were greeted by Gordon Pinsent, who, as a local boy who had already made his mark as a writer and actor on Canadian television, had been asked to be the official host for the festival. He was particularly nice to me and although we have never worked together we have been on friendly terms for over fifty years.

There followed a week-long round of daytime excursions to small towns and outposts and nightly celebrations. Away from home, the actors partied hard. I drank enthusiastically and danced wildly, liberated by the example of Jamie and Richard and inspired by the youthful high spirits of most of the cast, which included two pretty girls who added some excitement to the play's party scene. One was the current girlfriend of Robert Thomson and the other the sister of another actor. On one occasion we all attended a luncheon reception, which featured some pompous speeches. Bored and already a bit drunk, I suddenly hit the bottom of my empty glass and sent an ice cube flying into the air. It landed in the décolletage of the premier's daughter. Although the audience was unaware where it had come from, there was a round of applause when she retrieved it and sent it back into the air. "Whatever the final outcome, you have the satisfaction of knowing your actors love you," said Herbert Whittaker with some asperity.

There were other adventures. One of the male actors who was playing a homosexual propositioned Robert. There was also a scene in the play where one of the characters had a line about "three in a bed." This actor and I were sharing a room and I was awakened at about four in the morning as he made an entrance with one of the pretty girls. (Not Robert's friend.) He grinned at me and said, "Three in a bed. We're doing research. Care to join us?" It was not the first or the last time that I was to experience actors letting their characters' traits and habits spill over into their real lives. Indeed, I have sometimes wondered to what extent actors have what most of us think of as a real life.

The night of our performance arrived, and with it, a good deal of tension that had not seemed to be present back in Toronto. The set, which had been so effective at Hart House, did not fit the larger stage and looked as if it had not been finished. Then about five minutes into the act, the lights failed. Ten minutes later they failed again. This put a damper on what was meant to be a riotous party scene. It unnerved both the actors, who lost their original vigorous enjoyment, and the audience, whose response was much less enthusiastic than we had experienced in Toronto. The actors and audience left the theatre but Ron and I lingered. "We really bombed tonight," he said mournfully.

"Hard to judge," I replied. But I knew he was right.

On the final night, the prizes were awarded by the adjudicator, the highly experienced Quebecois director Guy Beaulne. He gave most of the awards to a French-Canadian play, *Le Pendu* by Robert Gurik. It was a fable in the tradition of Obey and Giraudoux, and although my command of French was not sufficiently accomplished to completely appreciate the quality of the language, I had to admit that the production was superior to ours and all the other entries in terms of its invention and theatricality. The artists of Quebec were already well ahead of their English-speaking compatriots in imaginative vitality, originality, and craft as Tremblay, Lepage, and Mathieu would soon make evident.

Terry Tweed received another best actress award and her scene with Robert was televised and shown on CBC, a first for both of them and an important step in their professional careers. I was summoned for a private interview by the adjudicator in his suite while he ate breakfast in a flowered purple dressing gown. He was graciously condescending and encouraged me to go on learning my craft. Meanwhile fog had descended on the Rock, and we spent two more leisurely days in St. John's, not able to see much, but enjoying the warmth and hospitality of the natives. I had dinner with my old friend Jimmy Armour and his family. He was enjoying a rather long appointment as the minister of St. David's Presbyterian Church, and it was nice to see that he had settled in comfortably. He was amused by parts of my play but disapproved of some of the racier bits.

It was interesting to note that there was a similar reaction from a number of audience members. They were less upset by the fact that two of the characters were homosexual than by the fact that the boy and girl went to bed together the first night they met. It was 1967, but of course the spirit of the '60s did not hit Toronto until the early '70s. My friend Ann Murray, who was by this time an actress in London, came home for a visit and offered to take my script to a producer friend in London. He returned it to me with a note: "I'm afraid I found it rather *vieux jeux*, though I can imagine it caused a certain *frisson* in the colonies."

My life returned to normal, more or less, as I went back to the office, business lunches, kids' birthday parties, skating at City Hall, visits to the zoo, dinner parties with friends and movies like *Zorba the Greek*, *Women in Love*, *Bonnie and Clyde*, *8½*, *Isadora*, *The Sting*, *Chinatown*, *The Accident*, and *Le Souffle au Coeur*. Films that would influence me in formulating a new artistic sensibility. Then one day the phone rang. It was Brian Parker asking, "How would you like to be playwright-in-residence at the university next year?"

My appointment to the Drama Centre was accompanied by a cheque for one thousand dollars. I told Brian Parker that of course I couldn't live on this for a year but would do whatever I could. What did he want me to do? He replied that he hadn't really thought about it; he just wanted to see if he could get some money from the Canada Council. I was free to do what I wanted.

The Drama Centre was set up by the university's president, Claude Bissell, to deal with the problem of Hart House Theatre. The longtime artistic director Robert Gill was drinking more and more heavily. He had become an increasingly isolated figure and was plagued by rheumatism, which meant he was in constant pain.

Some of his staff drew Bissell's attention to this situation and he responded by deciding to fire Gill summarily. His wife Christine intervened, pointing out that Gill had served the university for two decades and done much outstanding work. Bissell agreed to give Gill a long sabbatical and called a committee to consider the question of what to do about the theatre.

Several people saw this as an opportunity to set up a full-scale practical theatre training program at the university. Foremost among them was Herbert Whittaker, who canvassed a number of university worthies, most notably Robertson Davies, to support this idea. He was surprised to find Robert Gill opposed. Gill, a true professional, understood from long experience the extremely academic character of the university's arts faculty and the strongly entrenched tradition of amateur theatre on the campus.

Bissell was also opposed to the professional approach. Though I have never been able to get absolute proof, I believe that Bissell had come to an agreement with Murray Ross, the president of the newly founded York University, in effect stating, "Keep away from medicine and engineering and you can have the arts." In any case, York had soon set up a full scale practical theatre program, which flourishes to this day.

Bissell proposed to establish the Graduate Centre for the Study of Drama, which was to grant graduate degrees to students who wanted to teach theatre in universities under the joint chairmanship of Robertson Davies and Clifford Leech. The fact they disliked and distrusted each other did not contribute to easily agreed upon objectives. Both were busy men; Davies as master of Massey College and Leech as chairman of both the graduate and undergraduate English faculty, so that neither had much time to devote to planning the activities of the Centre. Fortunately they appointed a young professor, Brian Parker, as director of the Centre, which he led with energy, enthusiasm, flexibility, and openness to new ideas in its early years.

It was a time of relative prosperity and the university came up with a fairly sizeable amount of money to refurbish and run the theatre itself. Davies determined that there should be a professional season. He spoke to his old friend Tyrone Guthrie about kicking it off as he had Stratford. Guthrie, engaged with his new theatre in Minneapolis and various other ventures in New York and London, declined. A number of other professional directors from Britain and the United States were invited to consider becoming artistic director. It was often my job to show them the theatre, which was still in the process of renovation. While the new seats of the auditorium were brightly coloured and inviting, the fact that the theatre had no fly tower, very limited wing space, and no workshops for sets, props, and costumes could not be disguised. Not to mention a budget which, while generous by Canadian standards, was hardly munificent. All the candidates declined the offer and returned home to better facilities. In desperation, Davies and Leech considered the idea of a Canadian director and cautiously approached Leon Major.

Leon and I had been in the same year as undergraduates. He was a particular protégé of Robert Gill. Both Leon and Gill soon realized that Leon had no particular gift as an actor and Gill encouraged him to try his hand as a director. Leon directed an acclaimed production of Clifford Odets' *Waiting for Lefty* while still a student and won the first Ernest Dale Award, for which I was also nominated. I remember thinking he was a better candidate because he intended to pursue a serious career in theatre, which at the time I did not. On Gill's recommendation Leon attended Carnegie Mellon, but Gill told him he already knew everything he would be taught at the American university. At the end of a year, Leon realized Gill had been right and returned to Toronto to direct professional productions at the Crest Theatre. He gained considerable attention for his sensitive handling of an original Canadian play, Patricia Joudry's *Teach Me How to Cry*. Soon after, he left Toronto to become artistic director of the fledgling Neptune Theatre in Halifax.

Leon proved to be capable and popular in Halifax but he felt isolated and was anxious to return to Toronto, which offered a wider scope for his ambitions. He seized upon the opportunity to set up a professional company at Hart House and, encouraged by his academic masters to choose obscure plays that they wanted to see produced, elected to direct the Jacobean tragedy *The Changeling* and Goldoni's little known comedy *The Fan*. He was able to engage two well-known actors, Frances Hyland and William Needles, to head his company, and although both actors were miscast they helped attract other capable actors and audiences.

Brian Parker suggested to Leon that he employ me as dramaturge, and as I was willing and there was no money to employ someone else, Leon readily agreed. We had not had much contact as students but Leon was a genial, warm-hearted man who would give you a hug like a big Russian bear and make you feel he really wanted you to be part of his family of actors, so we got along well enough. We discussed possible actors and at least partly at my suggestion he hired actors Barbara Bryne, Colin Fox, and Rex Southgate.

I asked Leon what he wanted me to do and he pushed a translation of *The Fan* across the desk towards me. "Let me know what you think of it." I took it away and read it.

"It's terrible," I reported.

"Can you come up with something better?"

"I'll try."

At the first read-through Leon handed the actors the original translation. At the end he said to me. "You were right. It is terrible. We'll use your translation." He apparently had not read either version. The sudden switch confused the actors and made them distrust the play. Nevertheless, they dug into it and did their best.

After a week or two, Leon asked me if I could come up with a scene that would be funnier than the original. I obliged to the best of my ability. I watched the actors read the scene and was pleased.

"You're laughing," said Leon.

"Nothing like enjoying your own work."

"Absolutely. There's another scene I'd like you to have a look at." So I went back to my typewriter.

But there was a mild backlash. Hannibal Noce, the head of the Italian department, accosted me. "I hear you're improving on Goldoni." But he said it with a smile. Hannibal was a dignified, rather soft-spoken man who smoked a pipe and spoke with a slight drawl. He was asked to speak to the cast about Italian culture; Leon wanted him to inspire them to fiery flamboyance, but Hannibal was the absolute antithesis of what Leon was looking for: calm, rational, and dryly witty. In spite of his initial disapproval, in time Hannibal and I would become good friends.

In performance, *The Fan* was elegant and amusing, thanks to Martha Mann's graceful costumes, some clever business devised by Leon, and the skilful comic performances of most of the actors. I was pleased with my chance to be part of it, though I received neither credit nor payment. *The Changeling* was less successful. Leon had little feeling for the perverse or lascivious. The play could have benefited from some cutting, but Leon believed, probably rightly, that the academics wanted to hear every word of the text. Not so the audiences.

Leon said that one reason he had accepted the job at the university was that it offered him the "right to fail." This was a popular saying at the time and by it he probably meant the right to experiment. I suppose all artists have this right, but it doesn't make much sense in the theatre where a group of people work together at considerable expense of time and effort, not to mention money, in order to produce something of value for an audience. In any case, Leon did not fail. His first season was a moderate success and his second, in which he undertook the highly ambitious task of producing Eugene O'Neill's *Mourning Becomes Electra* with a cast that included Kate Reid, Anna Reiser, and William Needles, garnered him a good deal of favourable attention. Consequently when Mavor Moore suddenly resigned from his position at the newly constructed St. Lawrence Centre halfway through the first season, Leon readily took on the task of replacing him and his connection with the Drama Centre came to an abrupt end.

Leon braved out the largely ludicrous first season at the St. Lawrence that he had not chosen and over the next several years went on to do interesting work. He built an audience and offered them varied and often excellent fare including such warm-hearted comedies as *The Matchmaker* and *Trelawney of the Wells* and more serious works by Brecht and Solzhenitsyn. He employed director Kurt Ries and designer Murray Laufer to very good effect as well as a large number of budding actors including Domini Blythe, Marilyn Lightstone, and Richard Monette. He directed productions for the Canadian Opera Company and the Opera School. He was regularly lambasted by the critics. When he was passed over for the position of artistic director of the Canadian Opera Company he decamped to the United States, where he has had a distinguished career as a director in Baltimore, Washington, and New York. He is understandably somewhat bitter that he has been more or less forgotten in his native Canada, where he did much to develop Canadian theatre in the formative period of the '70s.

I had written a new play, which I offered to the Alum as a possible choice in a competition for a new Canadian play to be directed by Herbert Whittaker. He chose another script. Was this a payback for not directing *Out Flew the Web,* I wondered? In any case I decided to direct it myself at Hart House Theatre. This was a mistake. The new play which was called *Young Hunting,* a title I would reuse later, was an intimate piece for four actors, a young man and three women all of whom were infatuated with him: his sister, a chubby neighbouring girl, and an eccentric aunt. The boy did impersonations, sang and strummed his guitar, and behaved outrageously. The character was somewhat based on Jamie's friend Richard. Robert Thomson played the boy with charm, agility, and humour. Meg Hogarth gave a good account of the neurotic older sister and Claire Coulter was both amusing and pathetic as the neighbour. But my friend Annette Cohen was miscast as the aunt, which should have been played by Muriel Cuttle.

I was aware that if you manage to cast the right actors, half of your work as a director is done. If you get too many people in the wrong roles, there is only so much you can do to make the play work. I have once or twice done a production where I knew from the outset I did not have the actor I needed for a major part and it has always turned out to be disappointing. I have been lucky that I have usually been able to find the actors I needed and I take credit for possessing a certain instinct that allows me to recognize what actors can and cannot do. I was gratified that after the run of *Young Hunting*, Robert Thomson said to me, "You showed me I could do something I never imagined I could."

In any case, *Young Hunting* was not a great success. It attracted poor houses and was said to be derivative. I realize now I had been influenced by Tennessee Williams, whose work I greatly admired, though at the time this was unconscious. However, I was not discouraged and immediately set about working on another script.

Not surprisingly, there was a good deal of resentment from the students that their theatre had been taken away from them. Leon was not interested in working with students; he was building a career and he wanted the best actors available. In this he was supported by Robertson Davies and, of course, the critics. He was very aware of the physical limitations of the theatre and was interested in finding both rehearsal and building space.

One day Brian Parker informed us that the university had offered us the use of a small, de-sanctified church on Glen Morris Street that had been acquired when the Russian orthodox congregation moved to larger premises. Leon and I went to see it. The empty building was dingy and dusty with a small raised platform and a round apse at one end and a balcony at the other. It had a full basement with toilets and a kitchen. It seemed to me at once that it was suitable for performances in a small space. It could be painted and equipped with minimal lighting and sound equipment and stackable chairs for a very reasonable amount.

It would then be useable by the students in whatever way they wished. Hart House Theatre was a union house and students were not permitted to run lights or build sets. In this new studio space they could do both and not only act, but direct their own shows. It could still be used by the professional company for rehearsals in the daytime and the basement could be used as a carpenters' shop. Leon, sensitive to any political situation, supported the idea, as a way of getting the students off his back. Brian Parker, always open to innovative ideas and also saddled with listening to the brunt of student complaints, readily agreed. But who was to take responsibility for overseeing the running of it? "What about me?" I suggested.

We bought used lighting equipment from Ron Montgomery, a former Hart House lighting designer, and were given chairs by the Mirvishes, who were refurbishing the Poor Alex. The windows were sealed up, the interior was painted a uniform shade of charcoal grey, a grid was erected from second-hand steel scaffolding, and we were ready for business. Brian Parker suggested that I should direct the first play in the new space, and I chose Camus' The Just Assassins.

In the early years, the Drama Centre attracted a good number of students who had both talent and experience as performers, among them John Astington, Jim Bradford, Michael Fletcher, Maureen Fox, Leigha Lee, Tony Stephenson, Ross Stewart, and Graham Whitehead. Several of them came out to audition, but I also opened the auditions to undergraduates following in the tradition of Hart House Theatre. Brian Parker made no objection to this and I was able to assemble a strong cast that included Mary Caine, Maureen Fox, Paul Mulholland, and Robert Thomson. The play was set in the last days of imperial Russia and so seemed appropriate to the space. It offered good roles: characters of a Dostoyevskian complexity and the actors attacked them with verve and enthusiasm. Several of the actors had worked with me before and easily accepted my ideas.

The play drew a considerable audience because it was an interesting piece and because we didn't charge admission. This idea had been pioneered by Martin Kinch and Tom Hendry at Toronto Free Theatre on Berkeley Street. The Glen Morris Studio followed this policy for the first few years and it definitely established its reputation on campus and gradually to a wider audience. Herbert Whittaker, always interested in new ventures, wrote a favourable review. He also took Robert Thomson out for a drink after the show and persuaded him to completely alter his performance. I was not amused and said so, one of many dust-ups I would have with Herbie over the next decade.

Following *The Just Assassins*, there were two or three more shows in the Studio before the end of term. The students felt at home in the space and soon made it their own. In the spring they approached Brian Parker to ask if they could use the space to produce a season of plays throughout the summer. They had formed a committee consisting of Jim Bradford, Maureen Fox, and Tony Stephenson to take responsibility and supervise the season. Once again they would not charge admission but would rely on the costumes and props borrowed from Hart House and other theatrical organizations on campus. They asked me to direct one of the shows and I chose Brecht's *The Caucasian Chalk Circle*, a huge, sprawling fable and by far the most ambitious project I had taken on up to that time.

Designer Tom Dougherty divided the studio down the middle with the audience facing each other across an aisle. Stairs led up to the balcony on one side and a two-tiered platform in the apse, which gave me small, enclosed spaces for peasants' houses and barns. The play is something like a road movie. In the first part, the Governor's wife and her entourage flee, leaving behind her baby. The maid Grusha says goodbye to her soldier lover Simon, who departs for the front. Grusha finds the baby and sets out for the country fearing the revolution, which is all around her. She is taken in by various farmers, flees from rapacious soldiers across a tottery bridge which was lowered from the grid, marries a man she believes is dying, and is involved in his funeral led by a drunken priest. The corpse revives and claims his bride. Simon returns to find her with the baby and now married to a drunken lout.

In the second half, the revolutionaries find Azdak, a quick-witted vagrant, pull him out of his hiding place, and set him up as an itinerant judge. He travels around the country making outrageous decisions on the cases, taking bribes, and drinking brandy. He finally has to decide who will have custody of the child: Grusha has cared for him against the claim of his birth mother. Simon conducts Grusha's defence and engages in a battle of wits with Azdak. Delighted by Simon's performance, Azdak sets up a contest where the two mothers have to pull the child out of a circle drawn on the ground with chalk. Grusha lets go of the child's hand rather than let him be pulled apart, and she is given the child by Azdak. The play is fast-moving and its scenes range from elements of terror and pathos to farcical absurdity. Brecht's range as a dramatist is paralleled only by Shakespeare, and like Shakespeare, he doesn't concern himself about the mechanics of quick changes of scene or unprepared shifts in tone which challenge the imagination of both designer and director.

Even with some doubling the cast is enormous, but I was lucky to assemble a large company of effective players. From the Drama Centre came Harry Lane with his sonorous voice as the narrator and Maureen Fox, vain, imperious, and shallow as the governor's wife, and later suspicious and mean as a farmer's wife. Mary Caine and Robert Thomson played Grusha and Simon with simple honesty, providing the play with a strong emotional centre, aided by Marina Kovacs as the cook. I persuaded two Alumnae stalwarts, Ivor Jackson and Eileen Williams, to join the company and they brought weight and maturity to their roles of the fat prince and the addled mother of Grusha's bridegroom. John Browne, a classics student, was hilarious as a half-witted stableboy and the three soldiers of David Martin, Blair Mascall, and Jeff Piker were both terrifying and funny in their drunken threats and squabbling. Keith Mills, who appeared out of nowhere, made a wonderful Azdak, sly, boastful, corrupt, and charming, with a generous heart under his tattered gown. I looked forward to working with him again but he disappeared after the production.

The play has a number of songs, which had original music composed by an eminent German composer, but we decided to improvise our own music. The key figure was Peter Acker, a skilled guitarist who worked with my wife, Judy, playing several percussive instruments, and our four children, Sarah,

Ben, Guy, and Lavina, playing instruments borrowed from Margaret Galloway at the Institute. Both Mary and Judy sang and the children joined in the crowd scenes. And finally, we had a coach who trained us in Russian dance steps. Eventually the whole thing came together to form a rich, colourful tapestry, which in spite of its cynical moments was emotionally satisfying the way the best fairy tales always are.

We had a full house on opening night. Nathan Cohen attended and wrote favourably about it the next day. "This is the way Brecht should be performed, with full-blooded zest and enthusiasm," he said. Of course as a committed socialist he was sympathetic to Brecht's left-wing convictions. But there was another angle. The boy who played Grusha's peasant husband was a thoroughgoing hippy. There was a scene where Grusha has to give him a bath. It was not a surprise when he asked me at the dress rehearsal if he could strip right down to the buff. I readily assented. It was, to the best of my knowledge, the first case of full-frontal nudity on a Toronto stage. Cohen mentioned this in his review. The next evening I went to the theatre to find a lineup halfway around the block.

We ran the show for two weeks and never played to less than a full house. I had to sandwich in close friends and even Brian Parker. At the end of the performance he approached me and said, "Would you be willing to stay on next year? I think I could find two thousand dollars for your stipend." I readily agreed.

After the last performance, Judy and I gathered up the many items we had loaned the production for costumes and props. We had already put the kids to sleep in the back of our station wagon. At one thirty in the morning we set out on the five-hour drive to Marshall's Bay. About forty miles from our destination, I fell asleep. Judy, who didn't drive, took over at the wheel, guided by Ben, who was now wide awake. She drove along the country roads at thirty miles an hour. "Come on, Mom. You can pass that hay wagon. Step on the gas." And she did. She drove into the yard beside the cottage at a quarter to seven to be greeted by her astonished mother. "Well, dear, I always said you could drive if you really wanted to."

"Never again," said Judy. And she has stuck by it.

INHERITANCE

"Nice tie."

"Harry Rosen's sale. Five bucks. A week's salary in '39." Alex stuffed his brier pipe with Amphora and lit a match, then held his leather pouch out to me. "You want some?"

"I'm trying not to smoke till after lunch." I straightened the papers on my desk and stood up. "You haven't forgotten we're taking Lorne and Bill to the National Club?"

"We'll be lucky if they let that pair of four-flushers through the front door."

"They're going to get the Gage contract."

"I'm surprised at Gage doing business with them. He's a pretty classy guy."

"They're sharp operators"

Alex grinned at me through a haze of pipe smoke. "Takes one to know one."

"Takes one to know one." "Can't sell from an empty wagon." "Bullshit baffles brains." Alex had a ready supply of such maxims.

Alex tried to encourage me to see the fun in the game of selling: cozying up to the customers, listening to their problems, playing along with their little vanities, giving them a good argument but letting them win, subtly suggesting choices that would seem like their own, backing down rather than pushing too hard, always knowing that if an order was lost today, there was sure to be another one tomorrow. He understood we were dealing not just with dollars and cents but with a network of human connections. The important thing was not the individual sale but the building up and maintaining of long-term relationships. Alex cultivated not just the men he did business with but their wives and children, who likely as not would be running the shop tomorrow or the day after.

"You better get the Gage deal nailed down this week. K.M. wants you to go to the Warren meetings in Poland Spring."

"Instead of you?" I was surprised.

"I'm going too. It'll be fun. The Warren gang are a snotty bunch of buggers but they dish out pretty good grub along with all the hooey. Better than a holiday with the wife and kids."

My father and Alex almost never took holidays. It was like a point of honour with them, though in middle age K.M. had begun to go away for two weeks every winter with my mother. Neither of them enjoyed these expeditions much: Mother endured them because she thought Father needed a rest; Father thought Mother needed a change. The outings he really enjoyed were business trips: the Paper Trade meetings held in late summer at some grand resort like the Banff Springs Hotel or the Seigniory Club at Montebello; the American Paper Trade Convention in New York in the spring, and in mid-autumn the annual sales conference of the S.D. Warren Company at Poland Spring in Maine.

S.D. Warren was our largest foreign supplier and the grandest. They had headquarters in Boston and the attitude of their employees was shaped by that most elitist of American cities. They believed it was a privilege to be allowed to sell their products and they sent their sales representatives out to show their customers how to do it. These young men, graduates of Harvard or Princeton, wore Brooks Brothers suits and carried Mark Cross briefcases stuffed with elaborate sales aids. Stunning examples of photography and typography, dreamed up by leading designers and realized by master printers, they regularly won awards at graphic art shows.

S.D. Warren salesmen not only educated but policed their merchants; anyone caught cutting prices lost their franchise. They also took a very hard-nosed view of customer complaints, though on the rare occasions when they admitted that a printing problem was the fault not of a printer's incompetence but of their product not being up to their own rigorous standards, they made generous settlements. They thought of themselves as gentlemen first, businessmen second, an attitude that could either be seen as either admirable by someone like K.M., who admired their adherence to their principles, or pretentious by someone like Alex.

Heading downtown in Alex's Pontiac (he was shrewd enough to own a car one grade down from K.M.'s Buick) I quizzed my mentor, "What happens at these Warren wingdings?"

"Morning meetings telling us how great the Warren company is, afternoons on the golf course, evenings shooting the shit with a bunch of Hoosiers. Warren merchants are supposed to be the cream of the American trade. They'll tell us what shit-hot operators they are. The joke is, damn few of them sell as much paper as we do. The whole thing is an exercise in American bullshit. Nobody can pile it higher than the Warren guys. They think they invented paper."

"Doesn't sound like my idea of a good time."

"You're going to be a paper salesman, you better get used to it, kiddo."

"So we fly to Boston?"

"You kidding? Spend all that money on airfare? We're taking K.M.'s trusty Buick."

"The perfect car for a man in his position."

"Rich but not gaudy. No vulgar Cadillac for K.M."

"And no stereo. Not even FM."

"It's only a twelve-hour drive."

"You think even you can keep the gab going for twelve hours? K.M.'s not exactly a stunning conversationalist."

"I'm polishing up my stories. There'll be a few reruns. And I'm counting on you to get off a few good ones."

"I usually do better when K.M.'s not around."

"I've noticed. Well, he's counting on you being around for a while. You're a pretty good salesman."

"Am I?" Isn't it in your interest to say so?"

"Okay. You got the brains to see through me."

"Bullshit baffles brains?"

"At least you recognize bullshit when you step in it."

"So what's the deal here, Mr. Smith? You think K.M. might let the three of us buy him out?"

"Maybe over a twenty-year period."

"Do you think you and I and Llew could live together for another twenty years?"

"Good question."

"Llew resents you because he senses K.M. favours you, even though technically he treats you both the same. K.M. thinks he's being fair, but he's the one who defines what's fair."

"He's a smart old bugger, your father."

"Takes one to know one."

The Warren expedition got off to a bad start. I kept my father waiting for ten minutes when he picked me up at my house. An early start was called for so that we would arrive in time for the opening cocktail party. Because my tardiness had put them slightly off schedule, a cloud of disapproval hung over the first two or three hours of the twelve-hour drive. Father drove the first four hours without a break. He was a good driver and vain of it; he drove slightly over the speed limit but had never been caught by the state troopers, another subject of pride. Conversation circled around this topic interlaced with speculation about the likely placement of certain large printing orders in the next few months and the financial stability of some of our major customers. Alex made smart cracks about many of them, most of which I had heard before. I found it a long drive.

We arrived at Poland Spring at five fifteen, twenty minutes ahead of schedule, which was seen by K.M. as a triumph of his determination, but in practice was the result of Alex's audacious performance during the last third of the journey. "You're quite the driver," Father acknowledged as a bellboy staggered under the weight of our bags and golf clubs. Alex and I shared a room, where we showered and dressed for the opening reception. Although this was an all-male gathering in the depths of the country, a white shirt, dark suit, and well-polished oxfords were *de rigueur*. S.D. Warren maintained high sartorial standards, and woe to the poor benighted customer who turned up for dinner in a checked sport jacket with no tie.

Poland Spring had been a fashionable resort at the turn of the century, a Victorian pile, gabled and turreted with long porches overlooking immaculately kept lawns and flower beds, and an interior full of elaborate draperies and potted palms suggesting a distinctly eastern exoticism, a whiff of Turkey or maybe Morocco rather than Poland. It was not by the sea but rather located at the source of a hot spring. One could bathe in this healing water, though I doubted that anyone in the S.D. Warren party had ever attempted it. The spring water was bottled and could be purchased from fashionable grocers.

Alex and I came down the staircase together to find Father being chatted up by Chuck Kleber. He had bright blue eyes, a blond brushcut, and a boyish smile revealing not-quite-perfect teeth: a gap between an incisor and his eyetooth gave him a look that was both sexy and slightly feral. He turned to me and winked as he proffered a small square hand, his grip firm, his tone teasing. "Finally, I get to meet Junior. No sense trying to deny this one, Ken. He's got your long head. In more ways than one, from what I hear. Let me get you guys a drink. Your poison the same as the old man's?" He didn't wait for my reply but wheeled away to the bar.

I had heard my father talk about Chuck as the probable next president of S.D. Warren. Chuck had called on K.M. ten years ago and negotiated the franchise, but by the time I joined the company Chuck had been promoted into the ranks of management. He was now the youngest sales manager the company had ever had.

I could see why Father liked Chuck. He made everyone he talked to feel like an insider, one of the boys in a select company. His audacity in calling Father by his first name, which even Alex after thirty years in the company had never essayed, was balanced by a recognition of him as a significant player, a "long head." Chuck's flattery was subtle enough not to be objectionable. He was back in a flash with two Scotch-and-sodas. Alex had taught me the drill: two vodka martinis before lunch, two Scotch-and-sodas before dinner, two glasses of wine with the meal, two Scotches or brandies after. My constitution had gotten used to this; I could usually handle it and still not wake up with a hangover, which racked up points for me.

Chuck granted us another ten minutes, hinting that there was to be a major announcement in the course of these meetings and making sure we were in good hands before he moved on. We talked with other merchants from Chicago, Cleveland, Philadelphia, all of whom seemed more or less interchangeable, and a man from St. Louis named Sam who quickly picked me up on his pronunciation of the name. "Well, ah guess you Canucks cain be allowed to say St. Louie if you want, after all you founded the place, but those of us as lives there nowaday say Saint Louis with an S." He was a big genial man with the air of a Southern planter. He wore a light tan-coloured suit and a string tie and his grey moustache was stained with tobacco. He and K.M. seemed to be on genial terms, and he sat at the same table when we went into the dining room for dinner.

The meal was excellent, led off by a dozen oysters apiece, followed by clam chowder and lobster. There was a good New York wine, a fluffy chocolate dessert, brandy, and cigars. And of course there was a speech by the company president welcoming us to Poland Spring for the thirty-sixth consecutive year and stressing the long-standing ties that had been established and carefully maintained between "Mother Warren" and her merchants, a far-flung group of independent businessmen, leaders in their industry, dedicated to high standards of quality and service, stability but also innovation, and the search for an ever-more-efficient technology to contribute to the ancient and honourable craft of the printer.

The address wound up with a promise that whatever happened in their industry, the S.D. Warren Company was determined to maintain its independence, because only a small organization dedicated to quality could keep its integrity. "Lose that and we've lost it all." The ensuing round of applause was undercut by Alex whispering in my ear as he puffed on his cigar. "You have to hand it to these guys. They're so full of crap it comes out their ears but they've got great taste when it comes to stogies."

After dinner we were approached by the Koffler Brothers, two small, animated New York Jews who had inherited the most prestigious merchant house in Manhattan. The initial talk revolved around Leonard's tie, a gold and magenta designer creation.

"Would you believe anyone would pay twenty-five dollars for a thing like that?" His brother Lionel arched his beetling eyebrows.

"It's an artwork. You wouldn't understand. Only I've slopped chocolate on it. Ruined. I'll never wear it again." Leonard's face was a comic mask of angst.

"Listen to what I'm telling you. Wear a bow."

"I can't tie a bow. That's why I wear loafers."

"Loafers!" Lionel rolled his eyes.

"You got to try this liqueur, Millefiore. Fabuloso. I discovered it on a buying trip to Europe last spring. Plus I checked out a new source for handmade paper. This French company *Papeteries d'Arches.* Extraordinaire. I got them exclusive for the eastern seaboard, but you should tie them up for Canada."

"And it only cost you ten grand to find them."

"As Grandpa used to say, 'You can't sell from an empty wagon, bubbele.' People pay us top dollar and why? Because we've got product nobody else can match."

"What can I say, he's right. Leonard understands fashion. And you know what? More and more nowadays, that's the game."

The Kofflers came across a bit like a commercial version of the Marx Brothers. They flaunted their Jewishness in this wasp bastion, confident in the knowledge that they were urban aristocrats surrounded by provincial boobs. Their extravagance was calculated to astonish, but it was backed by the knowledge that when it came to high-priced and consequently profitable lines, they outsold everyone else in the room.

The evening wound down early. We were all expected to be in meetings at eight o'clock the next morning. Before I headed upstairs, Leonard came over to me. "Who you golfing with tomorrow?"

"I'm not much of a golfer."

"Me neither. Tell you what. Let's play hooky. I'll take you to lunch at a little place I know over on the coast. Meet me on the veranda at twelve thirty." He reached up to put a neat little hand on my shoulder and then bounded up the stairs two at a time.

Up in our room, Alex produced a bottle of whisky from a leather pouch and poured out two glasses. "Those Koffler Brothers are something, aren't they? Smart, though. Most of the guys here are not that bright. The thing is you don't need great brains to be a salesman. Just clean shoes, a big smile, and a lot of hunger."

"I'm surprised you'd say that. I always thought you really enjoyed what you do."

"It's called adaptation. I'm a chameleon."

"A smart chameleon."

"I wasn't exactly a brilliant student. I didn't have a special talent like your old man. He can literally make figures dance. I was just determined to get ahead. See, in the '20s and '30s everybody wanted to be a salesman. Just like in your generation everybody wants to be a lawyer. These things go in cycles. Next it'll be stockbrokers."

"Me and my friends wanted to be writers."

"Go ahead and write. Nobody's stopping you."

"I'm working ten, twelve hours a day and I've got three kids. I'm losing time. This isn't what I want to do for the rest of my life. I mean, it's different for you. You've achieved your goal."

"I've come to terms with my situation."

"What do you mean?"

"When I was a kid I thought I wanted to be a social worker. Then the war started and I wanted to be a soldier. I tried to enlist but I had such bum eyes they wouldn't take me. So I went to work for a munitions factory. Lucky for me. All the best brains were in the army getting their butts rained on for two years in England while I got catapulted into management in a few weeks and found out how the business world really operates. Simple. You set a clear target and you go after it. Most of the guys you work with don't understand that so you got a real advantage."

"Maybe that's what I need. A clear target."

"You really don't want to run the company?"

"You think I could?"

"Why not?"

"K.M. doesn't think I can handle it."

"You ever talk to him about it?"

"Not in so many words."

"Time you did then."

"I don't know."

"Don't get me wrong. I'm not in a big hurry, you know. I'm having a good time."

"You're not worried about where you'll be ten years from now?"

"I'll work for K.M. as long as he wants me to. And if he doesn't want me, there's other people who do."

"Would you work for me?"

"Depends what the deal is."

"You're a smart cookie, Mr. Smith."

"No smarter than you. That's why we can talk like this. You want another?"

"I think K.M. would take a very dim view of me going missing for breakfast the first morning here."

"Right." Alex put the bottle away. We climbed into our beds and within thirty seconds I was out like a light.

The next morning we were talked at by several Warren executives including a winking, smiling Chuck. A new line of coated paper especially designed for book publishers was introduced. A series of advertising and promotional pieces was unveiled. We were told once again how fortunate we were to be members of the Warren family. The virtues of the small, flexible, independent company over the rigid, giant corporation were hammered home once again. Then a panel made up of prominent Warren merchants regurgitated the party line.

We broke for lunch and I wandered out onto the veranda. The man from St. Louis offered me a cigar. "Y'all have a good meetin'?"

"You didn't go?"

"Naah. When you been at as many of these darn ol' clambakes as I been, gets pretty monotonous. Ah'm on their Council, see, so ah ain't goin' to larn much by goin' to meetin's. Ah just come here to be sociable."

Leonard bustled up to them. "How you doing, Sam?"

"Pretty good for an ol' fellow. That's some coat you got there, Lenny."

"Bought it on the Via Condotti in Rome. You like it?"

"Make a nice horse blanket."

"You're a character, Sam."

"Ah believe ah am."

"You work at it, am I right? Ready to travel?" Leonard didn't wait for my answer but skipped down the steps and across the lawn to his bottle green Jaguar convertible.

"One thing you have to give old Sam. He's got style. Nice jacket. But then I have a thing for English tweed."

"I think it's Irish.

"Never been to Ireland."

"It's a great place if you're into horses or theatre."

"You ride?"

"No, but I used to act."

"Why'd you give it up?"

"I didn't think I was good enough. I still do a bit of directing."

"You should try your luck in New York."

"I have this little family business I'm involved with in Toronto."

"I know what you mean. But don't let it get in your way. It's supposed to work for you, not the other way round."

We whipped through rolling hills and eventually arrived at a smallish resort town on the coast. White clapboard houses with shutters lined the streets. There were old-fashioned shops, a drug store, a candy store, a store selling nautical gear. We drove through the town and up a little hill to a sea captain's house with a widow's walk on top.

Leonard hopped out of his car and up the front steps, where he was greeted effusively by a middle-aged man wearing an ascot and a shabby blazer. "Leonard, dear boy, you should have told me you were coming. There's no one in the kitchen but me and young Danilo. I hope you're not in a hurry."

"We've got all afternoon. This is Martin, a friend from Canada. I want him to taste one of your soufflés. This man makes the best soufflés this side of the Atlantic."

"Come in and sit down. I'll start you off with a couple martinis, shall I?

"You bet, Henry."

We were led into a small dining room furnished with tasselled hangings and ornate nineteenth-century chairs. We drank martinis and smoked,

Leonard lighting one cigarette from another. He smoked Gauloises and the room soon filled with their pungent smell.

"Henry used to run a modern dance company. We met when I thought I wanted to be a dancer."

"Really? Why'd you give it up?"

"They didn't think I was good enough."

"Who's they?"

"Martha Graham and her entourage. I trained with her for two years. Henry encouraged me but I never succeeded in getting into her company. I danced for a short time with a somewhat less illustrious organization. My grandfather came to see me and told me I was making a fool of myself and he'd disinherit me if I didn't quit immediately and come into his business."

"You knuckled under?

"I was fired a week later when I dropped my partner and she broke her ankle. It seemed like a sign." He blew two perfect smoke rings that hung in the air between us.

After our third martini an exquisite sorrel soup arrived, served by Danilo, a striking but odd-looking young man with the erect carriage and slightly stilted walk of a trained dancer. He explained that he was working for Henry while he recovered from a knee injury. He lingered for a few minutes while he and Leonard traded gossip about the dance world.

"You obviously manage to keep up your connections with your old colleagues."

"I'm on Graham's board. She's a parody of what she was but she's become a huge success. What becomes a legend most? Answer: an early demise. Still, she has fun in her way and so do I. I decided if I couldn't be an artist, I was going to have a good time. And I do. Ah, here's the soufflé."

Henry brought it in himself and Danilo followed with a bottle of Sancerre. The souffle was indeed remarkable, light but slightly runny with a unique taste that neither Leonard nor I could identify but which Henry revealed was a combination of pumpkin and sage. Leonard regaled us with descriptions of several remarkable meals he'd had in Lyons, in Milan, in San Francisco. It was four o'clock when the dessert arrived, a crème brûlée with pears and blackberries. It was followed by two enormous snifters of cognac. Leonard suddenly asked me my age.

"Thirty-one."

"You could still do it."

"What?"

"Have a career in the theatre. You don't want to flog paper for the next thirty years, do you?"

"You can't make a living in the theatre in Canada."

"Come to New York. You could stay with me. I have quite good connections. I could introduce you to Kazan, Strasberg, all kinds of people."

"I do have a wife and children."

"So do I."

"Okay, but . . ."

"I'm not suggesting a liaison." He smiled at me through a haze of exhaled smoke.

We drove back by another road past some pretty old farmhouses and discovered we had a mutual interest in Stephen Sondheim. Leonard knew him and was putting some money into his next show, much against his brother's advice; Lionel had backed Cole Porter's *Kiss Me, Kate* and done very nicely out of it, but he was convinced Sondheim's work would never make money.

I was taking a nap when Alex came into the room in his golf clothes. As a golfer he was the perfect salesman; good enough not to embarrass his partner, but not good enough to be a serious threat. He habitually lost by a few strokes and did it with grace and good humour. Today, however, he'd been playing with three American merchants and he'd ended up with the low score. He didn't bother to hide his enjoyment as we showered and climbed into our suits.

After two generous Scotches dinner was a slightly hazy affair: a blurry procession of corn chowder, roast beef, and pumpkin pie washed down by a steady stream of California's answer to Nuits St. Georges. Again there was a speech from one of the senior Warren executives, this time anecdotal and jocular, drawing chuckles and guffaws as we sat over coffee and cigars. Somehow I managed to keep my eyes open but another thirty years of this loomed up before my addled brain as a decidedly gloomy prospect.

As soon as the speech was finished I stumbled out to the veranda to fill my lungs with sharpish night air. I was surprised by Chuck. "Not indulging in one of our Cuban stogies?"

"I figure I should go easy. Leonard Koffler took me over to Oqunquit for lunch and we polished off two martinis, a bottle of wine and two brandies."

"Manhattan style. Can't keep up myself. I'm just a poor little orphan boy from upstate Vermont."

"Really?"

"Yessir. So Lenny Koffler's taken you under his wing. He ask you to come stay with him in the Big Apple?"

"As a matter of fact, he did."

"Lenny likes to show off. Needs an audience. Lionel too. I guess it's natural to the breed. Lenny tell you he used to be a chorus boy at Radio City? His old man cut him off without a plugged nickel so he dragged his ass back home. Still, he's an operator. He and Lionel sell a lot of Mother Warren's product."

"I'll bet they do."

"You might learn a few things from Lenny even Alex Smith doesn't know about."

"I've learned a lot from Alex."

"He doesn't tell you everything he knows, I bet. You want to watch that guy. He's just a little too sharp for my money. I kind of hinted as much to Ken but he seems to really buy Alex's act. He's a shrewd bugger, your old man, but he's got his blind spots."

"When he likes somebody, he really likes them. You must know that."

Chuck winked at me. "It's funny with some of these older guys. It's almost like they get a crush on you, hunh? Ken and me, Lenny and you."

"Leonard can't be much older than I am."

"He's fifty-two, I happen to know. Of course he's had his face lifted. And his ass too, likely. Hair transplants. The whole bit. Anyhow it doesn't hurt to play along with these guys, as long as you don't let them get you alone in the shower, hunh?"

"You think that's what Lenny's after?"

"You're a good kid, Junior. Keep your eyes open. Especially with that guy Smith."

Chuck threw his cigar butt into the flower bed, gave me another wink and headed back into the saloon. I looked out across the wide lawn and up at the stars.

"Good advice. They dish it out like it was candy. It's almost like bein' back in school," came out of the darkness and I recognized the drawling accent of old Sam from St. Louis. "Thing is, ah wouldn't trust that kid Chuck neither. He's a bit of a twister himself. You havin' a good time here, young fella?"

"Okay."

"You don't like the paper trade, do you?"

"It's been good to me."

"Yo' daddy's business must be doin' okay if you got Chuck and Lenny courtin' you."

"It is doing okay."

"Enjoy it while it lasts. There's big changes comin'. Take my word for it. All that guff about small independent companies? The ones is any good is goin' to be gobbled up by big corporations within the next ten years. Maximum. Startin' with Mother Warren. They're negotiatin' a deal with a much bigger company right now."

"You sure?"

"Sure, ah'm sure."

"I guess if you're on their council, you ought to know.'

"You bet ah know. I tol' my grandson he better get into the brokerage business. The time you could make any real money as an independent merchant is oveh. The whole world's goin' to be run by about twenty big international giants befo' this century draws to a close."

"You think so?"

"Sure as shootin'. If you and yo' daddy are smart you'll peddle yo' business while it's still makin' a tidy profit. They'll let yo' run it for a while if you want to do that. Meantimes yo' invest in the stock market and get yo'selfs a nice tidy income. Yo' won't be sorry. Now you want to do me a favour, son? Yo' go in there and get me a triple shot of Jack Daniels. Yo' ever drink bourbon up your way? You should give it a whirl."

I went inside and got two triple bourbons. Sam was right about the whisky; maybe he was right about the future of the paper business too. By the time I got back to him he was already in conversation with another old codger. The conversation was about duck-hunting and I rapidly lost track of it. I staggered upstairs and fell into bed. I was almost asleep when Alex appeared. While he was undressing I told him about my conversation with old Sam.

"He's a smart old coot, that one."

"You think he's right?"

"I think we could sell the company for a pile of dough if we wanted to."

"If K.M. wanted to, but he doesn't."

"The key to the whole thing is what you want."

"How about what you want?"

"Okay. I'd like to be president, have a shot at running the place, sure. But I have a strong sense of obligation to your father. He arranged for me to buy shares and he gave me the job. As long as he's around I'll continue to honour that obligation."

"I guess I ought to feel the same way."

"You got to dope that out for yourself, kiddo."

"Yeah."

I lay awake pondering this but not for long. The day's alcohol intake caught up with me and in no time, Alex and I were snoring in harmony.

Next morning I woke with a colossal hangover. My temples were throbbing, my throat was parched and someone seemed to have driven a skewer through my left eye. I got up and showered, shaved, and dressed, then made my way to the breakfast table but it was no use. I managed to drink a glass of orange juice, then went to the washroom and puked. I crawled up the stairs and got back into bed. Room service brought me a bucket of ice. I wrapped some of it in a towel and put it on my forehead and lay there in agony for a couple of hours. My conversations with Leonard, Chuck, old Sam, and Alex slurred through my mind. I tried to think of nothing. Eventually I went back to sleep.

I was awakened by my father's voice telling me to get up. He looked at his watch. It was four o'clock in the afternoon.

"I didn't bring you here to lie in bed. I thought you had the sense to know when you've had enough."

"I missed one meeting."

"You've missed a whole day. Everyone's asking where you are."

"Can't you just say I'm sick? People do get sick."

"What do you think is going to become of you?" The thin tone of exasperation was an echo from childhood when my father had often posed this question to me, letting me know I had failed him, failed to be what he wanted in a son. Twenty-five years later nothing had changed. Except that now he added, "How do you think you're ever going to run a business?"

"You don't trust me to run the business?"

"I'd hoped that you and Bill between you might have the qualities, might complement each other —"

"Bill's never going to come into the business, you might as well face it."

"I thought you might persuade him, talk to him —"

"I have talked to him. Many times. He's made up his mind. You're not the only one with willpower."

"I won't pretend I'm not disappointed, Martin. I know you've worked hard at selling even though you're not a natural like Alex or Chuck. At least in the first years. But now . . ."

"Why don't you hire Chuck to run the business if you're so crazy about him?"

"While you run off to New York to dance around with a couple of Jewboys? Leonard Koffler talked to me about some idea the two of you cooked up. I didn't get the point of it."

"I could learn a few things from Leonard. Just like I've learned a lot from Alex."

"Alex is a good salesman —"

"You don't think he could run the business?"

"He doesn't have your education."

"He's smart, ambitious —"

"Alex owes everything to me."

"If you don't give him a chance to run the company, he may go over to the competition and take a lot of our biggest customers with him. Have you thought about that?"

"Has he told you that?"

"Not in so many words."

"I will have to consider this. I'll see you in my room after dinner. I hope you'll be sober." He turned and walked out of the room.

Alex came in half an hour later. "You picked a good day to lie low. A morning of complete crapola. I went golfing in the rain just to get away from the bullshit." He pulled the whisky bottle out of its leather sleeve and proceeded to pour out two glasses.

"I don't think I'd better.'

"Hair of the dog. Believe me, I know what I'm talking about."

"What the hell?" I rolled the first shot around in his mouth. It tasted great and gave me courage. Dutch courage, as they used to say. "K.M. came by and read me the riot act. Told me I'd never be fit to run the business."

"Really?

"I suggested he hire Chuck."

"You're kidding."

"No."

"What did he say?"

"Said he'd have to think about it."

"It's not as though I can't work for somebody else."

"Maybe I'll come with you. Start our own business."

"You're not serious?"

"No, I'm not. You know me. I'm never serious. That's one of the things about me that drives K.M. crazy."

"I think it's one of the main things you've got going. Get your duds on. We're having dinner with old Sam."

Old Sam hailed me as he came downstairs and motioned me over. In a voice like bourbon running over broken glass he whispered, "Smart fella, takin' the day off. Best thing about this shindig is bellyin' up to the bar come evenin'-time. Better have a shot of Wild Turkey."

I took a sip. It tasted good.

"Ah had a mighty interestin' talk with that fella Smith. Told him if y'all want to find a buyer stateside ah could probably find somebody who'd come up with a pretty sweet deal. 'Course ah'd want my commission." He gave a gleeful wheeze. "Ah'm serious, though. Yo' want to keep yo' eyes open in the next couple of yeahs. Like ah told you things is goin' to change right smartly."

Leonard came over briefly to tell me he'd had a word with my father who hadn't been very receptive. "He's a tough cookie. Well, it was just an idea. Keep in touch." He strutted off to greet someone else, highball glass and cigarette clutched in one hand, leaving the other free to gesticulate.

I enjoyed dinner, more oysters followed by lobster Newburg. I drank a fair amount of wine, thinking that as stone cold sobriety was no longer an option, I might as well face my father well fortified.

At ten o'clock, K.M. was sitting in his room wearing slippers and a dressing-gown. He indicated where I was to sit. "I've thought about our conversation. I hope you have too."

"Yes."

"I was hoping to take you to the Paper Trade meetings in Montebello next year but your behaviour here suggests your heart is not really in the business."

"I do have other ambitions."

"You don't want to run the business?"

"Are you willing to let me try?"

"Certainly not. Unless you're prepared to give it your undivided attention. And don't think I don't know about all your theatrical doings. You're out of the office half the time."

"That's an exaggeration."

"Unless you are willing to put the business ahead of everything else as I have . . ."

"I can't honestly promise that."

"If that is your decision, I hope you are prepared to face the consequences."

"I guess so."

"I've thought things over. I feel obliged to give Bill a considerable sum to compensate for the value of your shares. You know I've always tried to treat you two boys fairly."

"You don't think there's a chance he may not want to take your money? He likes to feel he's made his own way."

"That's one of the things I admire about Bill. Still, I can always set up a trust fund for him and his heirs. I haven't talked to Alex about any of this but I will when I'm ready."

"When do you imagine that might be?'

Father ignored the question. "It's obviously impossible for any of you or even all of you to buy out my interest unless I guarantee your loans and I don't believe it would be good for any of you simply to be handed the business like that. So I suppose I must start looking for an outside buyer."

"When will you do that?"

"I think first we should consider going public to establish a firm value for the shares. It could take two or three years but I have plenty of time. For now I expect you to carry on with your sales work. You have an obligation to me and of course to your family. Now I think you should go to bed. We should be on the road by eight in the morning if we're going to be home at a respectable hour."

I went back downstairs and had another whisky. The pressure had been replaced by a sense of emptiness, a widening gap I could have leaped over, could still leap over. I could go back up to Father's room and recant. Instead I ordered another whisky.

When I went up to bed Alex was already in his pyjamas. He poured us a final nightcap as I recounted the gist of my conversation with my father. Alex grinned at me.

"Sounds like if we all hang in for a bit everybody's going to get what he wants."

"Something like that."

"You're sure you're okay with all this?"

"Yes."

"You don't feel you're letting the old man down?"

"Are you kidding? After all my work he's just going to hand Bill probably a couple of hundred thousand bucks. And he tries to tell me that's fair."

"True."

"Well — it's his money. I guess he can do what he wants with it."

"He hasn't been able to buy what he really wants."

"You think I take some satisfaction in knowing that?"

"You've engineered this very neatly. You're quite the little schemer, kiddo."

"What about you?"

"Takes one to know one."

THE ISLES OF GREECE

In 1970, Father sold the paper company. I might have stayed on at a good salary and even risen in the ranks of the big conglomerate that bought us out; the competition among the younger executives didn't seem particularly formidable. Or I might have taken my nice little chunk of capital and turned my mind to making money on the market. Instead I decided to continue on in the rather ill-defined and poorly paid job at the University of Toronto. But before I faced the alfresco frolics and factional ambushes I was destined to encounter in the groves of academe, I decided to take Judy and the kids for a six-month sabbatical in Europe. My father was horrified that I was going to begin my new job with a half-year holiday, even though it was unpaid.

We opted to spend half of our time in Greece, half in Italy. We had no knowledge of either language, nor any very strong connections in either country, but somehow I felt this was a chance to explore our cultural beginnings. I had studied Latin for three years in high school, and even, for six months at special eight a.m. classes, classical Greek. I had read Plato and Euripides in translation and bits of Caesar, Virgil, and, by far my favourite, Catullus in Latin, but in choosing these destinations I was influenced much less by my Latin master Mr. Breslove or my philosophy professor George Grube than by Dorothy Goulding, director of the Toronto Children Players.

The plays we performed for Mrs. G. as children were often set in a halcyon Mediterranean world of her imagination. She told us the legends of Narcissus and Baucis and Philemon, showed us paintings by Botticelli and Fra Filippo Lippi, but her powerful perception of this world was idiosyncratic and unique. In my mind it had been augmented by images of Isadora dancing in the Parthenon, Savonarola burning the Vanities, Disney's azure gods and magenta nymphs frolicking to the strains of Beethoven's "Pastoral Symphony" in *Fantasia*, Fellini's sybarites draining life to the dregs in the rotting piazzas and palazzos of Rome. To some extent Judy shared this vision: together we would bring it to life for the kids. Whether they were ready for this was not a question we asked ourselves; how could they fail to be enriched by contact with the sources of Western culture? After all they were our kids, weren't they?

In fact the kids were the perfect age for this kind of excursion, out of diapers but not yet into drugs. Sarah was a rather serious twelve-year-old, a tomboy who played both the cello and touch football with her brothers: she was already doing bold and fanciful drawings full of eccentric animals and secret smiling angels. Ben was ten, an ebullient clown with an ability to charm adults even as he sent them up; Guy at nine was the faithful sidekick, but with a sharper, more theoretical cast of mind than his brother. The kids squabbled of course, but essentially they were friends and because we had both worked and left them to their own devices a lot they had developed their own ways of settling their differences. They ran a rough-and-ready little democracy among themselves that I thought Pericles would probably have understood and approved.

We went to New York to pick up our long flight to Athens. Judy's brother came out to meet us at Kennedy, his greetings full of undisguised envy, which I recognized as a sort of seal of artistic endorsement. We were the picture of affluent liberation: me in a suede Nehru jacket and tomato-red velour bell-bottoms, Judy in a hooded cape of black velvet, bordered with multicoloured braid and lined with aquamarine silk, the kids with their shoulder-length hair and outfits of faded denim, tie-dyed cotton and Indian silk. Judy lay down on the floor of the airport to take her nose drops, while the rest of us lolled on a bench giggling and gossiping, ostentatiously impervious to the curiosity of onlookers who were sure we must be international celebrities.

We were somewhat less perky by the time we arrived in Athens ten hours later. It was raining; the town was grey and bleak and the officials checking our passports were not impressed by our hip get-ups; in fact, they were down-right suspicious. Long hair had not yet hit Greece, but they had heard of drug-smugglers. Fortunately for us the Greeks do have respect for the family. If we hadn't had the kids with us, they might have given us a much harder time. After a certain amount of mutual incomprehension our passports were stamped, our bags collected, and we were on our way to a small hotel that had been recommended to us by some Greek friends in Toronto. It turned out to be a dump in a depressing part of town, Omonia, which, although we didn't know it, was the red light district. In any case, they had no rooms for us in spite of the fact we'd made reservations weeks ago. We were to learn that making reservations in Greece is a waste of time. The modern Greeks are empiricists; they don't believe you exist until you're standing in front of them.

I demanded to see the manager. He appeared after about twenty minutes. He made no apologies but immediately sat down and started to question the kids. When the boys insisted they were boys in spite of their long hair, he started to talk to them about football. He ordered up double shots of Metaxas for all of us. Liberated though we were, we didn't think the kids should be drinking brandy, so we corralled their glasses. Half an hour later we were amiably smashed and all chatting happily. The manager's brother joined us. He had been to Montreal to visit his wife's sister. It was a fine city, good food, beautiful girls, but too cold in the winter. After another three quarters of an hour it was revealed they had found rooms for us in another hotel, five blocks away. A very nice hotel, almost as good as theirs.

I asked them to call a cab, but they wouldn't hear of it. The manager's brother and two of his sons helped us carry our bags to the new hotel, where we were all offered more Metaxas. To refuse would have been unthinkably rude. The manager of the new hotel, a cousin of the other manager, had been to Toronto and had a cousin in the printing business, who printed menus for all the Greek restaurants there. Perhaps I knew him. Indeed I did. More Metaxas. We fell into our beds in an alcoholic haze at six thirty in the evening and awoke to the sound of chirping sparrows at seven thirty the next morning.

First the Parthenon. I think it was the British art critic and great cultural guru Lord Clark of *Civilisation*, his omnipresent television program at the time, who said certain works are so primary they have universal appeal. Nobody can remain unmoved by the Sistine Chapel, Handel's "Messiah," *Hamlet*. The Parthenon was like this for me. I had spent rainy afternoons peering at the tiny black and white illustrations of the *Discobalus* and *Laocoon* in the *Books of Knowledge* when I was in grade school; then my friend Dick and I happened upon the Dudley Fitts translation of *Lysistrata* when we were sixteen and fancied ourselves ultimate connoisseurs of dirty literature. I had read *Symposium* right through the night by candlelight in my third year at Trinity with my friend Troop, both of us turned on by a witty eroticism we were too stifled by schoolboy convention to emulate. It was thrilling just to be standing among those shattered marble columns looking out over Athens, though the modern city had a scruffy, rundown workaday air that did little to evoke the world of Phidias, Aristophanes, or Plato.

In the afternoon it rained. We hit the museum. I delivered lectures in front of the statues of Poseidon and the two youths pulled from the sea at Marathon and Anticythera. Guy asked about the Peloponnesian War and I delivered a streamlined version of what I could remember from Herodotus. Then dinner in the Plaka. Ben quizzed the waiters about the various dishes on the menu and immediately began to imitate their accents. He learned to say "please" and "thank you," "hello" and "goodbye," "yes" and "no," "how much," and "where's the washroom." None of us ever got much further than that with Greek. It was too far from any language we knew. Ben summed it up when he said, "It's like they've got a different word for everything."

Avid for Greek culture, we went that night to a small theatre to see a production of Aristophanes' The Birds done by the company of Karolos Koun, an avant-garde director whose name I had heard bandied about in academic theatre seminars. My explanation of the plot didn't mean much to the kids, but the production itself was quite a hit with them. All the characters wore fanciful bird masks and outrageous feathered costumes that exposed a maximum of bare flesh. The actors did pratfalls and played practical jokes on each other. They flew, battled in the air like spitfires, simulated copulation, and even released splattery bird droppings on each other. Sort of a cross between Sesame Street and the Folies Bergère with pop music and lyrics in classical Greek.

Afterwards, one of the actors rushed out and greeted us as we stood in the street. Alexis was a handsome young guy in his late twenties with a reasonable command of English and ambitions to work in North America. When he heard I was a theatre director, he became extremely expansive and offered to take us backstage where we would learn how the various trick effects were done. It was very crowded, so we couldn't all go at once. Perhaps the boys first, as the women in the cast took longer to get changed and would still be in their dressing rooms. Catching him stroke Ben's hair with a sudden deft flick of the wrist, I realized this might be a learning experience the kids weren't quite ready for. We thanked him and headed back to our hotel through a continuing downpour.

The next morning at breakfast, it was apparent the kids felt we had "done" Athens. I had figured on maybe ten days in this cradle of civilization, but my prodigies had sucked it dry in twenty-four hours. What now? I decided to phone Ian Vorres, my Greek friend from college days. Ian had seemed decidedly exotic even at Trinity, which encouraged the eccentric and arcane. He gave elegant cocktail parties and took out the best-looking girls, but obviously considered Toronto social life rather gauche. He let it be known that in Athens his father entertained on his yacht such celebrities as Melina Mercouri and Maria Callas. We thought this was bullshit. If Ian was so well connected in Greece, what was he doing in Toronto? Ian explained he didn't want to be a businessman like his father and brother, he wanted to be a writer. And he did indeed get a job as a reporter with the *Hamilton Spectator* and publish a book, a biography of his dear friend the Grand Duchess Olga, last of the Romanovs. Then his older brother was killed in a car crash, and he announced he must go home and run the family business for his aged and grieving father.

I had heard that Ian was not amused when people turned up at his front door unexpectedly, so I had written ahead saying we would be in Athens. Even so, I hesitated to call him. But at once he came on the line. "I have been expecting you every moment. You must come to my house in the country. It is not yet finished; it is a mound of rubble but you will forgive this, I know. An hour's drive. I send my car. Not my big car, forgive me, the little one, but it is quite comfortable, only there is no bar. I am giving a little lunch party. Very simple. Only thirty people. Some of them are quite horrible, but it is too late to put them off. And one or two are mildly amusing. So my car will call for you in fifteen minutes, yes?"

The car did arrive in fifteen minutes. It was a Rolls. We drove out into the country, climbing slowly up into the Attic hills through vineyards and olive groves tended by gnarled old men who saluted us respectfully as we passed. Ian's house was vast, and proved to be made up of two old farmhouses cunningly connected by a modern Greek architect. White plaster, natural wood beams, large areas of plate glass. Ian was at the door to greet us and take us inside where a collection of fashionably dressed people were standing around with glasses in their hands, chattering in half a dozen languages. We were introduced to the Italian ambassador, a Hollywood producer, the minister of finance. "Alas, Melina is not with us today. She is in love. Again."

Ian was delighted to see the children and immediately made friends with them. He took them through the house and out to the stables where they met his groom, Spyros, and the groom's three sons. In ten minutes they were all mounted on donkeys and were riding around the paddock. We headed back to the house as Ian explained how he had found this property. "It is the original farm of Demosthenes. When I hear this, I know that I must have it.

Ever since I come back to Greece I search like Demosthenes for an honest man. And like Demosthenes I am sorry, I do not find him. So I learn to live with the people I do find. But I can say I am happy here. The best is to go to the taverna in my village in the evening and talk with the old men. They are all philosophers. Now you must come and drink some of my wine. Frankly, it is the best wine in Greece." And frankly, it was the best wine we had in Greece, dry and light with a slight acerbic aftertaste, rather like Ian's conversation.

We did meet some amusing people; Americans, because we spoke English, and actors, because I was interested in theatre and so was Ian. When I told him about seeing *The Birds* the night before and meeting Alexis, he laughed. "Yes, a talented young man, but a little bit too desperate to be really the good salesman. But Karolos will teach him. A very clever man. Tough, sophisticated, relentless. You know that when I am sixteen I acted for Karolos. He was very charming then, not the dictator he is become today. Very charming, very sexy. He is the first man try to make me."

"And did he succeed?"

Ian brushed the question aside. "I would not be what I am today, if I had not known Karolos."

Ian seemed genuinely concerned that our stay in Greece should be successful. There was little of interest in Athens beyond the obvious attractions we had already taken in, and the weather would be uncertain for the next month. "You must at once fly to Rhodos. Take a house there. Don't worry about making arrangements, just get on a plane and go. Then visit Crete, Santorini, Hydra. Come back to Athens in a month. The weather will be better and you can tour the Peloponnese. I will see about a car. But tomorrow I must leave for three weeks. I go to Cyprus to talk with Makarios and then on see the shah in Tehran. It is very wearing, this little business of mine." Was he really on intimate terms with these people and, if so, what kind of business was Ian engaged in? It took me a while to figure this one out, but once I did it was obvious. He'd moved on from olive oil and beet sugar to more strategic commodities.

The town of Rhodes lay under a wash of spring sunshine, dreaming of a grander past. Gone its Colossus, its Templar knights, its Venetian grandees. The grey stones of its mediaeval fortress towered over streets that were empty, smelling of urine and neglect. The white sands of its beaches strewn with drying nets, ragged with dead seaweed, splotched with tar. Above the town the hills were coming to life, the almond trees white with blossoms. We feasted the first night at a restaurant run by seven brothers. We were the only diners. At one point all seven brothers stood around the table talking with us. They suggested various places we might stay on the island. At the end of the meal they set five bottles of Metaxas on the table, one for each of us, and sat down to talk. I don't remember how we got back to our hotel.

The next morning we hired a taxi to drive us to Lindos. We rounded a bend in the road and there it was sliding down a green hillside towards the blue-green sea, its medieval houses white and gleaming in the sun. As we turned into the town square a dozen idlers came to life and surrounded us, ready to hawk their wares. The most persuasive was a young man called Adonis. His face was worthy of his name. He had a house to rent on a cliff at the edge of town. He got into the taxi and we drove there through streets so narrow we scraped their sides, so bumpy we were bruised for days.

The house was small, four whitewashed rooms with tile floors, narrow beds, straight wooden chairs. A kitchen with a gas stove, a sink with a cold-water tap, and a plain wooden table. The only embellishments were the curtains, elaborate screens of handmade lace at every window. We rented the house for a month for, as I remember it, one hundred and fifty dollars. Adonis literally did a little dance of triumph as he helped us unload our bags. The taxi rumbled away over the cobblestones. Adonis told us he lived in the next house with his family. His mother and his sisters would visit us tomorrow and help us with anything we needed.

We sat on the steps of our little house and began to take in our surroundings. To our left, bordering the rocky road along the edge of the cliff, was a straggle of two or three other small villas and then the town, closely packed white houses, cobblestone streets, wisps of smoke ascending from chimneys, green branches sprouting into leaf. Above us to the right, a hill crowned with a ruin, broken pillars glinting in the late afternoon sun. Below us a path leading down to the Mediterranean, white sand and glimmering water. An arm of land reached out on either side encircling our bay, a natural harbour, calm and inviting. As old as time, but still as if untouched. We sat in a quiet row, drinking it in. This was what we had come so far to find.

There were no hotels in Lindos, nor even any restaurants, only the taverna, where the men of the town went in the evenings to play cards, gossip and drink. Women never went there, nor children. The first night when we turned up for dinner, one of the older men lectured me on the impropriety of bringing my wife and children into such a place. I didn't understand his words, but his moral fervour gave me a clear message. I argued we hadn't had a chance to shop and we were hungry. The owner took us to a dark corner as far removed as possible from the regular patrons and set places for us. We ate in isolation, ignored by the men as though we were invisible. We would eat there often, but no one ever came over to our table to talk or even greeted us when we entered the taverna. If, however, I stayed on after Judy took the kids home to bed, I was made welcome at the men's tables, offered Metaxa and ouzo, and encouraged to play backgammon. Sometimes there was music from the radio and once a very excited broadcast with a lot of shouting. I asked if there was some sort of insurrection going on in Athens and was met with looks of amused deprecation. What I was hearing was a football game.

After a week or so when the men realized the boys were actually boys, they began to take an interest in them. (I think they believed their long hair had some sort of peculiar religious significance; their own priests had long hair, though they did their best to hide it by tying it up in little buns like Mammy Yokum.) The men allowed Ben and Guy to watch their backgammon games, though not to play. Sarah was not even allowed to watch. She should have been at home in the kitchen learning to peel and scrub, they believed.

Some nights the men danced to the *bazouki* music on the radio. I was never able to figure out what got them started but once they began, the rhythm took hold. The dances were always slow to begin with, three or four of the younger men moving in unison in a line. Then the music accelerated and the men began to compete, swooping lower, kicking higher, leaping more recklessly into the air. The finest dancer was Kosta, a tall boy with bright red hair. Often at the end of the evening he would dance for perhaps twenty minutes by himself, showing off while the others shouted encouragement. He responded with trickier moves, flashier leaps, never acknowledging applause but remaining arrogantly conscious of his superior skills.

One night he came over to where the boys were watching a card game and offered to teach them the line dance, the *sirtaki*. They picked it up fairly easily in spite of the complex 9/8 rhythm and Ben proved to be not only a good imitator but quite inventive. In the next weeks he and Kosta often danced together, Ben grinning at his own accomplishment, Kosta never returning his grin but challenging him to try new moves, more difficult steps, higher leaps. I fantasized that Kosta, the dancing star of the taverna, had some sort of special status in the town. But no, he was a fisherman's son who went out to sea every morning at six in his father's boat like all the others.

Every day the men went to sea and the women stayed home together. They scrubbed their floors, washed their clothes and hung them out to dry, dug up vegetables and peeled them and made them into stew. And all day long they squabbled among themselves. We could hear Adonis's mother and sisters grumbling at each other in their gravelly baritone voices. And all of them berated the old grandmother as she sat patiently in the yard, her fingers working continuously with white thread and a little silver hook, for she was the maker of the lace curtains, the artist in the family. She took a shine to Sarah who used to sit and watch her working out her patterns. They never spoke but merely smiled at each other.

At dusk the men would come home and the women's voices rose to shrieks and yells. The men sat alone at the table rapidly downing their dinners while the women scolded them, then got up and went off to the taverna. They wove their way home after the women had gone to bed and rose with the first streaks of light in the sky, down to their boats before the women's tongues got going. As a pattern of domesticity it was not particularly admirable.

We settled in happily in our little white house. Every morning I would get up considerably later than the fishermen and trudge along the path to the store to buy milk and bread and oranges. We would sit in the morning sun and eat a leisurely breakfast and then go down to the beach. The Greeks would no more have thought of swimming in April than dancing the twist in the taverna, but we found the water warm and inviting. The kids were all good swimmers and were happy to spend several hours a day in the water. On the beach, we met the other visitors living in Lindos.

There were the Weissmans, Marshall and Olivia. He was a New Yorker with a graduate degree in art history. He had done a catalogue of the collection in the Palazzo Barberini in Rome, was a friend of the family, particularly the *principessa madre*, who was an American and, he implied, his former mistress. That was before he went to Oxford, where he met Olivia. She was a member of a titled family and, he intimated, a considerable heiress when her uncle died. Meanwhile they were living very simply in Greece while he worked on a major study of Cycladic art. They had two small sons, Piers and Roderick, who were delighted to tag around after Ben and Guy. They were uncertain swimmers and Guy in particular was very patient in helping them acquire greater confidence in the water.

Olivia and Marshall invited us to dinner in their sixteenth-century house in the centre of town. It was the closest thing Lindos had to a palazzo and Marshall gave us a rundown of its history, how it had been built for a noble Venetian who was recalled home before it was finished. Later, a Turkish pasha had lived here with his harem. He had caught one of his wives with a local Greek boy and walled both of them into the cellar to starve to death in each other's arms. The house had a pretty courtyard, which Olivia, who was a proficient gardener and had ambitions as a landscape architect, had planted with lemon trees in tubs and wisteria which was just coming into blossom. Their sitting room was sparsely furnished but featured some fine old Turkish *kelims* and paintings by Monticello and David Hockney. I had never heard of either of them but Marshall told me these were his investments for the future, and I expect he eventually did well with them. The meal was overcooked and tasteless beef and mashed potatoes, but the baklava bought from a local cook was splendid. After dinner, we played canasta for small but real stakes. Olivia won and was quite openly exultant at her financial success.

Several days later, Ben organized a special event for Piers and Roderick. He and Guy had discovered some paddleboats at the far end of the bay. They were chained together and there seemed to be nobody in charge of them. Ben asked Kosta about them and Kosta arranged with the owner for them to take one of the boats out. The four boys set out one day after lunch without telling any of the adults. They paddled well out into the harbour, but then discovered it was not so easy to get back. The tide was going out and they couldn't seem to make any headway against it. Piers and Roderick became frightened and started to cry.

Ben, the intrepid adventurer, got Guy to tell the younger boys a story. He jumped into the water and swam ashore, walked along the narrow path all the way to town, and found Kosta on the beach spreading out his nets to dry. Luckily he had returned early from his day's fishing. Kosta revved up the motor of his little boat and rescued them. He towed the paddleboat back to shore and Ben and Guy delivered Piers and Roderick to their parents, who were already frantically agitated, not knowing where the boys had disappeared to.

Ben and Guy had tried to persuade them not to tell their parents the details of this little escapade, but they broke down under Marshall's interrogation. Kosta managed to pacify Marshall somewhat, but he made a formal visit to me the next day and informed me that he and Olivia would appreciate it if in future we would keep our sons away from theirs. We didn't see them again for about ten days. Then one day I met Olivia in town shopping. She said hello pleasantly enough and asked about the children. "I'm sorry about what happened. I'm afraid Marshall gets carried away sometimes. He's alienated so many people, one way and another. It's not easy for me, as I'm sure you can imagine. I do hope we'll see you again." She turned quickly and walked away carrying her groceries in a pair of string bags.

A few nights later it was the full moon. We came home rather late from the tavern, and I'd had my usual three quarters of a bottle of retsina and two brandies. Judy and the kids went to bed but I decided to climb up to the Acropolis. It was brilliant in the moonlight, the broken shafts of the moon goddess's shattered sanctuary shone against the luminous sky. Down below, the surf rolled in between the two long arms of our bay. Over on the other side of the headland, the tiny, perfect landlocked circle of St. Paul's harbour sparkled with reflected moonbeams. I stood in a kind of dream and suddenly had a strong sense that I was not alone. Someone was standing just behind me, but it wasn't Artemis. Close beside me was Marshall Weissman. I could feel his breath on my cheek as we stood together looking down over my shoulder at wine-dark sea. He gave me a wry smile. "I suppose we're both looking for the same thing." Something reptilian, predatory in his manner put me off. I took one last look at the glimmering waters below us, the fluted columns above our heads, and headed home to bed.

There was also the Kastakis family, John and Paula and their children Anna and George from St. John's, Newfoundland. He was a professor of economics at Memorial University on sabbatical. John and Paula were Greek-Canadians who had grown up in Toronto. They spoke Demotic Greek fluently and had relatives near Sparta. They had taken a small house in Lindos for six months to take advantage of the weather and give John a chance to work on his new book. The kids were attending classes in the local school. They asked us to spend Easter with them.

This involved going to a service in the local church on Good Friday. We turned up at the appointed hour, about eight o'clock in the evening, but the church was already full. We stood in the square and listened to the singing flowing out of the church through the open doors. The voices were male; deep, sonorous sounds rolled into the square like musical thunder. Then the crowd in the doorway of the church parted and the priests came out carrying a sort of gilded coffin. They were surrounded by candles and incense as they started to make their way around the crowd, still singing. One by one the people in the square came up and kissed the coffin. I felt Ben's hand tug at my sleeve as it got closer. Suddenly he turned and darted through the crowd. I went after him through the empty streets till I caught up to him. "No way am I gonna kiss that thing." So we watched from a distance as the procession made its way through the town. It seemed that every house was blessed, every person kissed the golden box that stood in for the dead God. There was a sombre excitement in the air, an almost palpable satisfaction as if some deep hunger were being fulfilled. We walked home together not saddened but elated.

On Saturday the town was subdued, the stores closed, the streets empty. Even the taverna's doors remained locked. On Sunday morning the bells began to peal. We walked into the town to discover the streets filled not only with people but with white lambs. Every family seemed to have one with them. They had bought them from farmers in the countryside and were leading them into town on their skittering little legs. They shoved and trembled and bleated in their uncertainty. Suddenly the streets were running with blood. Almost simultaneously all the lambs were slaughtered: a primitive ritual that predated Christianity, yet somehow symbolized its central myth: the innocent lamb gives up its life for the salvation of the guilty. The dead lambs were given to the baker and the people crowded into the church.

The singing started: first the basses, then higher voices joining in, until the whole space was filled with the sound of rejoicing.

"Christ is risen."

"Yes, He is risen indeed."

Everyone was embraced, pulled into a celebration that seemed fuller and deeper than any religious ceremony I had ever experienced at home. I think because, at least for the moment, everyone seemed to give themselves over completely to the experience; nothing held back or kept in reserve. My Presbyterian forebears had beliefs they could explain and justify but these people had a different sort of commitment, not just intellectual but deeply emotional, physicalized in their voices and their sturdy embracings.

After the service, we collected our lamb from the baker and carried it warm in a pan to John and Paula's rented house. We drank red wine and afterwards sat around and talked about Canadian politics until eventually we were all dozing in our chairs. Paula sensibly suggested we should have a proper siesta. When we came to, the light was almost gone. John put some more bottles of red wine in a knapsack and we headed down to the beach. The whole town seemed to be there. There was *bouzouki* music, live this time, not coming from a radio. And gradually people started to dance. Not just the men; at Easter, even the women danced. They moved in concentric circles, not competing, not showing off their skills, just dancing for themselves, dancing as if to show their sheer enjoyment of being alive.

We stayed on another two weeks in Lindos. We went to the beach almost every day or played cards. I taught the kids the rudiments of bridge and we wrangled noisily. Ben sometimes tried to cheat and was denounced by Guy, whereupon he would throw his cards in the air and stamp out of the house. I chuckled to myself remembering bridge games with my parents, the tense silence while I counted points before bidding, the look of disgust on my father's face when I lost a trick because I hadn't kept track of how many trumps were out.

Occasionally we took a bus and made an expedition to a neighbouring town. We visited an ancient shrine to St. Paul, who was supposed to have preached there, and the Valley of the Butterflies. (But it was the wrong time of the year; the butterflies have their big reunion in the autumn.) The kids swam and Judy read to them. We read all Gerald Durrell's animal books and then began on Mary Renault's Greek books. I began working on a play about Alcibiades, in what I thought was a sort of neo-Brechtian style. It had plenty of intrigue and one or two good lyrics. I felt out of my depth, but was emboldened by the natural splendour all around me.

Before we left, we gave a luncheon party for everyone we knew. I went to invite Marshall and Olivia and discovered they'd packed up and left town. But the Karamatis family came and a few Greeks, Adonis and two of his sisters, and two French students who I'd talked to on the beach, where they seemed to be camping out in sleeping bags. It was they who told us what had happened to Marshall and Olivia. Apparently Marshall had tried to proposition Kosta and he suggested they clear out fast if they didn't want serious trouble. How the Frenchmen knew about this wasn't clear and it seemed better not to ask. However Kosta did show up at our party, rather late, and he and Ben danced together for the last time. The party spilled down onto the beach and we all danced as the sun sank into the sea, and up above us the crescent moon appeared through the broken columns of the temple of Artemis.

Once back on the mainland we rented a car and drove through the Peloponnese: Epidaurus, Thebes, Olympia. But the most memorable place for me was Delphi. We drove into the town after dark and checked into a little hotel. I woke early and went out on the balcony. I sat in the dark listening to the wind in the olive trees and watched the day break slowly over the Sacred Plain. I was keen to tune into the mystery of this place, determined to connect with the spirit of all the people who had come looking for inspiration in the last five thousand years. I left the others in bed and set out for Mount Parnassus. The sun got hotter. Finally, when it seemed directly over my head, I sat on a rock to catch my breath. Down below, I could see a broken circle of columns, the remains of the temple of Apollo. An eagle flew overhead, the shadow of its wings passing over me like a sign from the gods urging me on. I got up on my feet once more. I must have kept going for another hour, but I couldn't tell whether I'd actually reached the summit or not; Parnassus didn't seem to have an actual peak. Somehow this struck me as a perfect symbol of my struggle to find my aesthetic path. How was I to know if I was headed in the right direction? How could I tell when I'd reached the height of my abilities? The fact was I just had to keep on going.

It turned out this was the first of May, when all Greeks go back to their native town to dance in the streets. That night Delphi was crowded and the retsina flowed like water. We danced with the kids till they were tired and went to bed. Then one of the hotel waiters took us to a little disco hidden away in the hills, where we joined a bunch of handsome Athenians and boogied till dawn. I may not have connected with Apollo but Bacchus must have approved of my efforts, because the next day my legs were not even slightly stiff and I had no hangover. I drove to Athens and we caught a plane to Rome.

BELLA ITALIA

Going from Athens to Rome was like going from black and white to colour. The Greek capital had seemed haphazard and shabby; Rome might have been planned by a set designer. The shapes of perfect classical domes and symmetrical umbrella pines outlined against the brilliant blue sky, the people in the streets wore outfits chosen as carefully as theatrical costumes, startling and often revealing. Our taxi swerved through busy streets till it came to a full stop at the base of the Spanish Steps. Scarlet bloom spilled down in a brilliant cascade from the elegant obelisk backed by the baroque symmetry of the Santa Trinità facade. A throng of gypsies and hippies, hawkers and hustlers swarmed in front of us, sexy, good-looking kids flaunting their wares and their bodies. Casting by Tennessee Williams. Rome and the Romans seemed to give off carnal vibrations.

We checked into the Inghilterra, then still a slightly seedy family hotel. They gave Judy and me a front room featuring battered antique furniture and a view of the bustling Condotti, and put the kids in more rough-and-ready quarters on an upper floor. We were to learn that Italians have a very pragmatic attitude to kids: they don't expect or want them to behave like little adults, they pamper and encourage them but in return they expect kids to make room for adult foibles. Italians are realists; they don't expect either kids or their parents to be faultless, any more than they expect their priests or politicians to be incorruptible. Even the Pope is only infallible when he says he is. Perfection is for dead saints in gilded niches.

Our first afternoon in Rome was spent in the real heart of the ancient capital: not the Vatican Museum or the Imperial Forum, but the Piazza Navona. We sat at Tre Scalini and ordered gelati, the best ice cream I'd ever eaten, even surpassing the magical treats my grandmother cranked out by hand when I was a little boy. It set the tone for our gastronomic experience of Italy, which like my ascent of Parnassus would climb from height to height without every reaching a summit, something even more delicious being always just ahead. We fell into conversation with a lean American at the next table who turned out to be Norman Rockwell, who was entertaining his grandchildren for the afternoon. He suggested we all rent bikes. We wove our way through the crowds playing a sort of two-wheeled tag. The loitering crowd became interested in our game, cheering when one of the kids narrowly escaped, groaning when someone was caught. Two carabinieri appeared and I thought they might put an end to the game but they merely drew their swords and waved them encouragingly, cheering us on.

When the light was gone we went to a restaurant in Campo dei Fiori. Rockwell advised us to flee Rome, which was already suffering from a water shortage and would soon be in the grip of a garbage strike. The fountains would cease to play and the stone nymphs and satyrs would disappear under a mountain of vegetable peelings and plastic. Meanwhile, musicians serenaded us and people came up to gossip. Rockwell held court with charm and grace, a picture of the perfect cavaliere, the doyen of apple-pie Americanism giving us our first lesson in Roman style.

The next day I picked up our car. I had arranged to buy a Volkswagen van, big enough for all our stuff and for the kids to horse around in the back. It seemed ideal but I had not taken into account the fact that it was a standard shift and I had driven an automatic for the past twenty years. I was also not prepared for Italian driving. Italian drivers are unquestionably the most skilled I have ever encountered. They know what their cars are capable of and they drive them to the limit of their capacity. Most of them have learned to drive on scooters, which can and do go literally anywhere. When they graduate to cars they operate in the same mode, driving through narrow archways and up steep inclines, beating out slower vehicles which are expected to give way, offering no quarter to anyone. All are treated as equals: a priest in a soutane and shovel hat peddling his rickety bicycle along the Corso is the equal of an Alfa Romeo barrelling along at eight-five kilometres and may the best man or machine win. It makes for some very nimble priests.

We were to drive to a house we had rented on the coast of Tuscany just outside Porto Ercole. We set out in mid-morning expecting to make a two-hour trip and arrive in time for lunch. We drove down tree-lined streets trying to read their names on the sides of buildings, found ourselves speeding through tunnels under the Tiber and bridges over it, headed onto a super-highway that took us in the wrong direction, doubled back and found ourselves back in the teeth of city traffic. I became increasingly tense and tight-lipped. Advice was offered and disregarded. It irritated me that our van, which had the engine of a beetle but the chassis of a truck, was relatively powerless and almost everyone could go faster than me, a situation I was unwilling to accept. Drivers honked, flashed their lights, shook their fists. If I stopped on a hill, I had problems shifting into first. When I parked to get soft drinks, I forgot to put on the handbrake and the car started to roll away.

After two and a half hours we finally found ourselves on a good highway headed in the right direction. I resentfully stayed in the right-hand lane and watched the rest of the world sail past me. Eventually we got onto the road that was supposed to lead to our villa. We climbed a steep and narrow cow path full of hairpin turns as I ground the gears, shifting up and down. I couldn't find any of the landmarks that had been described. At the top of a steep incline I stalled, rolled backwards down the steep grade, steering with my neck craned out the window and rolled into a ditch. Totally frustrated, I cursed, tossed the keys into a neighbouring field, and walked off down the road leaving Judy and the kids in the car. Sarah was in tears. "Mummy, how much money have you got? Enough to fly home? I don't want to stay here with Dad if he's going to act like this."

Judy, accustomed to my irritability and propensity for self-dramatization, calmly got out a Thermos of juice and handed it round. After a bit, three Italian men stopped their truck and offered to help. They found the keys, pushed the car out of the ditch, and turned it around. They drove up behind me, stopped, and jumped out with gleeful grins. I fumed but controlled myself while in broken English they gave me directions. I took the keys with as much dignity as I could muster and got into the driver's seat. No one spoke. Ten minutes later we reached our destination and the villa's owners welcomed us. Fortunately they'd prepared a cold lunch and it was still waiting on the table. Nobody mentioned what had happened but it remained in our consciousness like a stain that wouldn't go away. It subtly coloured our time in Italy, giving it an emotional charge that was very different from the more contemplative and placid rhythm of our days in Greece.

Our rented house belonged to a prosperous Italian couple in their mid-sixties. Luxardo was a tall, imposing man with thick grey hair, a jutting nose, and twinkling, mischievous eyes. He was on the verge of retiring from running a substantial industrial plant in Parma. He was a Jew who survived the war, using false papers and running a chemical factory. "What I was to do? When I understand what is to happen, already is too late. They would take not only me but my daughters to the camps. So I must pretend. Always I wear gloves. With this I impress the Nazis. They think I am so much the gentleman." He chortled, delighted with his own duplicity. He had helped fellow Jews escape to Switzerland, then used his position to obtain classified information for the Resistance, before he eventually took off his gloves and turned his plant over to the advancing Allies.

His wife, Bianca, was an aristocratic Roman, handsome and languid. She would watch with a look of enervated scepticism as Luxardo talked expansively about his exploits or advised us about tiny, out-of-the-way restaurants, hidden beaches, and barely known ruins we should visit. Luxardo told us who made the best tagliatelle in the neighbourhood and who to bribe if the water ran out and what was the prettiest route to Siena. Later we discovered Bianca's carefully rationed energies were centred on shopping. She was already envisioning the flat they would move to in the centre of Rome when Luxardo retired. She sighed at the thought of how much work lay ahead of her, dealing with carpenters and plumbers, but she came to life as she described a wonderful piece of brocade she had bought for practically nothing in a little shop in Todi or the marvellous eighteenth-century mirror she discovered in a friend's attic and traded for a large ceramic lion, which though very pretty was definitely a fake.

Luxardo decided he must take us on an expedition the next day to see some of his favourite places, hidden treasures we might not discover by ourselves. We went down into Etruscan tombs near Tarquinia to view ancient pornography, graphically vivid paintings of orgiastic banquets, diners vomiting, and flute-players being sodomized. Then on to the Villa Lante at Bagnaia where we strolled through the terraced gardens built by a fun-loving Farnese cardinal. We sat on a marble bench which Luxardo assured us gave the best view of the lower gardens where fountains splashed and marble goddesses sported their charms. Suddenly jets of water rose in the air and soaked us. Luxardo was repeating one of the cardinal's little jokes, dousing his guests by stepping on a hidden pedal. His guffaws were an echo of intricately planned but essentially crude enjoyment. Renaissance ribaldry brought to life. For his finale, Luxardo guided us to a dilapidated chapel where he bribed a sinister-looking monk to unlock a rusty grill and let us view a dimly lit relic displayed in a tattered velvet box.

"What is it?" I finally asked.

"You cannot guess? My friend you are seeing before you the veritable prepuce of Christ." The old Jew shook with mirth as he led us back out into the bright light of a late spring afternoon and suggested we all have some gelato. The aging satyr rolled his eyes and smiled a mock-lascivious smile as we licked our dripping pink cones.

I gradually came to realize Luxardo's eccentric tour would also colour our view of Italy, insidiously affecting our sightseeing choices in the next month. I found myself seeking out the bizarre, the offbeat, even the perverse. More than the serene, perfect madonnas of Raphael and Perugino, the image that stayed in my mind was the sour face of the wilful young woman in Simone Martini's golden *Annunciation* in the Uffizi. "Why me?" she thinks as she glares balefully at the gimlet-eyed Archangel. Or Caravaggio's young *Bacchus,* his dark eyes stupefied by wine, his untried white body available for pleasure, his pretty, slightly stupid face presaging a life of profligacy, a brief future devoted to the pursuit of ever more elusive satisfaction. A world I'd already glimpsed in the early films of Fellini: *La strada, Le notti di Cabiria, I vitelloni.* These films had turned me on to Italy, though I thought *La dolce vita* seemed a bit over the top.

Luxardo and Bianca went back to Parma, but life definitely didn't relax into the quiet rhythm of Lindos. There was a different crackle in the air, a different energy in the speech and look of the people. The Greeks had been steady, sturdy, slow to come to the boil; the Italians were swift, sexy, and stylish. Clothes, food, and cars were used to express an attitude, make a statement. It was not just what but how you ate or wore or drove. What was important was not mere quantity or even value but the choices one made.

We began to frequent certain favourite places, such as a small, hard-to-find beach that could only be reached by a long descent down a rickety wooden staircase. A few other families began to make an appearance in the late morning, the mothers lying about in abbreviated swimsuits listening to their Walkmans while the kids played handball. They eyed us warily for a week, then began to make overtures, offering us eggplant sandwiches and chilled spumante. The terrace of the *Pelicano,* an exclusive little hotel in an isolated cove, was much too expensive to eat at, but ideal for a Campari at sunset. Here we became friendly with Claudio, a young symphonic conductor and his Viennese mistress Birgitta. They were friends of the Mussolinis: Claudio played jazz with one of Il Duce's sons, while Birgitta talked clothes and politics with his granddaughter, who was just beginning her career as a television personality. They were all neo-Fascists but nobody had started using that label yet. We often ate dinner at King's, an American-style bar in Porto Ercole. They catered to the children, supplying them with fresh wild fragoli and many flavours of gelato, before they retired to a cushioned loft and slept while Judy and I lingered over our chianti and bel paese or gorgonzola.

We had a car and we wanted to go places. Siena, Pisa, Assisi, Arezzo, San Gimignano, Lucca, Orvieto, Perugia, Spoleto. We took day trips to all of them, as well as spending three days in Florence. Sarah lingered as she took in paintings of grinning demons, strange wise-seeming beasts, and slyly smiling cherubs, but Guy was more interested in battle scenes; he wanted details about who was fighting on which side and who had won, which neither Judy nor I could supply. Ben, on the other hand, quickly became restless. He would corral Guy and they would go outside and try to join in games with Italian kids, but they found it difficult to communicate. Ben, with his quick ear and gregarious personality, managed better than his brother and he began to speak a sort of bastard lingo. I remember him saying, "Hey, padre, lissename, Ima learna parlo Italiano." But he wasn't willing to work at grammar, so this Chico Marx parody was about as far as he got.

The boys missed the rough-and-tumble of the schoolyard back home, though they didn't complain. As I negotiated hairpin turns or narrow streets, they played bridge and rummy in the back of the van. They told jokes and laughed a lot, but they were also often bored and scrappy. Life here was more stimulating than in Greece, but also more complicated and more frustrating. The Italians were actually less accessible than the Greeks, quicker to respond but also to lose interest. They were not as aloof, but also not as accommodating. They spoke their minds without concern for social niceties or bruised feelings.

In between our excursions, Bianca's housekeeper would come to clean and cook. Maria was a sturdy peasant in her thirties with four children at home. She would arrive at eight o'clock in the morning and immediately set about her work, dragging chairs and mattresses into the garden to air, scrubbing the tiled floors, washing our clothes and sheets and towels and hanging them out to dry. She would then take me shopping. I would drive her into town in my van and we would stop at one shop for fish, another for chickens, another for meat, still another for vegetables and fresh flowers, and another for bread. She was very particular, telling the butcher how to quarter a capon, demanding eggs that had been laid that very morning, pinching grapefruits and oranges to make sure they were firm, assessing the ripeness of strawberries by turning them out of their containers. I learned the words for various items of food and began to speak a little Italian, making many mistakes but much encouraged by Maria's appreciation of my effort to communicate with her.

When we got home, Maria would spread out the new provisions in the kitchen and proceed to cook us half a dozen dishes so we would not starve till her next visit two or three days later. She had a fantasy that Judy couldn't cook and encouraged me to learn how she made some of her own specialties, rich concoctions involving eggplants and artichokes and basil and rosemary. She let me watch as she deftly chopped and peeled, adding little pinches of special ingredients. Like my mother she never measured anything, but merely stuck her finger into the mix from time to time, licked it and then either smiled approvingly or frowned and altered the seasoning.

About the third time she came to the house we returned from shopping and Maria set out her fresh vegetables on the counter and handed me the knife. "Lei, vada cucinare," she commanded in her stentorian basso. I understood I was to imitate her efforts and produce a culinary delight on my own. She laughed openly at my awkward attempts to peel tomatoes or chop garlic, but she let me blunder on, occasionally testing my work with her finger and handing me some ingredient to correct my errors. Finally she was satisfied, took the dish away from me, and popped it in the oven.

Maria then whipped up a salad for our lunch, supervised Sarah in the setting of the table (in her view Sarah should do household chores, though the boys were exempt), ate standing in the kitchen while we sat at the table (she couldn't be persuaded to sit down with us), and washed the dishes. She took down the washing from the line and whatever was still wet she ironed dry. Then she summoned me to the kitchen and took my casserole out of the oven.

She plunged a sturdy finger into the hot concoction and tasted it, rolling it around in her mouth judiciously. She smiled triumphantly and commented on my work, "Bravo, Signor Martino." I offered to drive Maria home. She protested, but eventually gave in. We drove nine kilometres and I asked who drove her in the morning. She laughed and said she had walked.

After that I drove three mornings a week to pick Maria up as well as taking her home at night. I met her daughters and her husband, who asked me into the house and offered me grappa. I decided to ask the whole family to have dinner with us at home, but Maria seemed reluctant to do this. When I offered to take them out to a restaurant, however, they accepted and we all went together to a place they suggested in Bolsena.

We had a fine meal and a merry evening, short on talk but heavy on good-will and vino. One of Maria's daughters, a tall, plump girl called Serafina, was studying English at school; she and Sarah hit it off and she promised to visit us the next weekend. The bill proved to be about half what I'd expected and when I asked Maria if they'd made some mistake, she merely laughed and said, "Prezzo d'amico." Her husband drove home and invited us in for a final grappa. He produced a pack of Italian cards and proceeded to teach us how to play *scopa*. We drove home very slowly, about three in the morning, and left the car at the bottom of the hill so I wouldn't have to negotiate the hairpin turns in the dark.

The next Friday Maria's daughter came to stay overnight. She had a ringing voice about an octave higher than her mother's and told us she could run a mile in four and a quarter minutes. She was soon playing soccer with the boys. After dinner we all played *scopa*. The following morning Luxardo arrived with his granddaughter Carolina. She was staying with him and Bianca in Rome while Pucci, her mother, went to London to see a specialist. We all went to the beach and the girls swam together while the boys joined in a game of beach ball with the local *ragazzi*. I sat with Luxardo who held forth on the complexity of the politics of his family.

"Poor Pucci. She has scare by the doctor, but Italian doctors are not to take serious. Since Pucci is separate from Paolo, she is living in the West Indies with the other man. With Paolo she marries well but she will not be happy. She leaves her husband and now Bianca and I must help the child. We do but is not easy for Carolina, you understand? Now Pucci has found this illness and who knows what will be coming? Fortunately for us Pucci will listen at Gaia." Gaia was Luxardo and Bianca's model older daughter, bright, self-possessed, successful. She was married to a wealthy Englishman and divided her time between a splendid house in Regent's Park and a castle in Scotland. As a jour-nalist she wrote in two languages, trenchantly cutting through the Gordian knot of Italian politics for the benefit of subscribers of the *Daily Telegraph* and sardonically interpreting the intricacies of English mores for readers of *Corriere della sera.* She had published two acerbic if rather frivolous novels and a biography of Luchino Visconti and shown her watercolours in avant-garde galleries in Glasgow, Milan, and Hamburg. "Gaia is the lucky one. She inherits the cunning of her father and the fine taste of her mother. Poor Pucci has only the wilful nature and the body of Sophia Loren."

Luxardo's analysis of his progeny was interrupted by shouts from the boys. A little kid with sticking-out ears was taunting Ben, who retaliated by chasing him around the beach. A bigger kid stepped out in front of Ben and challenged him and a sparring match ensued. The boys circled the combatants and watched, shouting encouragement. The little kid with the ears snuck up behind Ben and tripped him. Serafina, who was half a head taller than any of the boys, grabbed the little kid, pinioned his arms behind his back, and held him for Ben to take a poke at. Ben grinned at him, tweaked his nose playfully, and offered to shake hands. This sporting gesture brought an invitation for the girls to join in the game. It was resumed and both Sarah and Serafina proved to be formidable players, so much so that they were soon separated and assigned to opposite teams.

Carolina declined to play and came over to sit with us. She was pale in spite of living in the tropics and apparently suffered from allergies, animals mostly, but also a variety of foods. As my kids also had allergies we compared symptoms, and for the first time she showed interest in the conversation. Luxardo then told us of a special anti-allergy medicine that he had learned how to make from his grandmother. "She was a very wise woman, you know. Una strega." He began to list the ingredients, which included such things as porcupine's milk and frog's spittle. He would take us out that very night on an expedition to assemble some of these magical ingredients, but we must gather them between midnight and the first cockcrow. It gradually dawned on me he just might be pulling our legs.

Nevertheless after dinner Luxardo began to organize his foraging expedition. Serafina and the boys were enthusiastic as he gave them instructions about what to do if they met a wild boar. "You look very deep into his eyes and then avanti. You plunge at him and hit him on his nose with a big stick." He produced substantial wooden clubs for all of them. He himself had a rather elegant cane with a bone handle carved in the shape of a ram. Judy stayed home while the rest of us set off into the clear, cool night under a vault of stars that twinkled down at us just like Luxardo's bright little eyes. Somehow we got split into two groups, I with the boys and Luxardo with the girls. We heard Serafina shriek nearby, though whether with fear or laughter was unclear. Then we saw a porcupine, a big slow-moving creature with very long quills swinging as it ambled along. Ben tried to catch it and got two quills in his hand. I couldn't see to get them out and decided we'd better go home.

We were upstairs in the bathroom extracting quills when Luxardo and the girls came home. Ben was making a fair amount of noise as Judy worked on his hand with her tweezers, so we didn't hear them. Downstairs I found Luxardo sitting by the fire with a large glass of grappa. His face was scratched and he had a bump on his forehead. He said he'd collided with a tree in the dark. His mouth widened in a rueful grin. "Le giovane, they miss the fun of being young. When I am young I laugh and laugh. Sempre rido. Ma adesso sono un scemo vecchio e piangio molto." Tears rolled down his cheeks.

The next morning when I came down for breakfast I learned Serafina had gone home, walking the nine kilometres back to her mother's house. Carolina had caught a chill and was in bed with a fever. Sarah was in her room, coaxing her to drink some camomile tea Judy had made for her. Luxardo was on the phone pouring out a flood of explanations, protestations, justifications. Finally he gestured dramatically, hung up the line, and joined us for scrambled eggs. He and Judy consulted and agreed that Carolina should stay with us for a few days till she felt better. He would return home and face Bianca.

Bianca phoned Judy later that morning to thank her for looking after Carolina. She felt however that she must point out that we had been just a little bit foolish in our dealings with Maria. Maria was a good woman but of course only a peasant. She had heard from a neighbour that Maria had hung our washing outside, something that only common people did, and which she herself never allowed even in the country. And our befriending Maria's daughter was setting a dangerous precedent. We were North Americans and didn't understand about these things. Italy was a very egalitarian country, but there were certain lines that were not to be crossed without upsetting the delicate balance of society. Luxardo sometimes challenged these conventions but it was her duty as a wife to restrain his unconventional excesses with an appeal to common sense and accepted standards of decorum. If we intended to live in Europe, we would have to come to terms with these things. We had showed exceptional discrimination but we still had much to learn. She spoke of course only for our own good. She knew we would appreciate her frankness. Till then we had attributed Bianca's comparative silence to a certain female deference in the face of her husband's dominating personality, but we now realized she was shrewder than we had imagined. Luxardo might be wily but Bianca was a worthy match for her mate, quite capable of undermining his exuberance with her own razor-edged innuendo.

The next two days passed quietly. Carolina and Sarah became friends, and she asked Sarah to visit her at her grandfather's house in Vicenza. On the third day she was so much improved we drove up to a tiny hill town for dinner in a family restaurant that contained only three rickety tables and an old piano. We seemed to be the only customers. A young woman, obviously the daughter of the house, came out of the kitchen and interviewed us. She was fascinated to learn that we came from Canada and wanted to know if we had ever seen a moose. I said, yes, once, in the Yukon some years earlier when I was mining for gold. She was delighted by this and volunteered the information that she had on hand some excellent venison. She asked how we would like it cooked, then disappeared into the kitchen to consult with her mother.

After ten minutes or so a younger sister appeared to consult about what vegetables we would like. We chose artichokes and potatoes and she too retired. Then a young boy of Boticellian beauty, perhaps fifteen, came in with wine and proceeded to set the table. He told us his name was Gianfranco and shyly enquired about the Canadian north. He dreamed of becoming a forest ranger. What were the prospects for him to get a job in Canada? He had always wanted to go to the Arctic and see polar bears and seals. He could sing the Canadian national anthem. A customer had taught it to him last summer. He sat down at the piano and played and sang "Alouette." We all joined in and by the end of the song the sisters and another smaller brother were standing in the doorway singing along with us. They wanted to hear other Canadian songs, but at this point Mamma arrived with the venison and we all went back to the table and tucked in.

After dinner, the sing-song resumed. Gianfranco played piano and the older sister played on a guitar. We alternated Canadian and Italian songs: "Santa Lucia" and "The Squid Jiggin' Ground," "Arrividerci, Roma" and "She Loves You." Also a song about Sacco and Vanzetti that was being sung every-where in Italy that year: "Here's to you, Nicola and Bart . . ." Carolina turned out to have a very sweet, clear voice. As she stood close to the piano, her hand rested lightly on Gianfranco's shoulder and I suddenly remembered it was she who had suggested we come to this restaurant. When it came time to go home, I asked Gianfranco to have dinner with us at our house the next night.

He consulted with his mother about borrowing her scooter and it was agreed he could visit two nights later.

The next day, Pucci arrived in her father's little blue Fiat. He was right: she did have a body like Sophia Loren. She wore jeans and a sweater and old loafers and still looked like an ad in Italian *Vogue*. She smoked incessantly and spoke broken but fluent English punctuated by many "dunque"s. She hugged her daughter impulsively as though she hadn't seen her for a year and told us the English doctors had pronounced her completely healthy. We must immediately do something to celebrate. We should all go to the baths at Saturnalia. It would rejuvenate us. We piled into the van and she undertook to drive, cigarette in hand, talking non-stop, taking hairpin turns without braking and making obscene gestures at other drivers who tried to pass her. We arrived at the baths in about half the time it would have taken me to get there and Pucci talked them into letting the children in free. This triumph was somewhat diminished by the fact that the children found the sulphur smell of the baths disgusting, but Pucci jumped into her bikini and rolled about in the murky brown water like some sea-nymph inviting Neptune to have his way with her. She launched into a detailed description of her medical and psychological problems for Judy's benefit, while I took the kids off for gelati.

On the way home we stopped at a little tobacco shop that had a tiny dining room in the back. Pucci insisted they made the best gnocchi in Tuscany and she was proved right. They also produced a clear white wine with a slight sting to it that was the perfect complement to it. I tried to discover its name but without success. Pucci told Carolina she was sending her to their grandfather in Vicenza for the next month. She had promised to take her to Africa to the game parks, but now this was impossible. Carolina said it wasn't fair; their father had promised to take them to Egypt to see the pyramids the year before but then had cancelled the trip. "Poor Paolo, he couldn't help it. He fell in love. Dunque, now I must to disappoint you. Mi dispiace, mia cara, but you see — I am incinta. You are going to have the little brother or sister. *Dunque*, just in time for Natale." Pucci laughed and lit another cigarette as her daughter stared at her in disbelief. When we got back to the house, Pucci packed up Carolina's clothes and piled them into her little car. They must return to Rome that night. She was sorry, but it had to be. Carolina begged us to come and see them at their grandfather's house in Vicenza and we agreed we would. Pucci kissed us all effusively and clambered into her car. She waved her cigarette at us as she lurched through the gate, accelerating as she turned into the first curve of the road.

The weather improved and we drove to the beach every day. The boys swam and played beach ball. The Italian kids accepted them but verbal communication remained minimal and I couldn't help but realize they were bored, ready to move on. We held a family pow-wow and this was confirmed. We agreed that we should start making plans for our trek north. But I wanted a few days in Rome. My friend Gilbert Reid had promised to try to get me an interview with Fellini. And Pucci had given me her address and promised to introduce me to her ex-husband Paolo who was a producer for RAI, the Italian broadcasting system. Judy felt the kids would be bored while I trailed around gladhanding and offered to keep them amused at the house while I went up to Rome on my own.

On the drive, I picked up a hitchhiker, a lean, handsome youth called Silvano who told me he was an art student in Venice. He was learning to restore paintings, specializing in the Mannerist style, which he claimed had been invented by Michelangelo in his *Last Judgment* in the Sistine Chapel. He was going to Rome to meet with a master restorer and examine this painting, which was to be revamped in the coming decade. Perhaps he could be part of the team working on it. We stopped for gas and he warned me to keep an eye on the attendant because they often rang up phony figures when they filled the tanks of tourists. My German plates were a dead giveaway.

On the way into Rome, Silvano talked knowledgeably about how classical forms had modified the early simplicity of Italian painting, replacing sincere belief with sinuous sensuality. I dropped him near the Termini and we agreed to meet for a drink the next night at seven on Via Veneto. It was only later I realized he'd swiped fifty thousand lire from me. He must have taken it from my wallet when I got out of the car to make sure I was not cheated by the service station attendant. But why hadn't he completely cleaned me out?

"Ah, that is very Italian," said Paolo. "He didn't want to spoil your evening, so he left you your cards and some cash." We sat on steel chairs in his apartment surrounded by the bits of a broken obelisk, a bubble-pipe, a mummy case, and a large stuffed camel. "I call him Ptolmey. He is rather fun, no? This whole room I decorated in my Egyptian period. I am bored with it now. In the autumn I will change everything but in this moment I have too much work, so I must live with it. Besides, I must pay school fees for Carolina. You must tell me, do you think she is happy living with Pucci?"

"Pucci's been scared. They thought she had cancer."

"Poor Pucci. Always she must dramatize her life. She has her father's energy. Also his appetite. In a man this is amusing, but in a wife, it becomes exhausting. When I was with Pucci, sometimes I did not have the energy to get out of bed for many days at once."

I had called the number Pucci had given me, expecting to meet her for a drink, but Paolo had answered and insisted I come over to his apartment immediately. He had to fly to Tunis in the morning, but we had been so kind to his daughter. He would never forgive himself if he did not at least offer me a cup of tea. "I love Luxardo," Paolo went on. "He is like something out of the Old Testament. Noah perhaps in a fresco by Signorelli or Lorenzetti. Or King David in his old age. He is also very Italian. Like Gianni Schicchi. But it is very difficult for the girls. They try to keep up with him. Gaia is madly ambitious. She paints, she writes. She travels to Moscow and Nepal and Peru. She gives the smartest parties in London and still she is restless, unsatisfied. Pucci cannot compete, so she is the bad girl. She smoulders like Mount Vesuvius. One sits and waits to be destroyed like the poor citizens of Pompeii." Paolo's long, folded face crinkled into a grimace of resignation at the prospect of a hopeless situation. "Now, what do you want to do in Rome?"

"Meet Fellini."

"Difficult. The pope, the president, these I might arrange. But Federico is in the middle of shooting a film. Unless yours is the perfect face he is seeking in this moment, he will not see you. Literally. You will not be there for him. Federico is a monster. But then all Italians are monsters. That is why life in Italy is one long horrifying, and beautiful fairy tale. It is still the land of Dante and Tasso and Boccacio, where anything can happen and probably will."

An hour later I was sitting with my friend Gilbert drinking Campari at his favourite café near the Pantheon and telling him about my experience with Silvano. Gilbert shrugged dismissively. "Italians are not bad people. But they do consider any foreigner fair game. Right, Franco?"

"Certo," agreed his friend Franco, an aspiring moviemaker. "You must understand that if you are not family, it is acceptable to steal your car, cheat you at cards, sleep with your wife. If you cannot accept this, you shall stay away from Italy. Si, è vero. In Italy you have the individual and you have the family. This is the largest social unit we Italians can comprehend. You must remember that a hundred years ago Italy was still dozens of tiny states, each ruled over by a noble family. If there were two rival families in a town, they fought to the death. Think of *Romeo and Juliet*."

"But there were also republics. Venice was a republic."

"Venice is not Italy. It is a trick, all gilt and reflection to dazzle the eyes of the outside world. Venice is trade and pageants, navigation and opera and art shows. It is the most sophisticated tourist trap and also the grandest mausoleum in the world. A place to play and a place to die. Every showman, every artist wants to die in Venice. Like Diaghilev. But who wants to live there? Even that indefatigable adventuress Peggy Guggenheim could only hack it for a few months of the year. She had to go home to the peace and quiet of Manhattan to recuperate."

"You could argue that all Italy is a mausoleum. Look over there. The Pantheon."

"And we sit across from it, but we are not lost in contemplation of it. We plot movies and meals and affairs. Rome may be a collection of monuments, but Rome itself is not for the dead. Fellini is right, the Romans may be nothing but children, but they dance and drink and make love in their graveyard. The tourists provide an audience but even without them, Via Veneto and Piazza Navona would still be thronged every evening. And a hundred churches would celebrate mass every morning."

"For two or three old ladies."

"Where one or two are gathered together, the Spirit is in their midst. Ah, you will ask, what Spirit? The Spirit of Christ, the ultimate individualist and therefore the quintessential Italian."

This dissection of the Italian character was swept aside by the arrival of Giovanella, an agent who handled the professional affairs of the French actress Catherine Deneuve. She had huge grey eyes and a cascade of black curls. She was accompanied by Marie-Christine, a coffee-coloured modern dancer and the daughter of Katherine Dunham from New York, six-foot-two and slim as an eel. Marie-Christine slid into place beside me when I told her I had once seen her dance in my brother-in-law's company. Gilbert fixed his attention on Giovanella, who prodded and poked him playfully with one hand while she chatted up Franco, teasing little nibbles of movie gossip out from behind his saturnine smile.

The two women exchanged giggles and glances periodically, as if sharing some sort of hidden agenda, which it gradually became apparent was that we should buy them dinner. As I felt Marie-Christine's long, smooth legs slithering across my shins under the table, this began to seem like a good idea and before long plates of mussels and clams appeared followed by pasta and salad and bread, several bottles of vino bianco and then a bottle of Strega. This was emptied and the girls began to talk about moving on. "Why don't we all go to Trastevere for a nightcap. You want to see Fellini. He's supposed to be shooting. Maybe he'll be hiring extras."

We went out into the street and flagged down a taxi, Giovanella and Marie-Christine and Gilbert and I. Gilbert rode in the front with the driver and I sat squashed between the two women. Marie-Christine slid her hand into my pants pocket. I lay back and closed my eyes as we careened and caromed through the maze of Roman streets. Then I felt my fly being undone and realized from the number of hands in play that at least one of them had to be Giovanella's. Somewhat shy of an orgasm, I heard Gilbert suggest we get out and walk the rest of the way as traffic was obviously at a standstill. I zipped up and rolled out of the cab. We wove our way across a bridge and down a couple of small streets, until finally we stood across from the old church of Santa Maria, its mosaics glittering above the floodlit piazza. A group of grotesque diners, their faces glazed with boredom, stared grimly at the clusters of bottles and mounds of spaghetti spread out before them. High above them riding a crane sat the master filmmaker in his broad-brimmed black hat, totally absorbed in a discussion with his cameraman. Finally he turned his imperious gaze towards the weary revellers and gave them the word, "Adesso, mi bambini, mangiate come domani sera la fine del mondo."

They sprang into sudden life slurping and slavering as they shovelled great forkfuls of pasta into their mouths, talking and gesticulating as salsa dribbled down their chins and stained their shirtfronts, laughing and cursing and shrieking and belching like the figures in some *quattrocento fresco* come to life. The crane swooped down, bringing the director within a few feet of his performers. Fellini rode it like Vittorio Emmanuele on his monument, conducted like Toscanini on the podium at La Scala. He himself was giving a consummate performance to inspire and exhilarate his actors, provoking them to ever greater excesses and improbabilities.

"Where does he find these people?"

"In cafés, in markets, in the street. He collects people wherever he goes, uses them then moves on. He's quite Jovian in his attitude," said Gilbert admiringly.

At this moment, Fellini caught sight of Giovanella and Marie-Christine and gestured to them to join the scene. They moved in, squeezing in on either side of a grossly fat man who registered their appearance with open-mouthed delight. Marie-Christine reached over and flipped spaghetti back into the fat man's mouth. Fellini grinned with delight.

"Brava, bravissima," he roared approvingly as the crane swung him overhead and on down the table.

"They'll be even more impossible now they've caught the maestro's eye," Gilbert sighed unhappily. "Stay here, I'll see if I can round up another bottiglia." I stood and watched and once more felt a hand slide into my pants pocket. I realized it couldn't be Marie-Christine this time, turned my head and found Silvano standing close behind me. He didn't make any effort to extricate his hand, but boldly stroked my thigh.

"You've got a nerve."

"I'm sorry, but I had great necessity of money this morning and I know you do not need."

"What do you know about what I need?"

"I know. Come." He took my hand and pulled me after him through the crowd and out of the square. He shoved open a little door and pulled me into a shadowy passageway. He pushed me up against a wall, and stuck his tongue into my mouth. I was surprised, not just at the audacity of it, but at my own excitement. "This morning as we drive into Rome in your car I want do this, but I am fear I might too much excite you." He started to undo my belt. I moved my hand to stop him, but soon gave up. Suddenly a light was switched on down the passage and we hurried back out into the street, scrambling with zippers and belt-buckles as we staggered along.

Silvano led me to a little bar. "Senta, mi amico, I want buy for you a grappa." We sat and smiled at each other across the little table and made a further date to meet for drinks on Via Veneto. We walked together to the bank of the Tiber and kissed goodnight. I watched Silvano turn and walk away under the plane trees, turn a corner, and disappear. I crossed the bridge and had the idea I wanted to toss a coin into the river for luck. I reached into my pocket and realized I had been robbed a second time. Fortunately I'd left my wallet with my cards and my passport hidden in my hotel room. I'd lost the equivalent of about twenty dollars. I looked at my wrist to see what time it as and my watch was gone. Oh well, only a Timex.

I resolved to get up the next morning and drive back to Porto Ercole right after breakfast. I didn't really blame Silvano; he'd given me something in exchange for my money and my watch. Or had they been taken by Marie-Christine? Well, she'd given me a good time too. I'd been brought up to think of prostitution as being just slightly less wicked than murder. But of course this was silly. These people were just selling what they had to sell. I was used to paying for meals and movies, so why not for this other form of pleasure? They didn't take it all that seriously, so why should I? It was just part of the Roman life I had wanted to experience. La dolce vita. I realized Fellini's vision wasn't over the top at all. But maybe it was time for me to move on.

I arrived at our villa to be greeted at the gate by Ben in a state of outrage. Apparently Luxardo had made a surprise visit while I was away and finding Judy alone in the pergola, had propositioned her. Ben had surprised Luxardo on his knees on the flagstones while Judy was shelling peas. Luxardo, far from apologizing, had offered Ben money for gelati if he would take his brother and sister off to the beach. Ben had responded by rushing into the house and returning brandishing a poker from the fireplace. Luxardo then proposed to take the entire family to a restaurant for lunch but Ben indignantly ordered him off the property, even though he owned it. Luxardo had resignedly climbed into his sporty little Fiat and driven away.

"Of course I really didn't take him seriously," Judy said. "Especially when I had to help him to his feet after he knelt on the grass. And he was so upset by the grass stains on his trousers. He kept saying, 'You understand, this is not serious. Just a little fantasia, while your husband amuses himself in Roma. He will understand, no? What he does in Roma? Un piccolo divertimento. So for you is la stessa cosa, no? What you English call the fair play.'"

I decided it would be a mistake to reveal the accuracy of Luxardo's perceptions. Luxardo was right. None of this should be taken seriously. A divertimento, let's leave it at that. After lunch, Bianca phoned to say that they would not be coming down on the weekend. She would be grateful if we would not overtip Maria. She knew she could rely on our discretion in this and other matters. After all, it was not our fault if we were somewhat too open and unguarded in our manners. We would doubtless learn to correct this if we wished to be accepted in good Italian society.

This barbed little speech enraged Judy. "That smarmy old hag. Who does she think she's talking to? And I wonder exactly what happened that night you all went hunting porcupines. I'll bet Luxardo tried to put the make on Serafina. I hinted about it to Maria. She became very thin-lipped all of a sudden. The old goat." I remembered Luxardo's scratched face and the bump on his forehead, Serafina's shriek in the dark and her hasty exit the next morning. "Poor old Luxardo. At least he has a sense of humour."

"Sense of humour? You didn't have him running his creepy old paws up and down your thighs or you might not be laughing. I'm supposed to take it as a compliment and be flattered by the gallantry of it all. If that's what's meant by European civilization, they can keep it."

That afternoon we went to the beach. It was a very warm day and three Italian boys actually went into the water even though it was only the end of May. Our three kids challenged them to a game of netball and won handily. I offered to buy soft drinks for the *ragazzi* and they showed Ben and Guy the rudiments of Italian billiards, which was played on a small table without cues. Sarah insisted on having a turn and beat them at their own game. Then we went to King's for dinner. We ate pasta and the kids retired to the loft while Judy and I finished our wine.

There was a long table set for a large party and the guests began to assemble. One of them, a handsome woman in her early fifties, I was sure was Mary McCarthy. Judy was a big fan and I persuaded her to go over and speak to her. The hostess graciously invited us to join her party and we squeezed in at the big table. Mary McCarthy was holding forth on Tuscan cooking, advancing the theory that the finest dishes are created from scraps that anyone else would throw away and commending Tuscan austerity and reserve. She regarded Judy's somewhat flamboyant outfit with a certain hauteur and asked what we were doing in Tuscany. It turned out that she knew Gaia but had never met her family. Judy could not resist rendering a full-length portrait of Luxardo culminating with a description of his amorous advances in the pergola. McCarthy listened with obvious delight. I understood Judy was paying Bianca back for her toploftiness and had no doubt McCarthy would put the story to good use.

The next day we packed up our camper and headed north. We stopped near Bologna for lunch and managed to reach Vicenza in the late afternoon. We had decided to take Carolina up on her invitation to visit her grandfather's house.

It turned out to be a splendid Palladian villa with classical columns crowned by Greek-style pediments surmounted by statues of dwarfs. The house was perched on the edge of a hill overlooking a broad and fertile valley. We rang the doorbell and waited. Eventually, a fiery-faced old man opened the door and stared blearily at us. We asked for Carolina. He belched, shook his head, and slammed the door in our faces. We headed across the broad lawn towards the gate when suddenly Carolina came out of the house and called to us. She greeted us warmly, notably more at ease than she had been at Porto Ercole.

She explained that the butler was drunk as usual, but her grandfather tolerated his outrageous behaviour because he was very sympathetic to the working classes. "Nonno is Communist. They call him the Red Lion of the Veneto because his speech is very fierce. You are lucky he is home, because he lives mostly in Rome. He stays in a very old hotel in Trastevere. Always the doorman says to him, Signor Marchese, we have as usual reserved for you the poorest room in the house."

Carolina led us around to the back of the villa and through French doors into an eighteenth-century salotto decorated with Tiepolo frescoes of girls in swings being pushed by turbaned blackamoors and serenaded by masked harlequins strumming ribboned mandolins. On a shabby gilded sofa sat a balding man in vest and shirtsleeves. He rose to his full height of five-foot-four and smiled cordially. "Welcome to my house. It is beautiful, is it not? Even though it is falling around my ears. But when I am dead and gone, Carolina will look after it better than I. She loves this house, don't you, mia cara?"

"You are not to talk of dying, Nonno."

"The contemplation of death is the proper business of men of my age. It is not in my power to have faith in the afterlife, so I must finish off this life as gracefully as possible. Let me get you some tea, while Carolina shows you the house." He padded down the hall in his carpet slippers.

Carolina led us through a series of rooms, each more prettily painted than the one before. The furniture was obviously original, gilt-framed sofas with frayed silk coverings, ormolu cabinets on which rested a clutter of photographs, many of Carolina, a few of Paolo, mostly on horseback, a stunning wedding photograph of Pucci trailing yards of antique lace and several photographs of a breathtakingly beautiful woman in a series of fashionable gowns in the style of the '20s and early '30s. "This is my Nonna. She was a famous singer."

"She's very beautiful. Did you ever hear her sing?"

"She stop before I am born. She had the horrible accident and came here to recover but she is never leave the house again. That is why Nonno will not change anything. For twenty-seven years he is mourning for her."

"But you want to change the house?"

"It is my dream to bring back this house to its first glory."

"Maybe your father will help you. I met him in Rome."

"He is very handsome. They call him Belpaolo. But he and Mamma are very foolish with money. He spends on horses and she spends on clothes. Fortunately her new man is very rich. But I will work very hard and I too will become rich."

"Maybe you'll be a singer. Like your grandmother. You sang very nicely that night in the restaurant."

"I have a true voice but it is not very big. I think rather I will become a music publisher. Perhaps like Ricordi, I will discover a musical genius. The new Puccini."

'Perhaps Gianfranco?" She blushed like a ripening peach. "He turned up for dinner after you left and we had a very nice evening singing together. I know he was very disappointed to find you gone."

Carolina smiled happily and led us back to the salotto where the Red Lion was waiting with a tea tray. Carolina poured and handed round the cups. I asked him about the re-emergence of the Fascist party in Italy.

"It is useless to discuss politics with stranieri. It is not possible they should understand. La politica Italiania è totalmente pazza."

"But I'm told you have devoted your life to Italian politics."

"Non è vero. I have devoted my life to beauty. First my wife, now my granddaughter. I live for the past. But my politics are for the future. This is how we are in Italy. The past teaches us despair but still we hope. An Italian can only survive if he is an incurable optimist."

The door opened and the drunken butler staggered into the room. He let out a stream of abuse, picked up the tea tray and tottered down the hall cursing. We heard a horrendous crash at the other end of the hall, more curses, and then silence. "Poor Mario. He will be so sad. Those were his favourite dishes. I must go and console him. It was so kind of you to visit me. Please to come again."

The old marchese kissed Judy's hand and disappeared. Carolina walked us to the gate and said goodbye. She promised to visit us if she ever got the chance to come to Canada. She stood framed by the tall pillars of the gate and waved till we were out of sight. We drove on to Verona and spent the night walking through the streets of the medieval city where Romeo and Juliet had lived out their fatal passion. But we'd had enough of life and love Italian-style.

The next morning we crossed the border into Austria. For the next week we skimmed through Austria and up into Germany, eating knödel and knack-wurst which made us feel stuffed and snoozy, looking at castles and church-spires whose intricacy caused us to marvel at their ingenuity, and sleeping under huge feather comforters that activated our allergies. We saw and smelled and tasted but didn't really take it in. Germany was a blur. We spent two days in the Hague and then, rested and ready for our next adventure, we loaded the car on a ferry at the Hook of Holland and barged across the North Sea.

THE SWINGING '70S

Arriving in England felt like coming home, not just because of the language and the fact that both Judy and I had actually lived here fifteen years earlier, but because we were going to stay with my old friend Annie Lazier and her new husband Michael. Annie had been a mythic figure of my late adolescence, the epitome of the Party Girl. Half my high school friends had their first drink in Annie's kitchen and many had their first sex in her basement. Though not with Annie; while they were unhooking and unzipping in the dimly lit rec room she would be upstairs drinking stingers and dancing a loose-jointed Charleston or a tortured quirky tango, demonstrating the joys of sheer abandon. A sort of suburban Lady of Misrule. Annie was at the same time slinky and manic, her trademarks a half-tamed mane of honey blond hair, thick glasses with rainbow-coloured frames and a laugh as relentless as Woody Woodpecker's.

Annie moved on from a disastrous first marriage that produced two sons when she inherited a substantial fortune from her grandfather, who was, I think, a lumber baron. Her next husband, Michael, was an econometrician so brainy he claimed to have been totally bored until he entered graduate school at the age of nineteen. When Michael was made a fellow at Balliol at twenty-six, Annie bought a sixteenth-century manor house that once belonged to Lady Ottoline Morrell, installed her two sons and her new daughter Trinity, and at once began giving parties where she mixed university dons with a variety of strange characters who took her fancy as she drove around the country lanes of England in her Aston Martin searching for antiques and the remains of Roman roads and Druidic holy places.

We landed at Southend and drove straight across four counties until we found her mellow, red-brick house on the outskirts of Oxford. We rang her bell at about three o'clock in the afternoon and eventually Michael came to the door in pyjama bottoms and a raccoon coat. "This house is intolerably cold, even in July. Do come in. Had lunch? Annie's still in bed but I'm sure I can rustle up some grub." He led us into the cavernous kitchen, where he produced a joint of cold beef and a bottle of Chambertin. We ate and drank and after a while Annie came downstairs flaunting an embroidered silk dressing gown which she claimed had belonged to the Dowager Empress. She insisted on toasting our arrival and in very short order we went through three bottles of Taittinger.

We settled into life at the manor house with differing degrees of ease. I was happy to rerun old jokes with Annie and delighted to discover she had saved every issue of *Salterrae*, a scabrous weekly newssheet that I had edited when we were both undergraduates at Trinity. I was happy to accompany Annie on her forays into the countryside in her nifty little car. She peered from under her wide-brimmed hat through her thick glasses, grazing hedgerows and narrowly missing gateposts. She picked up all hitchhikers, though many of them were clearly nervous of her cascading laugh and erratic command of the wheel; they would make preposterous excuses to get her to stop so they could make their escape, and one poor lad actually jumped out of the back seat and ran down the road with Annie pursuing him in the car shrieking with delight. He finally got away when she swerved into the side of a small bridge and stopped with one wheel dangling over the edge. She was still laughing when a local farmer came along and helped pull the car back onto the road.

Occasionally, Annie and one of her itinerants would take to each other and become instant intimates. One such was a middle-aged woman in a bright ankle-length dress and matching bonnet obviously of her own manufacture. She announced straight off that her name was Jennet and she was a witch, and not just a white witch either. Her appearance was not very witchlike, however; she was fat and jolly with a chortling giggle that counterpointed Annie's own distinctive laugh and she carried a large string bag full of various kinds of homemade sweets, sticky and oozing with syrup, which she popped into her mouth at frequent intervals. She seemed to know a lot about ancient Britain and when she discovered Annie's current passion of mapping ancient Roman roads, she poured out a long litany of place names, none of which could be found on any map. Not to worry, she would herself devise a map; map-making was one of her special skills; she had inherited it from an ancestor who was chief cartographer to James I, who was himself a witch, having been inculcated in the fraternity by his mother, that last of the great royal witches: Mary, Queen of Scots. Jennet came home with us and became part of the household, tending various pots that she kept boiling on the stove, stuffing her sickening sweets into young Trinity's eager mouth, and working away on her map which she drew in special ink made out of goat's dung and sheep's blood on a large cowhide stretched out on the floor of the library.

On rainy afternoons, which were frequent, Annie stayed home and painted. Her paintings were a curious mixture of the geometric and the surreal, of op and pop. On a receding or spiralling or knotted checkerboard, there appeared images of Virginia Woolf, Chiquita Banana, Chairman Mao, a Model T Ford, Clarabelle Cow, the Taj Mahal. The paintings were carefully structured, meticulously crafted, quite unlike the rest of Annie's life. And she was totally unlike herself when she worked on them: silent, focused, calm. There were perhaps a dozen finished canvasses stacked at one side of the library, enough for a small show, and I couldn't help thinking they were shrewdly geared to the taste of the time, but when I mentioned this to Annie she merely shrugged and went on painting.

There were also days when Annie didn't get out of bed. Then I would go into Oxford with Michael, browse in the Bodleian or the Ashmolean and then have lunch at high table, preceded by sherry of unprecedented dryness and followed by port of incomparable nuttiness. Obviously in Oxford one did not do any serious work in the afternoon. Instead we would walk to the Botanical Garden or Parson's Pleasure and discuss politics. Michael was a fund of information about people in high places and loved to disclose who Edward Heath or Lord Snowden were currently sleeping with, who was the masked butler at a certain scandalous sex party in Soho, the real reason a certain Labour politician had been forced to become a peer and retire to the House of Lords.

Meanwhile our kids reacted very positively to the change of scene. They got on well with Annie's two sons: John was a big fourteen-year-old, outspoken and aggressive. Jimmy was skinny, silent, and sharp-eyed. They rarely spoke to each other but seemed happy to be with our kids. They all bunked in together on the third floor, which was like an animal warren, full of small rooms and long passageways. They were allowed to take food to their rooms and had midnight feasts of roasted marshmallows and swiped champagne; storytelling competitions at which Ben and John competed to see who could most effectively scare the others, and strip poker games in which John's aim was to see Sarah in the buff; she effectively frustrated him by wearing unexpected bits of jewellery borrowed from her mother's suitcase. They played elaborate practical jokes on each other involving whipped cream, corn syrup, and various small animals, alive or dead, in each other's beds, sudden outbursts of firecrackers or dousings of water, which on one occasion brought down the ceiling in Annie's bedroom.

The kids' big epiphany came one night when Annie and Michael persuaded us to watch some new British TV show they'd discovered. It turned out to be *Monty Python*. Ben and Guy were instantly smitten. In the parlance of the day, *Monty Python* blew them away. Ben had inherited the Byers knack for mimicry and he soon began to sing *Monty Python* songs and take on some of the characters, extending their routines and recycling their jokes. Guy, as always an ardent fan of his older brother, imitated Ben's imitations. Expressions like "right, then" and "know what I mean?" "upper-class twit" and "poofter" began to shape and define their entire system of verbal communication. John and Jimmy and Sarah struggled to keep up and even their practical jokes began to take on a Pythonesque character.

Judy was less happy at the manor house for a number of reasons. She found it impossible to accept Annie's virtually non-existent standards of housewifery. On our second day in the house she undertook to clean out the refrigerator and discovered an ancient piece of uncooked meat that smelt like carrion and was literally crawling with maggots. She decided to throw out everything and start over. Annie drove her to the neighbouring butcher shop and ordered up saddles of mutton, sides of beef, and haunches of venison. When Judy protested that this too would go bad before we got to eat it all, Annie merely turned to the butcher and commanded, "Send this to the manor house, my good man," and stalked out. Judy pretended to be shocked, but may actually have been miffed at finally meeting someone who could top her own extravagance.

Her concern for young Trinity was, however, more altruistic. Trinity wandered around the big house virtually on her own, often scantily dressed in garments pilfered from her mother's cupboards, foraging for herself and living largely in a make-believe world of her own devising. She was lively and imaginative, but also given to sudden tantrums and rages and indifferently toilet-trained. Judy decided to take her on as a project. She spent long hours reading to her, making her special treats in the kitchen, teaching her nursery rhymes and finger-plays, and taking her shopping for real little girl's clothes. They became fast friends and had little to do with the rest of us. Annie was not jealous. Indeed she barely seemed to notice. This further confirmed

Judy's notion that Annie was unfit to be a mother and led her to intensify her efforts to reclaim Trinity to a life of comparative order and respectability.

Almost every night there was a party at the manor house. Michael bade his colleagues, Annie found eccentrics on the road or sometimes invited people whose names in the telephone book caught her fancy. I remember on one occasion she phoned someone called Peregrine P. Plunket. He turned out to be a long-haired and rather spacey young man who kept bees. He had been named for the hero of an eighteenth-century novel by an intensely literary father and retaliated by never learning to read at all. On another occasion Annie invited five different people whose names ended in Bottom (Ramsbotham, Higginbottom, Sidebotham, Winterbottom, and her favourite, Wyglebottom) and when they were all assembled announced, "I'm sorry but I have to tend to something in the kitchen. Perhaps you could all introduce yourselves to each other." She then reappeared with a tray of martinis and brightly commanded, "Bottoms up." Mrs. Winterbottom left in a huff, but the others thought it was funny and stayed on into the small hours, periodically slapping their thighs and bursting into guffaws. No one laughed harder than Annie.

After a bit, Annie's parties began to merge into each other. They all began in the drawing room in a rather civilized way with her excellent but deadly martinis and hors d'oeuvres of smoked trout or Russian eggs or tapenade ordered up from a local foodstore. The guests eventually wove their way into the dining room and found places at the table and made their way through soup and pheasant or roast beef or rack of lamb liberally washed down by good claret. It was not uncommon to see guests with their faces in their plates by the time dessert was served, and sometimes when we repaired to the library for port and cognac we left several people passed out on the dining room floor.

The evening would end with Annie dancing in the living room sometimes on a table surrounded by admirers who egged her on, sometimes alone, choreographing a major work to the strains of "L'après-midi d'un faune" or Ravel's "Bolero." Michael, meanwhile, would be constructing some intricate intellectual defence of an impossible philosophical or political position for the benefit of his befuddled colleagues among the brandy fumes and cigar smoke of the library. They would argue on, becoming increasingly impassioned but irrational, imaginative but inarticulate.

The kids would be out in the garden. John had just discovered pot and had a rather erratic supplier, Lord Timothy, an aristocratic undergraduate at Michael's college and a thoroughly affected young man who had obviously read *Brideshead Revisited.* He also sold vintage wines to Michael and was a frequent visitor at the manor house. Though effete, he was decidedly heterosexual, and several times tried to lure Annie out onto the terrace. When she refused, he solaced himself with whatever other female company he could muster, usually frustrated lady academics many years his senior. Sometimes they would wander back into the house at two or three in the morning looking weak and bedraggled, sometimes they just disappeared, never to be seen again.

About ten days after our arrival we organized a day-long expedition to Wiltshire to visit Wilton House, Stonehenge, and Avebury. Annie and I sat in the front of the van. Jennet, whom Annie now referred to as "the family witch," rode in the back with the kids. Judy stayed home with Trinity. At Wilton, I introduced myself and Annie as Canadian Shakespearean scholars from the University of Saskatchewan who were working on a book about the Bard's infatuation with William Herbert, an ancestor of the owners of the mansion and a major patron of poets, whose sister married Sir Philip Sidney, and who was considered a likely candidate to be the Mr. W.H. of the sonnets.

We were soon handed over to Dr. Chloe Reeves-Wilmot, a rather aggressive young bluestocking from the University of London who happened to be working in the library of the house. She pooh-poohed the idea that the young earl could possibly be Mr. W.H.; she had another much more plausible candidate but was not at liberty to divulge his identity. To get back at her, I advanced the theory that the original production of *Much Ado About Nothing* had been designed to be performed in the gardens of Wilton, when the London theatres closed because of the Plague. William Herbert was to have played Claudio and his fiancée Hero, though this meant she would have to pretend to be a boy during rehearsals. Shakespeare himself was to play the villain Don John and would get to denounce his lover's girlfriend. The whole project was stopped by the young earl's mother, who sniffed a scandal in the making. This was an on-the-spot fabrication on my part. I had chosen this play because I knew the text well, having twice acted in it and directed an outdoor production in Toronto, so that I was able to quote from it at length. (This was of course long before the film *Shakespeare in Love.*)

The novelty of the idea appealed strongly to Dr. Chloe, who went into a scholarly tailspin, trying to cast the other roles and make sense of the dating of the play in relation to the other comedies and the exact timing of the Plague. Just as I was beginning to realize my academic knowledge was too skimpy to permit me to hold up my end of the argument much longer, Jennet burst in on us to say it was vital that we move on. She was counting on us getting to Stonehenge before five o'clock when the shadows cast by the stones would be of particular significance from a witchy point of view. She had rounded up the kids who were waiting in the car. Annie extended a dinner invitation to Dr. Chloe, and we bade her farewell as she promised to ransack the Wilton library for clues that would support my theory and get back to me "with all deliberate haste, as Malvolio would have phrased it."

Annie and I jumped in the van and we took off for Stonehenge, which proved to be a mob scene. There were twenty-odd tourist buses, innumerable hot-dog vendors, and a huge party of Japanese, including several monks in saffron robes being addressed through a loud-hailer. We therefore went on to Avebury, driving down the processional avenue lined with stones till we reached the monument where Jennet took charge. She had changed into a tent-like robe that trailed along the ground and she made strange sounds, which Annie suggested were ancient Druidic runes. The rest of us stood and watched while she hopped and darted across the field, sometimes stopping abruptly and reversing direction, or prostrating herself on the ground and mumbling to herself. She beckoned to us to join her. We all took hands and began to dance in a ring and it was then I suddenly realized Ben and Jimmy were missing. Nobody had seen them since they were all playing hide-and-seek in the gardens back at Wilton.

I cut through the wiccan ritual by announcing I had to go back immediately and find them. Jennet countered that if I left in the middle of the ceremony I would bring down a serious curse upon all of us. Not being at all superstitious, I didn't care. Annie suggested I go back and she stay with the kids. Guy elected to go with me. He was pretty sure he knew where Ben and Jimmy had been hiding. When we got to Wilton, they were in the gatehouse. It was obvious from their dirt-streaked cheeks they had been in tears. Fortunately the gatekeeper was a kindly old gent who had fed them sweeties from a glass jar. He had some sharp words for me, but they were nothing to the tirade I got from Judy when we finally got back to the manor house. Ben had phoned her from Wilton and told her what had happened.

Judy announced that she had had enough of Annie's self-indulgent eccentricity. She didn't find it amusing and she was sick of trying to run a twenty-room house and care for six kids and five supposed adults, each of whom was more irresponsible than the kids ever thought of being. And that went for me too. I realized the rebuke was at least somewhat justified and promised to drive up to London the next day and see about renting a flat. Judy insisted we should all go and when Trinity burst into tears, suggested that Trinity should come with us. Annie, who was mixing up the second batch of martinis, raised no objection. In fact, she'd be happy to send the boys up to visit us in London, once we got settled.

So the next morning we packed up the van. I dropped Judy and the kids at Regent's Park zoo and went to see a house agent in Beauchamp Place. She showed me a variety of high-priced flats fashionably decorated with glass tables, oriental screens, and gilt commodes. None of them seemed likely to stand up to the ministrations of six kids and my agent was becoming distinctly snappish, when she suddenly thought of a place she knew about in Earls Court. It was a rambling apartment with four bedrooms and two baths, a huge kitchen, dining room and drawing room, all decorated in the height of fashion of about 1936, but now shabby and neglected. It was about half the price of the other places we'd seen. "Of course you *couldn't* ask anybody in, but as a place to camp out, I suppose it has certain advantages."

I immediately signed a month's lease and we moved in that afternoon. In the next four weeks I calculated we entertained some two-hundred-and-seventy-odd visitors. None of them objected to the decor, not even Lord Timothy who drove John and Jimmy down from Oxford the next weekend and pronounced as he presented us with a complimentary bottle of Chateau d'Yquem, "Delicious, my dears. The whole thing is simply too, too original." We ate hamburgers and he took the kids off to a party in the King's Road, from which they returned alone in a cab well after the Tube had stopped running and smelling distinctly of cannabis.

During the weeks that followed, we were entertained by Canadian friends living all over London. Our childhood acting buddy Powell Jones lived in a vicarage in Islington. Rodney Archer had just acquired an eighteenth-century house with the original panelling but no plumbing or electricity in Spitalfields. Together they were just beginning to write plays combining outrageous old-fashioned puns with a highly advanced sexual outlook. Garrick Hagon and his wife, Lisa Ross, lived around the corner in a flat belonging to Canadian sculptor David Partridge: his compositions were constructed entirely out of thousands of steel and copper nails. Garrick and Lisa spent hours polishing tiny tacks and huge spikes between sessions doing voice-overs for sexploitation movies. Robert and Liz Troop had a small house in Barnes, where he was working on a screenplay for Peter Hall based on his novel *The Hammering* and she was halfway through her first book, *Woolworth Madonna*. Ann Murray was bringing up her children in Kensington and had already started to conduct historical walks through the City of London for American tourists erudite enough to know who John Aubrey and Sir John Soane were. Miranda Davies had acquired a substantial middle-class house in Chiswick and was preparing to be a child psychiatrist under the aegis of a famous Jungian analyst. It soon proved too complicated to get all of us to all these far-flung places and get home again, so after the first week they came to our flat for dinner and many of them stayed long into the evening and sometimes through the night.

The one person who never seemed to find time to visit was my friend Dick Williams who rarely left his studio at Soho Square, where he was working on his animated version of Dickens' *A Christmas Carol*. It would win him his first Oscar a year later.

Every Friday he and his staff screened the week's work and we would go with the kids and watch in a little basement projection room. Dick paid close attention to the kids' reactions and once when Ben asked, "Didn't we just see that a minute ago?" Dick flew into a rage. A young animator had used one bit of footage twice to save time and Dick insisted the whole sequence be done again, even if it set back the work by nearly a week. On another occasion, we were joined at the screening by Alastair Sim, who was supplying the voice of Scrooge. He cackled delightedly throughout but insisted on redoing three sequences. He was a perfectionist, as was Dick. With this project as with several others, the producers eventually took the film away from him, realizing that if they waited until he was completely satisfied, it would never be shown at all.

The last time I'd seen Dick had been six years earlier in Toronto, where he spent an evening with Judy and I and the kids at home. He had just won a prestigious award at the animation festival at Annecy for his film *The Little Island*, but that victory had cost him his first marriage. His wife, Tep, had become completely fed up with a life that involved meticulously copying animation cells fourteen hours a day and then sitting in a pub listening to Dick play trumpet with his musician friends. Dick was shattered, though not, I think, utterly unconsoled. During his visit with us in Toronto, he seemed much impressed by the joys of family life as we embodied them. He was fascinated by Sarah's early efforts at drawing, by Guy's appreciative giggles when Dick told one of his outrageous stories alternating between a Russian, a Japanese and a southern accent and by Ben's spontaneous and deadly accurate imitation of him. Less than six months later he sent us an invitation to his wedding to Cathy. She and Dick now lived in Hampstead with their two young children.

Dick was anxious that we should meet them and arranged for us all to have Sunday brunch together at a smart restaurant in Mayfair. Cathy greeted us regally: she was a beauty and well aware of it. She had been educated at a fashionable English girls' school while her father, a highly placed American diplomat, was travelling the globe, then had a brief career as a model before marrying Dick. She had arranged for her children to attend this lunch with their nanny, who whisked them away home after the first half-hour.

She had also invited some neighbours introduced as Bernard and Araminta. He was a financier with interests in the Middle East, she another former model who now had a shop where she sold Indian embroideries and tribal African jewellery just off Sloane Square. They had a flat in Cairo, a houseboat in Kashmir, a chalet in Gstaad and a beach house at Santa Barbara. Bernard questioned me about the possibility of buying property in the Canadian Rockies and when it became apparent I knew nothing about this, turned his attention to Cathy. Araminta interrogated me on the subject of Amerindian crafts and resolved to go to the Canadian West Coast to meet the native carvers. It became clear as she spoke she was interested less in crafts than in ethnic craftsmen. Meanwhile, Dick was at the other end of the room blowing his horn, reprising old Beiderbecke numbers like "Goose Pimples" and "I'm Coming, Virginia" with the rest of the band. Cathy was telling Bernard that she was considering some sort of import business of her own. She had been to Morocco with Dick and had been very taken with the silverwork and blue cloth of the Berbers. Perhaps they should go on an exploratory buying trip.

By the time we'd been in London two weeks, the kids were travelling the Tube on their own every day with John and Jimmy. They went to the zoo, the tower, and Madame Tussaud's, played pinball machines, and hung out at the Great American Disaster, an upscale fast-food eatery offering twenty-five kinds of burgers. Judy and I went to the Victoria and Albert Museum, the Tate, and the Hayward, foreign films, plays at the Aldwych and the National, and explored fashionable new restaurants. The first of these we encountered was Parkes. The head waiter handed each of us a white orchid and led us to a booth where we sat together on a mound of purple velvet that was less like a banquette than a double bed. A tall, willowy young man sauntered over and sat down beside us. "Hello, I'm Alastair. I'll be looking after you tonight." We ate an extraordinary meal that seemed to be mostly flowers: nasturtiums, violets, more orchids. We received a bill that should have covered taking Alastair home for the night. I would have suggested it, but was afraid he might say yes.

Two days later we went to lunch at the Reform Club with Hamish, an old friend of Judy's from her stay in London in the '50s. He had been a colonel in a Scottish regiment in the war and still sported a splendid military moustache. He consulted gravely with a horse-faced waiter and ordered for us: game pate, cockieleekie, mixed grill, and a savoury. He and Judy didn't seem to have much to say to each other, which struck me as curious, because she has never been exactly tongue-tied. Fortunately we had Guy with us; he had overslept and the other kids had gone off without him. He asked Hamish about his experiences in the war and the rest of the lunch was a prolonged account of the Italian campaign with mustard pots and salt cellars pressed into service as tanks and artillery pieces.

When we parted, Guy and Hamish made a date for the next afternoon and they saw each other almost every day for the next two weeks. They visited the War Museum, various military monuments, Hamish's old mess, and finally Sandhurst. Hamish became convinced that Guy had a military future and offered to put him up for his regiment when the time came. Little did he suspect that Guy would eventually become a peace activist and socialist candidate. I realize now it was the politics of war that interested him, not the pomp and circumstance, the honour and the glory. Judy seemed delighted that Hamish and Guy had hit it off and often joined them for tea in the late afternoon while I was having a drink with Troop or one of my other old buddies.

Troop was trying to convince me I should settle in England. He was hopeful of getting into the script-writing business and thought I too should take a crack at it. We had collaborated successfully in the past on *Salterrae* and I remembered our Sunday afternoon sessions typing out scandal and scatology on his old Olivetti as some of the most entertaining times I'd ever spent. The prospect of picking up where we'd left off fifteen years before was very inviting. Troop tried several times to arrange lunch with Peter Hall, but it always seemed to fall through. Still, the seed of the idea of writing for movies stuck in my mind like a burr and was fertilized every time I visited Dick in his studio and listened to his movie talk. He would sit at his drawing board, endlessly sketching and scheming, snickering as new and more outrageous figures took shape on the paper before him.

One afternoon as I sat watching and listening to him in Soho Square, George Dunning came in. I hadn't seen him since 1957; he was a bit fleshier, a bit greyer, but still elegant, offhand, with his characteristic slow, sliding speech, as though he was reluctant to part with each syllable he uttered. We left Dick's together and walked to the Savoy, where George ordered a bottle of Nuits St. Georges and offered me an Egyptian cigarette. He told me he had begun a movie based on the Beatles. (It would eventually become *The Yellow Submarine* and every frame of it would reflect George's keen wit and skewed erudition, his quirky juxtapositions of unexpected styles and deep anarchic love of mischief for its own sake.)

"So here you are again, fifteen years later. Not quite the shock-haired Colonial boy I remember, but still an intriguing specimen." He reached across and laid his hand on my knee, left it a moment, and then withdrew it. "If I had kept my hand on your knee that evening in Mayfair ten years ago for another say, three minutes, what would have happened to you? You might now be an up-and-coming film director and the intimate of whom? Cecil Beaton, John Gielgud, David Hockney?"

"I have no regrets."

"Good. Never regret, never regress. Dick tells me you're thinking of settling in London?"

"I have a job to go home to."

"But you've got caught up in the glamour of swinging London? You envy Dick working with Mike Nichols, Tony Richardson, Woody Allen. You know he's fought with every one of them. But then, you don't have Dick's ego."

"I don't have his talent."

"You have your own talent. But unless you also have Dick's commitment to talent — your own talent — at the expense of everyone else's —"

"You think that's important?"

"It's essential. I didn't know it when I was twenty-five. At least not consciously, though maybe even then I knew it in my bones. Dick knew it when he was nineteen. I remember him at our studio in Kleinburg —"

"Even earlier than that. When we used to do shows together — puppet shows, high school revues, he had to be the star."

"And you let him be the star."

"Yes. I suppose when I really like someone, really believe in them . . ."

"Ah well, there you have it then. The truth is — you're just not enough of a shit." George smiled across at me like a sleek, drowsy panther and poured himself another glass of burgundy. Then, "If you really want to stay here, you can come and work for me."

I looked at my watch and realized Judy and I were supposed to be having tea with Hamish and his wife Prudence at their flat in Knightsbridge. "That's very generous of you, George."

"Not really. I could use you."

"I'll call you before the end of the week, okay? Now I've got to go." George exhaled through his nose and cocked his eyebrows at me through the smoke as I made my way across the lobby.

It was nearly six when Prudence showed me into her chintz drawing room and said briskly, "I sent Judy and Hamish off to Fortnum's for tea, actually. It was their old haunt, you know. If you like I could make you some fresh, but I suspect you'd rather have a spot of whisky. I know I would."

She poured us two stiff shots of single malt and we sat in wing chairs facing each other across the empty fireplace. "I do think it's nice that Hamish and Judith have met again after all this time. He's greatly taken with your son Guy. Poor Hamish always wanted a son and all I seemed to be able to produce were girls. They rode and Jilly even learned to shoot, but it's not the same. Hamish wants to take Guy fishing in Scotland the week after next. Do you and Judith fish?"

"We're supposed to be going home."

"I can't honestly say I'm sorry to hear that."

"Why?

"Seeing Judith again has been upsetting for Hamish. He has a weak heart, you see."

I looked at Prudence's upper lip tremble. I didn't know what to say, what she expected me to say. I waited. After a moment she got up and left the room. She came back carrying a small cardboard box. She held it out to me.

"Please take this."

"What is it?"

"Letters Judith wrote to Hamish after she went back to Canada. I intercepted them. I suppose it was naughty of me, but I didn't know what else to do. Hamish and I have never talked much about things. I mean other than what schools the girls should go to and whether we could afford to recover the furniture. That sort of thing." I took the box. "Thanks awfully. That's a load off my mind. Can I drive you to your flat? I'm a very capable driver. I drove ambulances all through the blitz, you know."

I declined her offer. At the door we shook hands solemnly and then suddenly she gave me a quick peck on the cheek. She shut the door and disappeared. I walked into the park and opened the box. The letters were all opened. I was astonished to discover I didn't want to read them. I took them home and found Judy sitting waiting. She had declined Hamish's offer to take her to dinner at Simpson's. I gave her the letters and left her sitting on the sofa in the living room turning them over in her hands. I came back into the room five minutes later with two drinks, a vermouth for her and a Scotch for me. I wanted to ask her about Hamish but somehow understood this wasn't the moment. We went out to dinner at the Ritz, came home rather drunk, and went to bed. After breakfast the next morning I was drinking coffee in the drawing room and realized the ashes of the letters were in the grate.

We had seen a number of plays in London that summer. The most successful was Peter Brook's production of *A Midsummer Night's Dream* with its acrobatic, sexy, menacing fairies, its foolish volatile lovers, and bumbling, vulnerable clowns. Ben in particular loved this show and wanted to see it again but tickets were difficult to get. I remembered that Chloe, the young Shakespearean scholar at Wilton, had told me she had an in with the RSC. I called her and indeed she was able to get us additional tickets. She also wanted to talk to me again if possible. She would be in London in a few days and would get in touch.

Ben was even keener on Brook's production on second viewing. He was also keen to see Brook's film version of *Lord of the Flies* but was refused admission because of his age. I argued with the theatre manager, saying that the picture was about kids exactly Ben's age so why would they ban kids from seeing it, but this had no effect. Then one evening we were having dinner with Chloe, who arrived in London and announced she was completely revising her thesis as a result of our conversation at Wilton about *Much Ado About Nothing*. She begged me to come up to Oxford with her to meet her supervisor Una Ellis-Fermor. I would have been interested to meet this formidable scholarly dame but realized I would undoubtedly be unmasked as a fraud in the first ten minutes. I also realized Chloe's interest in me and my ideas was not totally academic. I suggested maybe I could drive Annie's kids home the following weekend. Judy said I could go if I wished; she had no intention of going back to Annie's even for one day. I caught the flicker of triumph in Chloe's eyes and wondered if Judy saw it too.

At this point the doorbell rang. It was two policemen in tall blue hats delivering Ben and John back home. Apparently they'd sneaked through a back door into the cinema where *Lord of the Flies* was showing. They'd seen the last three-quarters of it and planned to stay through the next showing when they were intercepted by the manager and turned over to the law. I thought this was amusing, but the policemen didn't. They gave us a solemn lecture about the responsibility of parents to provide a good moral example to their children. They would let the boys off with a warning this time. They refused our offers of coffee and cookies; fortunately I'd suppressed my instinct to offer them a drink. As soon as they'd gone, John and Ben made milkshakes laced with Scotch and downed them happily. Judy gave me an ominous warning look.

The next day I held a family council. I explained that I'd had a job offer from George and wondered whether I should take it. I had discovered we could get a long lease on our flat at a very reasonable rate; it would contain a clause that if the owners, an ancient Danish couple in their nineties were to die, the lease would terminate, but they might go on for years. The kids seemed to like London; they were starting to know their way around and make friends. And Judy seemed to enjoy her life, shopping at Harrod's, tea at Fortnum's — I looked at her narrowly.

The kids began to ask questions. Could John and Jimmy stay with us in London? I was prepared for this one; I had spoken to Annie and Michael the night before. Annie was willing to let Trinity stay on with us a while longer but Michael had paid school fees for the boys in Oxford and wanted them home by the weekend. School. The kids had almost forgotten about it. I said of course there were schools in London for them to go to. Would they have to go to schools if we stayed here? Absolutely, said Judy. Sarah said she didn't mind trying out an English school, in fact she liked the idea, but the boys were adamant about wanting to go back to their old school at home. So their vote was cast. Judy considered; she'd enjoyed looking after Trinity, but she'd be better off at nursery school. Judy could teach in England but she'd not had a very good experience when she'd taught here fifteen years earlier. She'd rather go home. Wouldn't she miss Harrod's and Fortnum's? Perhaps, but there were more important things than tea and sympathy. I felt disappointed and also relieved. As I had fifteen years earlier, I saw that London, so stimulating, so stylish, was not really open or accepting. The hierarchy, the gamesmanship. Oh, I knew I could learn to play the game acceptably, but was that what I wanted? To be an acceptable player?

We decided to give a bang-up party in our flat before we left. We asked everybody we could think of. The first arrivals were a pair of squat, greyhaired gnomes in frock-coats who might have been twins: one wore a clerical collar and the other a necktie. Their accents were impenetrably upper class. It gradually dawned on me that the clerical one was an old friend of Judy's brother Jamie, a rural dean whom we'd been trying to track down since our arrival in England; the one with the tie was his sister, the headmistress of a highly regarded girls' school. Annie and Michael arrived next and Annie immediately invited both the dean and his sister to dinner at the manorhouse. As the evening wore on, she invited most of the rest of the guests as well. And of course she danced on the dining room table, though I missed it. I was in one of the bedrooms talking to George.

"So you've decided to give Canada another chance. I think you're the generous one, dear boy. I hope Canada will be suitably grateful. Though frankly, I doubt it. Still, the truth is, although some places are much more amusing to be idle in, one can work anywhere. And you do seem to be committed to the notion of work."

"I don't work as hard as Dick does."

"Nobody works as hard as Dick does. But then as you said, almost nobody has his talent. It's funny, talent and work seem to be symbiotic. They feed each other. The work gets better and better because the talent develops through use. And the fact that the work is always improving means one wants to go on working. That's true even for a sybarite like me. I think I want to sit about and do nothing, but I can't. I keep getting ideas. One thing leads to another. Horrible. Do you have any decent wine? This is disgusting."

"I think I've got something tucked away." The bathroom door opened and out came Cathy and Bernard. She looked at me coolly. "Dick had to fly to L.A. this morning. He said to tell you be sure to call next time you're in London. Lovely party, but I'm afraid we have to be going." She didn't even let go of Bernard's hand as she turned away.

I looked at George who shrugged. "Does Dick know?" I asked.

"I shouldn't think so. He's not particularly forgiving, as I have reason to know. He'll find out soon enough."

"You don't think he'll be upset?"

"He'll be outraged. He won't see that he's to blame, leaving the poor girl alone all the time. And he'll find consolation. As he always has in the past."

I went in search of a bottle of Pommard I had hidden in the broom closet. In the kitchen I found Chloe pouring herself a drink. She asked if we could postpone our trip to Oxford as Lord Timothy had invited her down to his family seat where there was an interesting collection of Elizabethan manuscripts. I said I would be going home in a few days. She didn't seem greatly disappointed.

On the way back to the bedroom Hamish stopped me in the hall, tumbler of Scotch in hand. "I just wanted to say — I'm so glad she met you. I couldn't have given her what you have." He shook my hand gravely. "I gave her a little gift. I know you'll understand." He looked at me like a bloodhound who's lost the scent. He shook my hand and headed for the door. When I got back to the bedroom, George was asleep on a pile of coats. I took my Pommard back down the hall. In the drawing room, the crowd was thinning out. Michael was carrying Trinity who was asleep in his arms and trying to interest Annie in rounding up the boys. I helped her find them and we all went downstairs and stood around the Aston Martin. There was a fresh breeze that gently shook the leaves above us. Jimmy was asleep and John was tipsy but Annie was in top form. Her laugh rang out through the summer night. I could still hear it as the smart little car pulled away and sped down the Old Brompton Road.

Back upstairs, Judy was emptying glasses and ashtrays. Everyone else had gone, even George who had awakened and presented her with a present, a rather ambiguous drawing called *Leda*. We tried to figure it out.

"It might or might not have been a depiction of swan-fucking. I hear you also received a present from Hamish."

I opened the bottle of Pommard. Not that either of us needed another drink, but it was our last night in London. Or actually our last morning. The first faint glow of dawn could be seen above the swaying trees of Redcliffe Gardens. We clinked our glasses.

"Do you want to see?" Judy opened a velvet-covered jewellery box and displayed a large clear, yellow stone in a silver mount. "It's a cairngorm."

"A what?"

"Semi-precious Scottish stone. He used to wear it in his dress sporran."

"How appropriate."

"Don't be snide."

"You won't miss him?"

"Yes. I'll miss him and Harrod's and Fortnum's and the Café de Paris. But that's not life. Life's the kids and school and our parents. Life's Eaton's and hockey practices and cast parties and summers at Marshall's Bay. You know that as well as I do."

And the fact of the matter was, I did know it.

HITS AND MISSES

About two months before we took off for Europe, I attended a meeting at the Drama Centre at which Leon Major announced, "Martin doesn't know it yet, but he is going to direct a student production at Hart House next month." This was typical of Leon's seat-of-the-pants way of doing things, but it would be my first full production on the Hart House stage and I jumped at the chance. Following the success of *The Caucasian Chalk Circle* I opted for an early Brecht work, *A Man's A Man*. A much less accessible work, it has interesting roles and I was able to recruit some good actors: Jim Bradford, John Brown, Jim Cox, Michael Fletcher, Maureen Fox, David Rotenburg, and, in his stage debut, Ray Conlogue, who at one point got stuffed into a wooden crate where he had to stay for half an hour, which may have been a formative influence in his future career as the *Globe and Mail* drama critic. I had discovered as a student director that it was easy to persuade attractive girls to play whores and our production featured some stunning young women.

Again I worked with Tom Dougherty as designer and as we had virtually no budget we built a set out of old crates we scavenged from a dump, mounted a prop gun made from a mop handle on a janitor's wheeled bucket, and borrowed a baggage wagon from Union Station. Ross Stuart, my assistant director and I rolled it up University Avenue and were initially denied access to the campus but we went to another gate and it functioned effectively onstage as a railway car. I revised the Eric Bentley translation to my own liking and completely rewrote his lyrics, which were set to music by Clifford Ford, a young student composer at the Faculty of Music, who assembled a small orchestra of his peers to play live on a platform at the rear of the stage. The staging relied on various pratfalls and sight gags, including two actors under a blanket impersonating an elephant. While it did not have the warmth and humanity of the later Brecht play, the audience responded favorably, Leon pronounced it an enjoyable entertainment, and Brian Parker complimented me on my audacity. He asked me to come back next year for the second term at double my old salary and to direct another student show. And off we went to Europe.

I had proposed another Brecht show, I think *The Good Woman of Setzuan*, but

I was informed on my return that I would be directing *Serjeant Musgrave's Dance*. It was not for me to select the repertoire, which was and would continue to be controlled by a committee of staff and student representatives. *Musgrave* was a challenging script and I set to work on it with the help of Martha Mann as designer. We decided to use the turntable that Leon had constructed for his production of *Mourning Becomes Electra*, which would revolve against a backlit cyclorama on which we would project images of industrial England, a scheme which we were unable to realize because of the technical limitations of the theatre staff. However, the turntable allowed the soldiers to march doggedly onward while it turned in the opposite direction, an effective technique I had lifted from the Berliner Ensemble's production of *Mother Courage and Her Children*. I was determined the soldiers should be taught proper British army drill and consulted two or three retired officers, all of whom seemed to have completely forgotten the appropriate military moves, but I finally turned to Jimmy Hozack, who had been a warrant officer in the Second World War, and he readily responded. Jimmy obviously enjoyed this experience and my stock went up a bit in his estimation.

I was once again able to work with some good actors: students Ron Davies, Peter Froelich, and John Taylor, and several faculty members: Michael Tait, Alan Toff, and Al Masters. This established a precedent of using not only students but anyone who had a university connection, thus giving me access to a number of more mature actors. Again the play had songs and this time Judy and our children acted as street buskers, playing on tin whistles, tambourines, and some instruments borrowed from Margaret Galloway at the Institute of Child Study. This is a dark play, but we tried to bring out whatever humour we could find in the text. At the time the theatre's box office was run by a handsome actress, Eleanor Beecroft, with whom I had worked at the Alumnae. She persuaded Herbert Whittaker to take her out for a drink after he came to the show, and I have always believed that she influenced him to write a more favourable review than he might otherwise have done. In any case, the show consolidated my reputation as a director of students.

During the run we had a visit from the playwright John Arden, who said little but seemed to enjoy our production. Not so his wife Margaretta D'Arcy, who was highly critical, particularly of the actors' accents. It was apparent that she had taken charge of her husband's career and indeed he never wrote anything as powerful as *Musgrave* again.

The Drama Centre had a number of celebrity visitors and it was one of my jobs to look after them. Soon after a celebrated American playwright was invited to speak at Convocation Hall. Just as I was about to leave for the airport, my phone rang and a voice said, "This is Edward Albee. I'm at . . . where are we, darling? Some place called the King Edward. Could you pick me up there?" I obliged and was told that he had two wishes: to buy a sheepskin jacket and to visit the Chinese collection at the museum. We then repaired to the Massey Common Room for tea, which he pronounced was the quietest place he had been in North America. We were joined by a very good-looking graduate student, who offered to take Albee out for supper.

I collected him the next afternoon and he gave a highly political speech to a packed auditorium. There was a dinner at Massey from which he slipped away early and the next day a lunch was arranged at the Faculty Club for Albee to meet Marshall McLuhan. Unbeknownst to Brian Parker, the two had already met and taken an instant dislike to each other. After the exchange of a few barely veiled incivilities, Albee turned to me, "Don't we have a plane to catch?" I agreed we did and we set out for the airport. As I took his bag from the trunk, my hat blew off. He gracefully retrieved it, set it back on my head and said, "I've had a marvellous time here in Toronto. Many thanks." He gave me a kiss and was gone. I later heard that he had met his life partner during his short stay, but whether it was the graduate student or his bedfellow of the night before, I never learned.

Brian Parker was now in his last year as director of the Drama Centre and let it be known that he did not wish to extend his term. There were two likely successors who were attached to the Centre. Fred Marker was an American who had graduated from Yale and recently joined the University of Toronto along with his wife Lise-Lone, a Danish theatre historian who taught the only compulsory course offered by the Centre. Ann Saddlemyer was a rather jolly woman who specialized in Irish studies with a particular interest in Synge and Yeats. I got on well with both of them and both told me that if they were elected they would want me to stay on with increased responsibilities. I have no idea how a decision was reached but as it turned out, the job went to Ann.

She was as good as her word and immediately invited me to return Hart House to a fully functioning student theatre. She thus abandoned the idea of a professional company and although I didn't know it at the time she grabbed a large chunk of the theatre's budget, which she would use to fund a journal called *Modern Drama,* to be edited by Fred, and also to hire visiting scholars and directors. She offered me a salary of ten thousand dollars a year and although I tried to up the ante to twelve thousand, she held her ground. I would learn that Ann was a tough bargainer, determined to get her own way, which she usually managed through a combination of charm and bullying. I would sit through many a meeting which Ann would prolong until she got what she wanted. After three or four hours many of us would give in, thinking, "I don't care anymore. Do what you want, Ann."

I wanted to do an initial season that would have broad appeal for both university and senior high school students and we settled on a bill of Molière's *The Misanthrope,* Ibsen's *Rosmersholm,* and *Hamlet. Rosmersholm* would be directed by Fred, who was an expert on Scandinavian theatre; Robertson Davies once quipped that the Markers believed they owned Ibsen and Strindberg. Davies proposed that Donald Davis be invited to direct the Molière. I had met Donald before and we had several amiable get-togethers at my house and his where a good deal of Scotch was consumed. Then he went away for the weekend to New York and returned saying he had acquired the rights for a wonderful new play which he wanted to substitute for *The Misanthrope.* I read it and discovered it had three characters, none of them young and a very large part for a middle-aged American general, which of course Donald wanted to play himself. There was also a good part for his sister Barbara Chilcott, though of course she would expect to be paid. This seemed to me to completely defeat the purpose of what I was trying to do and I met with Ann and Rob, who agreed with me. Rob sighed and said, "The Crest Theatre was eventually destroyed by Donald's caprice." He undertook to inform Donald that it was too late to change our plans.

Donald sulked and we no longer met for friendly drinks. However, he put together a very skilled cast including Bradley Bernstein, Irene Blum, Rita Davies, Bie Engelen, Harry Lane, and Robert Joy, all new students at the Centre. They worked reasonably happily with Donald for two weeks, although he had picked on one young actress as his whipping girl and told her he was recasting her part. At this point he announced that he had an offer to do a part in New York that he couldn't refuse, and took off. Before he left he entrusted the production to John Wood, a rising young Canadian director. It was a happy solution. Donald was inventive but changeable; John was even-handed and meticulous, a demanding perfectionist. The result was a production of a very high order. The play received excellent notices, including a laudatory lecture from the *Star's* newly installed drama critic Urjo Kareda. It got our season off to a good start, and both Ann and Rob were pleased.

Rosmersholm was another matter. Fred was a rather prickly character and decreed that no one would be allowed to attend his rehearsals. He had cast Ray Conlogue as Rosmer, and although he looked Scandinavian with his red hair and tall angular frame, the part was well beyond his capabilities as an actor. I was invited to the dress rehearsal, by which time it was too late to make major changes. I remember Ray asked me for some pointers. All I could say was, "Learn your lines." It was part of a plan Ann had set up to integrate the Drama Centre's critical study of texts with the theatre's practical work, to have a post-mortem after each production. Kareda's comments on *The Misanthrope* had got this off to a good start. The question and answer session set up with Fred in the hot seat was less successful. He fielded a few fairly mild questions before he was attacked by David Gardner, an experienced actor and director who had just joined the Drama Centre as a student. Fred bridled noticeably and walked off the stage. He would spend the rest of the term licking his wounds and waiting to pounce.

Meanwhile, I had held a week of open auditions for *Hamlet,* which drew a good number of undergraduates as well as Drama Centre students. There was a whole new gang at the Centre including a good many Americans, some who were avoiding the draft, others who were attracted to the university by the lower fees and the chance to study with renowned scholars and writers Northrop Frye, Clifford Leech, and Marshall McLuhan. Hart House Theatre has always been at its best when it attracted a variety of interesting students, immediately after the two world wars, when returning veterans enriched the make-up of the student body, and again in the early 1970s when baby boomers and Americans contributed new variety and depth of experience to the campus.

Very early on in the auditions I was confronted by a slim, androgynous young woman with a slight accent who presented herself for the role of Hamlet. She gave a highly intelligent reading of one of the soliloquies and I could see she was a real actress with a distinctive personality and unique quality. Instead of casting her as Hamlet, I determined to do build a production of *Medea* around her, which I would direct at the studio. I had seen Judith Anderson perform the role in the Robinson Jeffers translation in New

York several years before. I took Jeffers' translation and reworked it, cutting it severely, interpolating bits from Seneca's version of the myth and adding several mimed scenes from Medea's backstory, where she helps Jason get the golden fleece and kills her brother. I was aided by a new student named David Moe, who designed a simple and effective set, by painting a circle in the centre of the studio floor and hanging ropes from the ceiling grid. He also lit the show with striking geometrical gobos and devised a soundtrack of electronic music.

Bie Engelen gave a stunning performance as Medea, full of dark fury and stinging scorn, impassioned eloquence and the coiled athleticism of an enraged cobra. David Sutherland was her tall, beautiful, and totally uncomprehending Jason, who watched while his beautiful new wife Francesca Mallon was set ablaze by the golden robe that Medea sent her, and my two sons Ben and Guy played her children, whom she strangled with the dangling ropes that the chorus of women had twisted and knotted as they watched the drama play out. I was extremely proud of this production and it was the beginning of my long collaboration with Bie, a remarkable artist and friend, whose abundant talent never quite received the recognition that in my opinion it deserved.

Then on to *Hamlet*. I had been approached before the auditions by Rod Beattie, an actor with some experience, who obviously had the necessary intellect and wit to play the role. This meant that I went into the auditions with confidence I could cast the play, my first crack at Shakespeare as a director. Among the many actors who auditioned, I was impressed by the variety and range available. I would eventually cast John Taylor as Claudius, Arlene Perly as Gertrude, Richard Plante as Polonius, Jim Duggan as the Ghost, and Tim Fort as a Gravedigger, all new Drama Centre students. The undergraduates included Reed Needles as Laertes and his brother Dan as Horatio, Seana McIvor as Ophelia, and Marvin Karon and David Dowling as Rosencrantz and Guildenstern. Rod's brother Douglas was also in the cast, which may have provided an early entente which would eventually lead to the combination of talents that produced the highly successful series of Wingfield plays.

At the very end of the audition week, a slim, hollow-eyed young actor appeared and auditioned for the title role. Robert Joy presented me with an interesting alternative: nervy, quick-witted, and unpredictable. Although I was more or less committed to Rod, I pondered this possibility for several days until Robert phoned to tell me he had landed a role in a film and would not be available to play Hamlet. So that solved that problem. A few weeks later he came back saying he had completed his film commitment and could he still be in the show? I offered him Osric and a Gravedigger, which he played with great verve and spirit. Ten weeks before the show opened, I began working with Rod. As a result he not only knew the whole text thoroughly, but we were able to explore a variety of interpretations.

Martha Mann designed our *Hamlet*, which was beautifully costumed although she could not deliver the set I had asked for, which involved a huge curtain that could be used to reveal or conceal the machinations of the central characters. Ten days before the opening, it was clear that the show would not be ready on time. I summoned the theatre staff. "You are supposed to be the professionals. What are you going to do about this?" They cut back on the designs and somehow the show was ready on opening night. This confrontation impressed the staff, but at the same time they resented it, and it built up a feeling of antagonism that I would have to deal with in the years ahead.

Rod Beattie was a highly idiosyncratic Hamlet, mercurial, posturing, possessed of a wicked wit, and quite possibly a bit mad. He played several scenes in a sort of jester's outfit with a foolshead and had a wonderful exchange that he devised with Rosencrantz and Guildenstern in which they played an imaginary game of tennis. He and Reed Needles were boyhood friends and they worked for several months on the duel scene in the last act, which was truly spectacular. Bearded and rather scruffy of dress, Beattie was a far cry from the elegance and melancholy nobility of Gielgud or the pseudo-Nordic grace of Olivier. The originality of this performance eluded the critics, particularly Urjo Kareda, who upbraided me in print for daring to produce a *Hamlet* without actors who possessed the skills of the great British players of the era.

I had a very clever assistant, an American girl called Debbie, who was greatly helpful in coaching some of the actors and staged the players' scene with skill and assurance. She had a crush on Rod and one night after rehearsal, confessed to me her frustration over a drink in a nearby pub. I pointed out to her that whenever I saw her with Rod, she seemed absolutely miserable, whereas when I saw her with Ed, a young actor playing a courtier, she was completely at ease. Many years later, I ran into her when she was acting as a story editor at Sullivan Films. I asked her if she ever saw Ed and she replied, "Oh yes, Ed and I have been living together for fifteen years." Although initially I was wary when students came to me with their personal problems, I had learned that they would only listen to what they wanted to hear. Consequently I could advise them, "Yes, I would jump out a window if I were you," knowing they would not follow my advice.

The post-mortem following the production of *Hamlet* involved an appearance by Joseph Papp of the Public Theatre in New York who happened to be in town directing his production of *Two Gentlemen of Verona*. Robertson Davies, mindful of the fiasco following *Rosmersholm,* set it up as a conversation between me and Mr. Papp. The theatre was full and I knew the audience had not come to listen to me, so after a brief exchange, I withdrew and turned the session over to our guest. The audience showed their appreciation by clapping and Papp proceeded. He impressed me with two stories about his experience as an artistic director. He had seen a production of *Troilus and Cressida* at Yale, which greatly impressed him and he asked the director to bring it to New York. After three weeks of rehearsal, he went to one and said, "This is crap. We are not going to open it." He paid off the actors and sent them home. On another occasion he was planning to direct a production of *Much Ado About Nothing*, when a young director came to him and asked if he could direct the show. Papp said no, but then asked the director to explain his idea. "Your idea is better than mine, you go ahead and do it." It demonstrated the flexibility that is required to run a successful theatre. I drove Mr. Papp to the airport and he said, "Nice meeting you, kid. If you're ever in New York, call me." I said, "Thanks, Mr. Papp, but I doubt if I'd get through to you." He grinned. "You're right. Have a good show."

The attendance at the three shows of our first student season was gratifying, but trouble lay just ahead. To assuage Fred Marker's disappointment at not being named director, Ann set up a compulsory first year course for him to teach on the nature and practice of theatre. I was asked by Fred to sit in on the course as the voice of a working director. I was also asked to sit in on Fred's smaller course on playwriting. Fred was not himself a playwright and to the best of my knowledge none of his students ever wrote a play that was produced. I gave my opinion when asked and sometimes when not asked, occasionally differing from Fred's ideas and theories. Shortly after the production of *Hamlet* closed, I was summoned to Robertson Davies office where Ann and Fred were waiting. Fred accused me of belittling and ridiculing him

in front of his students. He did not specify which particular piece of impertin-
ence he was objecting to but stated that the situation was intolerable and he
was ready to resign from the Centre. As it paid a high percentage of his salary,
this was rather daring of him. He left the room. As I was not sure exactly what
I was being accused of, I did not attempt to explain myself, but also offered
to resign. I too left the room.

I was summoned to a private meeting with Ann a few days later. She told
me she valued my work at the theatre. I was no longer to attend Fred's classes
and only such Centre meetings as I was specifically invited to, beginning with
a planning meeting for the next season. I was prepared to stake out my position by saying I wished to direct two major plays next year, one in each term.
I was anxious to direct another Shakespeare and also a Canadian play. I also
gave it as my opinion that students should be allowed to direct plays at Hart
House, if they had demonstrated ability by directing at the studio. Davies was
opposed to this, but agreed as long as I would supervise their work. Ann was
supportive, as it would save her directors' fees. Ann announced that she had
asked Fred to direct another play in the coming season and he had chosen
Peer Gynt. She also announced that I had expressed a wish to direct a play
by Robertson Davies. I could hardly demur but said the Shakespeare I had
chosen was *Troilus and Cressida.* The meeting adjourned with everyone getting
most of what they wanted, a credit to Ann's undoubted skills as a negotiator.

Robert Gill and I had adjoining offices above the dressing room behind
the theatre. He had been very complimentary about my *Hamlet,* comparing it
favourably with his own production twenty years earlier, starring Tony Grey.
He thought my use of the stage with stairs built into the alcoves an interesting
and effective innovation and commended my ability to bring out the comedy
in the piece, something he had admired in my student performances years
before. I got to know Bob Gill in quite a different way at this stage. He was
frail and nervous, but friendly and full of interesting advice. He thought my
choice of *Troilus and Cressida* was unwise, being too obscure, but commended
my ambition. "You are going to bring this theatre back to what it was in my
early days, I'm sure of it," he once said and indeed I took his work as a model,
although my style and taste were different. He was right; I was much more
attuned to comedy than he.

The week following the meeting, I was invited by Robertson Davies to
lunch with him at the York Club. Rob and his wife Brenda had already been

very welcoming to Judy and me, inviting us to private dinners with the likes of Raymond Massey and George Steiner at Massey as well as Christmas dances and the annual Gaudy Night, which featured Rob telling his annual ghost story. But this lunch was something more intimate, and of course the purpose was to discuss which of his plays I should direct. I had read virtually all of them and even reviewed one of them for the *Varsity* years before. Even in the early '70s it was the received opinion that his plays were no good, but in the '50s he had been widely produced and entertained audiences with a series of neo-Shavian comedies, whose characters were sometimes two-dimensional caricatures who expressed too obviously the opinions of the playwright, but were at the same time colourful, witty, and representative of the social structure of the day.

Rob strongly urged me to attempt an unproduced play about Casanova called *Intimate Confessions*, which he had written more than a decade earlier for the Davis brothers and their sister Barbara Chilcott to produce at the Crest Theatre. It was scheduled for production in 1957, when the Davises suddenly rejected it in favour of a play that J.B. Priestley had written for them, which they subsequently took to London's West End. (Hence Davies' remark about Donald's "caprice.") I read and reread the play, which was dense and intricately plotted with a strongly Jungian flavour. It also called for three mature and highly accomplished actors whom I did not have. We discussed his other plays and I finally said the work I would most like to do was the adaptation of his early novel *Leaven of Malice,* which played in Toronto, Boston, and New York with the title *Love and Libel* under the direction of his friend and mentor Tyrone Guthrie. It was well received in the first two cities, but the Manhattan critics condemned it and it closed abruptly. Reportedly Davies put some of his own money into it, which of course he lost. He initially refused to consider the idea, but I persisted, and eventually he agreed. I persuaded him to add a few new bits from the novel and set about casting.

The cast assembled on the Hart House stage on a September evening. Davies arrived with sad news: Brenda, who was to have played Molly, had been called away to look after her aging mother in Australia. Ann Saddlemyer stepped into her place and the cast read the text. I had assembled some good comic actors: Rod Beattie, Irene Blum, Tim Fort, Francess Halpenny, Marvin Karon, Reed Needles, Michael Sidnell, Rex Southgate, Maarten van Dijk, and my wife, Judy. They gave a good account of themselves and Robertson graciously acknowledged his satisfaction. I believe Ann hoped that I would cast her in Brenda's place but I chose an Irish actress named Felixe Fitzgerald, whom Rob soon took a scunner to, which I suppose was inevitable.

The play contains a comic dream sequence, which various people thought I should cut, but which the audience loved. The play takes place around Halloween and moves quickly through a number of settings: a bedroom, a street, a cathedral, a library, and a park, among others. Reed Needles not only played Solly, the hero, with considerable charm, but proved to be a wonderful prop-maker. He built a single set-piece for each location and assembled six different beds on wheels, but his masterpiece was the front-end of a Volkswagen Beetle with headlights that could be turned off and on. Beverley Miller was my choreographer and supplied six of her ballet school students who were sort of spirits and moved a good deal of the furniture. Like all dancers they did what they were told, but I don't think they enjoyed the experience. Larry Schaffer, a new student at the Centre, created a series of shiny silver screens with clever images that evoked the various locations. His frequent use of plastic materials earned him the sobriquet Mylar Mary. Martha Mann created some highly amusing costumes, circa 1948.

The cast was critical of the play, in a way they wouldn't have been if it had been written by, say, Ben Jonson or Richard Sheridan, but they turned to and gave cleverly inventive performances. Although I had asked Rob to interpolate a few brief scenes from the book, I did a substantial amount of cutting. One night at a rehearsal of a scene I had chopped fairly severely, I was horrified to discover that Davies had tiptoed in and was sitting at the back of the house. There was a short, leaden silence and then he came over and sat beside me. "I just want to tell you, that you have edited that scene much more cleverly than Tony Guthrie did." I breathed a sigh of relief and went on brandishing my scalpel. In the end, I realized I should have cut a further ten minutes from the text.

My other main contribution, apart from moving the large cast about and encouraging them to keep the tone light and lively, was the introduction of music. The show opens with an academic procession and contains a rehearsal in a church as well as the dream sequence. One of the principal characters, an odious, out-of-place little Englishman with cultural pretensions, splendidly played by Maarten van Dyck, sang "O Promise Me" to a ladies' tea party and a bawdy duet "The End of My Old Cigar" at a smoker. (He also played a hilarious seduction scene with his landlady, a deliciously foolish Irene Blum.) To run between the various scenes and accompany the songs I persuaded Giles Bryant, the college organist at Massey to record some baroquely styled tunes ranging from "Gaudeamus Igitur" to "What the World Needs Now is Love" on the organ at St. Mary Magdelene. This almost turned the show into a musical.

This was one reason the show was highly popular. Another was the fact that it had a university setting, which the audience enjoyed seeing gently satirized. The show had excellent reviews from both Herbert Whittaker, who was a close friend of Davies, and Urjo Kareda, who would probably like to have been. Like most critics, they were both, to some extent, star-fuckers. I have observed that when a writer or performer reaches a certain eminence where a small-time critic is powerless to destroy his reputation, they prefer to climb on the bandwagon and salute the brilliance of the artist. While I was pleased with the positive attention these reviews brought to the theatre, I was more pleased that Davies genuinely enjoyed the production. He came several nights and his guffaws could be heard above the more restrained laughter of the rest of the audience.

Davies had already been very positive about my efforts, but in the wake of this production we formed a closer bond. I knew he enjoyed a good gossip and discovered that he would often be in his office immediately before lunch after he had finished his morning's writing. Once or twice a month I would knock on his door and he would invite me into his inner sanctum where we would enjoy a glass of sherry as we dished the dirt. About a year later the Shaw Festival decided to mount *Leaven of Malice* in Niagara-on-the-Lake. I wrote to Tony van Bridge, who was then artistic director, offering to send him my cut script and production notes. I received no reply. We went to the Shaw opening, which was rather dreary, and Urjo Kareda came up to me at intermission to suggest that we send for Rex Southgate and Rod Beattie to take the next bus to Niagara. Davies wrote me a kind note to say how much more he had enjoyed the Hart House production.

The next play of the season was to be David Rabe's play *Sticks and Bones*, which had just had a successful run in New York. Initially we were refused permission to produce it by his agents. When I inquired why, they told me they expected there would be a professional production mounted in Toronto. The only possible producer was Ed Mirvish at the Royal Alexandra. I phoned his office and was told that if I wished to speak to Mr. Mirvish, he would be at his restaurant on King Street from noon until one-thirty. I went for lunch at noon the next day and Ed Mirvish was standing by the door in his habitually impeccable blue serge suit. He said if I wanted to talk with him he would come over to my table in half an hour. In precisely half an hour, he sat down across from me. I explained my problem and he said, "I have no intention of producing that play. I will not put anything in writing, but you can tell that to the agent." I did and we obtained permission to proceed with the production. Mark Diamond did a fine job as director and established the entitlement of students to direct at Hart House Theatre. This was not greeted with enthusiasm by the theatre staff, who were already up in arms at the idea of mounting three large productions and two smaller ones in one season. I expected this would cause me some grief in the future, and it did.

I was not familiar with *Troilus and Cressida* when Debbie Nathan suggested it to me. She would certainly have been involved if she had stayed on at the Centre. There are a large number of male parts, which demand good actors. I auditioned perhaps thirty male students and was delighted by the calibre of many of them. There was a considerable range of physical types and I gradually devised a pattern where the Trojan princes were tall and fair and the Greeks smaller and darker. Then there is Cressida, who must be pretty, sexy, able to converse wittily with her Uncle Pandarus, and yet naive. I knew as soon as I saw Barbara Stewart that she filled the bill. After a week of auditions, I had cast most of the roles but still lacked a Pandarus and a Thersites. At the end of a long day on Friday two short, bright Italian guys stepped out on stage. Michael Macina was the Thersites I had been looking for. Damiano was not Pandarus but was obviously bright and experienced as a director. My putative assistant Barry O'Connor suddenly said, "Why not ask Damiano to be your assistant and I'll play Pandarus?" So I had a cast. The Greeks included John Cartwright as a level-headed Agamemnon, Rod Beattie as a devious and highly articulate Ulysses, Bradley Bernstein as a darkly handsome and arrogant Achilles, Tim Fort as a rather buffoonish Ajax, Graham Harley as a humorously wise old Nestor and Peter Robertson as a confident and sexy Diomedes. The Trojans included Scott Baker as a tall, poetic and clear-spoken Troilus, Timothy Brook as a handsome but weak-willed Paris, David Sutherland as a proud, dashing Hector and Reed Needles as an elegant Aeneas. As for Damiano, he proved to be a very insightful assistant. He went on to direct a highly intelligent and colourful production of Camus' *Caligula* in the next season and eventually became the director of radio drama and features at the CBC.

Troilus and Cressida contains some of the most complex verse in Shakespeare's canon and I worked on it with the actors over a six-week period, demanding that the early scenes be played for fast-paced comedy alternating with sensuous lyricism, before the darker side of the story takes over and the cynical Greeks prevail. Michael Macina and Rod Beattie were particularly effective in colouring their characters through comic inflection and inventive business.

The moment Larry Schaffer learned that I was producing this play, he demanded to be allowed to design it. I told him I wanted two moving towers and he said no, I will give you one fixed, metal skeletal structure upstage that your actors can climb on and two smaller fixed structures at either side of the proscenium. I accepted his dictum on the condition that they were built early on so we could rehearse on them. Larry proceeded to design costumes, spectacularly draped dresses for Cressida and Helen, and for the soldiers, harnesses that exposed a good deal of male flesh. He stood in the sewing room upstairs as the cast, stripped to their underpants, were fitted, and he obviously considered this a suitable compensation for the endless hours he spent supervising the seamstresses. It was mid-winter and all the men wore body make-up, which had to be washed off and re-applied every night. I told Larry we should consider selling tickets to the showers.

The other person who contributed hugely to the success of this production was Reed Needles. Not only did he construct almost single-handedly more than a dozen crested helmets to be worn by the Greek soldiers, but he trained all the male actors for the huge fight scene at the end of the play. They worked for an hour three nights a week, and the cast not only more or less mastered the demands of fighting with broadswords but were noticeably energized in performance. In the end the climactic battle between Achilles and Hector proved so dangerous that I decreed it must be done in slow motion. Reed and I decided that we would start the fights up to speed and gradually slow them down. This was a technique that had been used in several movies but, not to my knowledge, on stage. The play ended with the fighters ·in frozen positions silhouetted against an orange cyclorama, evoking the patterns on an ancient Greek amphora. We received a somewhat grudgingly positive notice from Kareda and a visit from Robin Phillips, newly arrived in Canada, who would invite Rod Beattie and Barbara Stewart to become members of his Stratford company the following season.

Clifford Leech was also very taken with this production, and as he was an internationally acknowledged Shakespearean scholar, I was pleased and flattered. We became quite good friends and sometimes dined together, during which time we imbibed freely. One evening we set out for home in my car when I became aware that a glaring light was shining in my rear window. I stopped and a police car pulled up beside us. "Don't you stop when you hear a siren wailing right behind you?" asked the cop. Clifford sat up and in ringing British tones replied, "Officer, this young man is driving me home and it is imperative I get there as quickly as possible." There was a silence in which I thought we would both be spending the night in the slammer. Then the policeman got back into his car and drove off, leaving us to weave our way to Clifford's apartment.

The Hart House season ended with a production of *Marsh Hay*, written by Merrill Denison for Hart House Theatre in the '30s but never produced. It is a grim depiction of rural Ontario life that was probably influenced by the early work of Eugene O'Neill. It was given a sound production directed by Richard Plante and an elaborately detailed set by Marion Walker. Merrill Denison was still alive and was very gratified to finally see his play on stage. So ended one of the most ambitious and varied seasons the theatre had ever put on the boards. Ann asked me to sign on for another season at a somewhat larger salary.

I still had ambitions as a playwright. I wrote a three-act play about a dysfunctional middle-class family (is there any other kind?) in which two brothers compete for the same woman. I gave it to a young up-and-coming director called Martin Brenzell who rejected it as "too Arthur Miller–ish." I then gave it to Bill Glassco. I had known Bill slightly in our teens and reconnected when he came back from Princeton and Oxford to be an English lecturer at Victoria College. He had directed a student production of an obscure Jacobean comedy, which I thought was a mess and concluded he was yet another academic who fancied himself a theatre practitioner. Soon after this, Bill went to New York with his wife Jane to study directing at NYU. He returned two years later and fairly quickly they founded Tarragon Theatre, the first professional theatre in Toronto devoted almost exclusively to presenting Canadian plays. Thus the tables were turned; Bill was the professional, and I the academic.

Bill had asked me to send him a script. He read my play and suggested I come and discuss it with him in the study of his house in Rosedale. After an exchange of theatrical gossip he told me he thought the play had promise but needed work. He was undoubtedly right. I made some rather flippant remarks. Bill looked at me sternly and said, "I'm sorry. I thought you were serious. Let's forget the whole thing." Foolishly, I didn't apologize but went on my way. Bill would prove to be a very skilled dramaturge who would coax fine scripts out of inexperienced writers. If I had had the good sense to submit to his criticism, I might have become the dramatist I still hoped to be.

During my time working for Brian Parker I had been asked by the University Women's Alumnae to develop a script in a workshop. They had been funded by the Canada Council for this purpose and they paired me with one of their members, Joan Shaw. I had known Joan as an undergraduate actress but had no knowledge of her work as a director. Off the top she said to me, "I don't want you to write any more neurotic women characters." We decided to recruit a number of teenage actors, which included Timothy Brook, Tim Jocelyn, Jeffrey Cohen, Sandy Mayzel, and David Rotenberg, among others. We met twice a week in a church hall and the kids improvised a great variety of scenes. I enjoyed working with them and found much of what they did amusing. Joan was less impressed and declared the whole enterprise to be nothing but a pile of clichés. She was not entirely wrong. I told the Alumnae ladies that we had not been able to construct a play and told them to keep their thousand Canada Council dollars. Ah, the arrogance of the young.

Nevertheless I began working on a script that used some of the material we had developed in the workshop. My play was called *Flowers of Paradise* and was set in a church and concerned a bunch of hippie kids who came under the influence of a female faith healer. Jeffrey Cohen had a band and I wrote some lyrics, which he set to music as well as incorporating a number of well- . know hymns. I put together a cast that included David Rotenberg and Sandy Mayzel from the original improv group, undergraduates Ron Davies and David Sutherland, Hugh McKenzie, and Alumnae actresses Valerie Grabove, Francess Halpenny, Beverly Miller, Juliana Saxton, and Jackie White, who gave a wonderful bittersweet performance as a lonely spinster. I remember saying to Ann Scrannage, my stage manager at the dress rehearsal, "Probably nobody will come to see this." But in fact we played to full houses and young people liked the show, partly because of the music and partly because it picked up on the freewheeling, tie-dyed exuberance of middle-class kids of that era. My parents came to the show and hated it. I suggested that in future they not come to see my shows, and they took me at my word. The lyrics I wrote were salty and betrayed the influence, though not the genius, of Bob Dylan.

"You used to run through fields of daisies
Laughing like the other crazies
Letting the fresh wind blow you
Then you'd crash and cool your ass
In the long green grass
Until one night you caught pneumonia.

You made your home
In a geodesic dome
With constant humidity and temperature control
You're no longer zonked and spastic
But your bubble of bright plastic
Makes the cutest little package for your soul."

My next play was based on the exploits of the outrageous Athenian soldier and politician Alcibiades. It contained some fairly explicit sexual material, a number of songs and a sizeable cast. Although I had enjoyed directing *Flowers of Paradise*, I thought it would be a good idea to have someone else direct this play, which I titled *Charisma*. A recently graduated Drama Centre student, Tony Stephenson, agreed to take on this chore. He assembled a cast and had a read-though while I was away at the cottage. The cast was highly critical of the play which was long, sprawling, and contained a mixture of highly colloquial and more formal language. Tony phoned me to say he had decided not to do the show after all. I later gave it to Urjo Kareda, who commented, "You have obviously been influenced by Brecht and Shakespeare. You have structured the story quite cleverly and there are some interesting characters. But your models have a gift for language. You don't." He was probably right. Urjo was a sharp and pithy critic and fearless in expressing his opinions. I abandoned my playwriting ambitions and concentrated on adaptations for some time to come.

The next season at Hart House I led off with the revised version of James

Reaney's *The Kildeer*. I had worked backstage on Pamela Terry's production of the original script and been fascinated by Reaney's intensely imagistic language and his intuitive understanding of the often cruel comic twists of rural life as I had experienced it as a child visiting my relatives on eastern Ontario farms. The original play fell into two distinct halves that seemed almost unconnected. There were also two divergent halves in the rewritten script, but they seemed to me to complement and complete each other. Again the role of the buttoned-up but fanciful farmwife was played by Francess Halpenny, who originated it in the earlier production. She was joined by my wife Judy as her eccentric companion, and the scene where they dance with life-sized cutouts was weirdly magical. The romance between the humorous delivery boy played by George Komarowski and the Egg Girl, a pretty, introverted Joan Calderera, was like an improvised country dance. There was also a luminous performance from Howard Clarke as the emotionally damaged farm boy dominated by his sinister hired man.

Howard had grown up in Stratford where he worked backstage as a dresser at the Festival. He appeared at Hart House with his shoulder-length red-blond hair in a braid and said he would like to work in the prop shop; he was good with his hands. In conversation with him I sensed he really wanted to act and encouraged him to audition. He played Patroclus in *Troilus*, where he looked stunning, but it was in *The Kildeer* that he played with real sensitivity and a surprising simplicity. I praised his work and he asked me as many others would, "Should I consider being an actor?" "Not if you can be a doctor." (I knew he had just been admitted to the medical school. Today he is a highly skilled plastic surgeon at Sick Kids Hospital, where he repairs the scars of children who have been badly burned.)

I had expected to direct another Shakespeare, but the committee who chose the plays for the season commanded me to direct an Aristophanes comedy to please the Classics department. I was annoyed at this interference in what I was beginning to think of as my theatre. I read most of Aristophanes' works and had trouble working up any excitement about any of them. I admired *Lysistrata*, but it is a one-joke play and Herbert Whittaker had fairly recently done a production at Hart House. I settled on *The Frogs*, which is essentially a satire on various kinds of ancient Athenian drama. I decided no one would get the jokes and so I completely rewrote the text and set it in modern times, though following the episodes of the original.

The central characters were Hercules, Dionysus, and Xantius, a slave. These I recast as a jock, a gay man, and a lovesick girl. Instead of parodies of Greek plays we introduced send-ups of Michael Ondaatje's *Billy the Kid*, Michel Tremblay's *Hosanna*, and David French's Newfoundland plays, the current hits of the Toronto alternative theatre scene. There were recurring scatological jokes and songs that parodied "Begin the Beguine" and "Over the Rainbow." I wrote the lyrics and Glen Morley, then a student at the Faculty of Music, supplied the tunes. A typical lyric (move over Cole Porter):

> "We're dancing in the dawning
> To the tinkle of far guitars,
> Under an awning
> Of fading stars:
> Dancing in the dawning
> Of a new desire
> We've caught fire.
> Soon the broom
> Of another humdrum day
> Will sweep the magic away.
> But right now it's entrancing
> To be dancing
> Like leopards leaping
> Or salmon spawning:
> Dancing,
> Chancing anything
> Come what may
> Just at the break of day
> Dancing in the dawning."

The two authority figures of Greek dramatists were shameless parodies of Robertson Davies and Ann Saddlemyer. The chorus of frogs was a girls' French-Canadian hockey team who commented on the action in outrageous Quebecois accents. Michael Macina proved himself a gifted comic and was especially brilliant taking off Richard Monette as Hosanna and Pierre Trudeau. Kareda pronounced the show "dated and dumb." The Classics department stayed away in droves, except for Desmond Connacher who said, "It doesn't have much to do with Aristophanes, but I found it highly entertaining." And the audience laughed a lot. If I was to some extent venting my frustrations as an underpaid outsider in academe, I was at least entertaining people in the process.

Though the set was unimportant, the cleverly designed and executed costumes by Martha Mann were a major element in the show. I had known Martha since shortly after I graduated, and we had by now worked together on at least four productions at the Centre. I had great respect for her taste and knowledge not just of clothes, but of the theatre generally. Her father had been an actor at Hart House in the early days and theatre was in her blood. A strikingly beautiful girl in her twenties, she had always dressed in a distinctive manner and continued to do so. She had a deep voice, a salty wit, a huge appetite for the good things in life, seemingly endless energy, and a razor sharp tongue that was highly critical of one and all, so much so that her costume room came to be known as "the stitch and bitch pit." When Ann announced she had appointed Martha resident designer, I was delighted. We would remain firm friends and work together often over the years.

Ann had somehow contrived to be away during *Frogs,* but I have no doubt that she got an earful from some of her colleagues when she returned. She did not call me up on the carpet but instead suggested that I take six weeks of paid leave and go away somewhere. And so on a February morning I set out for India, where my daughter Sarah was attending school in a remote hill town.

HEAT AND LUST

I felt very sorry for myself as I sat on my piled-up bags in the huge marble lobby of the Bombay Taj Hotel and sneezed violently. I'd picked up a heavy cold during my four-day stopover in London and although I'd made reservations two months ago, the clerks behind the desk would have nothing to do with me. No, they couldn't find accommodation in another hotel. All the hotels in Bombay were full. They were always full. I watched glumly as an Arabian sheik was welcomed effusively; it dawned on me that perhaps he was getting my room when I saw one of his retinue hand the reservations manager a sheaf of colourful banknotes.

Before I had time to protest, I caught sight of my sixteen-year-old daughter Sarah. She was deeply tanned, her brown hair hung in a braid halfway down her back and she wore khaki shorts, a silk shirt, and one heavy silver earring which tinkled as she moved towards me.

"Hi, Dad."

We looked at each other and shook hands rather formally; for the first time since she'd been born, we had been separated for over six months. Sarah had been a quiet, almost introverted student at North Toronto Collegiate until a year ago. She had announced that she was fed up with grinding out "dumb" essays and wanted to go abroad. I'd heard about the astronomic costs of Swiss finishing schools. But it turned out what Sarah had in mind was a school called Woodstock in Mussoorie, a hill station in the Himalayas. She'd heard about it from a friend who was a missionary's daughter. We wrote to the school with a covering letter from our minister and she was accepted. The fees were affordable and at the beginning of the September term, off she went.

Now here she was in India. She'd survived her first term and looked healthy, but different somehow — thinner, more sensuous, and at the same time more remote. I wasn't quite sure what to say to her.

"That's — quite an earring."

"I had my ears pierced. I thought of having my nose pierced too." She grinned as she took in my expression. In the mid-'70s nose piercing was not yet a common practice in Toronto. "What's the matter, Dad?"

I told her about my hotel problem and she shrugged. "Why don't you get rid of a couple of those bags and stay with me in the hostel. We can probably get a room to ourselves.'

There didn't seem to be any alternative. I quickly re-packed in the lobby and we went outside. Sarah was in the process of engaging a bicycle rickshaw, haggling in Hindi until the driver came down to about a third of the original asking price. I realized I should simply put myself in Sarah's hands and stop worrying.

The street was so full of people it seemed impassable. Our driver was small and scrawny and looked about seventy. I thought he might have a heart attack at any moment. I was concerned about his ability to pedal both of us until I saw other rickshaws containing families of six or eight people pass us. Boys with wooden crates on their heads yelled at each other, donkeys staggered under the weight of huge loads as their drivers beat them continually, motor-scooters wove in and out, honking raucously. Women held up things for sale, embroidered vests, silver bangles, sticky sweets. Beggars stretched out imploring hands. I dug in my pockets for coins. "Don't give them anything or we'll be mobbed," said Sarah. I tried to ignore the intense, piteous faces, the withered legs and mutilated hands.

I had come to India for two reasons: to visit Sarah and to live out a longstanding romantic fantasy. Since boyhood I'd been fascinated by the mysterious Orient; I'd identified with Kipling's *Kim*, Sabu in *The Thief of Bagdad*, even Bob Hope in *Road to Morocco.* I'd made a sudden decision and set out, feeling guilty because I hadn't had time to make adequate preparation. As I looked at the teeming life around me, I realized nothing could have prepared me for this. I'd just have to take it as it came.

After our precarious rickshaw ride (we had traveled six blocks in half an hour) the Salvation Army hostel seemed a haven of peace and certainly less of a flea-bag than I expected. We checked in, and I had a shower while Sarah chatted with a couple of sunburned boys from New Zealand. I joined them but quickly became bored with their conversation, which was mainly about the price of meals and dope. They had been cheated; they had been robbed. This was to be the common complaint of all the young Westerners I encountered in India.

Sarah and I went out to a small Indian restaurant and she came up with a knowledgeable selection of dishes. The strong curry attacked my cold and I downed three beers in a vain attempt to conquer my dry throat. Consequently,

I had little difficulty falling asleep once we got back to the hostel in spite of an endless rendition of "The Foggy, Foggy Dew" from the New Zealanders down the hall.

Next morning, Sarah and I made our plans. She had ten days before she had to be back in school. She'd already spent two weeks working in Mother Teresa's orphanage in Calcutta and a week on the beach in Goa. So we decided to head for Rajasthan and check out Moghul monuments: Fatehpur Sikri, the Amber Palace, and the Taj Mahal.

The railway station was a madhouse. At the ticket counter people yelled and sobbed, pushed each other, and shook their fists. We struggled vainly to get the attention of a ticket-seller, until an enormous Indian in a pinstripe suit saw us and loudly ordered people to make way for us. "You are a disgrace to our country. No wonder the rest of the world despises us. A nation of ignorant, mannerless peasants," he exclaimed passionately. It occurred to me he might be a politician.

We bought second-class tickets to Jaipur (Sarah having pronounced first-class a waste of money) and made our way to the platform. There was no train in sight but the platform was already crowded with people. After about half an hour, the train backed warily into position alongside the platform. Even before it came to a stop, people started to board through the open doors and windows. In no time, all the compartments were filled. We waved our tickets and demanded seats but this time no one came to our rescue.

We went from car to car looking for a conductor. Finally we found a strip of corridor that no one else seemed to want. We settled down on our bags for the long trip ahead. It would be sixteen hours but at least we could take up a semi-recumbent position and sleep. My mouth was muzzy from the beer-drinking of the night before. Fortunately Sarah had thought to fill a water bottle, but she rationed me; we had a long way to travel.

At the second stop, Sarah rolled down the window and bought some chai from a vendor. The tea was very sweet and left rather a sickly taste in the mouth, but at least it was wet. While we were enjoying it, a turbaned head appeared in the open window, gave a cry of delight, and before we knew it a family of twelve had invaded our corridor.

They crammed themselves into what we had come to think of as our space and the train started. There was no longer any prospect of stretching out; there was barely room to sit. The baby began to cry and the mother unwrapped it so that it could pee. I closed my eyes, leaned against my bag, and willed myself into a state of semi-coma. Was this, I wondered, the beginning of the path to transcendental meditation?

When I opened my eyes Sarah was dandling the baby on her knee. The mother was feeding sweets to another child. She offered me one and the old granny nodded encouragingly. I decided it would be rude to refuse. The sweet was gummy and tasted of perfume. I closed my eyes and returned to my pursuit of nirvana.

Twenty hours later, we arrived in Jaipur. Smelling of urine and sweet tea, with cramps in my legs and a two-days growth of beard, I decided we should stay at the best hotel in town. Ignoring Sarah's protests, we drove to the Rambagh Palace, an elegant Victorian mansion. The head porter took one look at us and suggested loftily that we try a smaller hotel. Enraged, I made a scene, picking up, I suppose, on the example of the politician in the railway station. I cursed and kicked my bag in fury to the astonishment of several well-bred guests. Suddenly, a handsome middle-aged man in riding breeches strode through the lobby and up to the desk.

"Send them to the Raj Mahal Palace," said the man and disappeared. Within five minutes we were politely shown into a large chauffeur-driven car and whisked to the edge of town where we were installed in a sprawling English-style country house, surrounded by a well-tended garden full of fountains and peacocks. Upstairs, a manservant wearing a scarlet turban ran me a bath and unpacked my clothes. "Dinner will be at eight, sahib. There will be drinks in the library at seven fifteen."

An hour later in the library an odd assortment of people was already gathered. Sarah and I amused ourselves trying to figure out who they might be: a pale, fair-haired man in a rumpled linen suit reminded me of the young Alec Guinness; an androgynous-looking punk with fuchsia-dyed hair reminded Sarah of Boy George; a sinister-looking Japanese gentleman might have been Yukio Mishima; and a middle-aged American couple could almost have been Maggie and Jiggs. Maggie and Jiggs came over and greeted us.

"Say, isn't this *something*? Those peacocks out on the lawn. It's like *Gone With the Wind*. I just hope they don't keep us awake all night with their squawking. And those waiters. Don't you just *love* their outfits? If you give them five rupees they'll take off their turbans and show you how they tie them up. *Fascinating*."

She took a quick swig of her martini and rattled on. "Say, how'd you find out about this place anyways? Charley met Bubbles playing polo in Virginia. He says Bubbles is one of the smartest little polo players he's ever come across."

"Bubbles?"

"That's what everyone calls him. Don't you just *love* it? It's right out of Noel Coward. Here he comes now. That's his mother. Just *look* at those emeralds."

The man in riding breeches from the Rambagh Palace came into the room with two handsome Indian women both wearing beautifully embroidered saris and breathtaking jewellery. He came over and introduced himself as Colonel Bahadur Singh, maharaja of Jaipur. "Everyone calls me Bubbles. My nickname at Sandhurst. I've never been able to shake it, so I suppose somehow it must suit me. You come from Canada? I shall go there next year to play polo with Mickey Sifton. You know him?"

I was able to say with honesty we were at school together. (In grade five for one term.)

"Excellent. Do you play? I can offer you an excellent mount. I had hoped to have a *chukka* with Charley, but the silly fellow has put his back out. Not very sporting of him, what?"

His accent, like his nickname, seemed to belong to a vanished British past. I asked him if he still visited England. "I play polo with Philip Edinburgh. He is an excellent fellow, but his ideas are a bit too advanced for me. I leave politics to my mother. Raj Mum, as we call her, is mad about politics. She was a member of our congress and a great chum of Mrs. Ghandi's until they threw her in jail. Poor Raj Mum. They found a roomful of rubies and emeralds in her palace. They said she was trying to avoid taxes. But of course she didn't even know the room was there. When one lives in a palace with three hundred rooms it is easy to overlook one little room, what? But India today is full of fanatics."

At this point two extremely beautiful women came into the room. In a second, Bubbles was at their side. They accepted his attentions as no more than their due. A younger Indian woman came over and introduced herself to us as Miss Singh; she was Bubbles' cousin. She explained that the other women were *Vogue* models. The magazine was photographing a spread for its spring issue. The Japanese man was the photographer, the fuchsia-haired punk was a make-up artist. The whole crew was going up to the Amber Palace the next morning along with some of the maharaja's elephants. "It's nice they have something to do. Bubbles has two hundred elephants and it's difficult to justify their keep in these hard times. But one can't just turn them out of doors, poor beasts."

We went in to dinner and Bubbles talked about the good old days when his father used to entertain his guests with tiger-shoots. He'd had to give this up but at least he was better off than his friend Freddie Bharatpur, who'd had to turn his game park into a bird sanctuary for tourists. Bubbles seemed to pay particular attention to one of the models whose name was Chloe. It dawned on me that this whole evening had probably been laid on to impress her.

During dessert, Raj Mum decided to draw out the fair young man who had so far remained silent. It seemed he was a British movie producer looking for locations for his next film. At once the model sitting beside him, who had not even glanced in his direction up to this point, did a one hundred and eighty degree turn in her seat and flashed her beautifully capped teeth at him.

"What sort of palace are you looking for?" asked Raj Mum.

"Something small, isolated, a bit decayed perhaps."

"I doubt if we have anything. The water palace is certainly decayed but it's completely submerged in the rainy season and the smell is quite heinous. You might have a look at Peter Bundi's place. It's a sweet little palace with an enchanting purdah gallery. Peter's off in Switzerland being analyzed but Bubbles will lend you a car. And you could go on to Tonk after lunch."

Dinner was followed by coffee on the terrace. Maggie Jiggs came over and hissed in my ear, "There goes Bubbles off into the garden with that Chloe. I thought she had her eye on him."

I watched the maharaja disappear into the shadows, not without a twinge of envy. Miss Singh wondered if I would like to see the lily pool. I hesitated for just a moment, and she suggested that Sarah and the Englishman might join us. We strolled in a leisurely fashion among the perfumed bushes and heard the call of the bulbul, which Miss Singh explained was a cousin of the English nightingale. As we stood in the luminous dusk like figures in some Persian miniature, Miss Singh placed a featherweight hand on my sleeve and smiled at me enigmatically.

Next morning I came down to breakfast to find Chloe alone on the terrace having coffee. "God, I hope we get finished up today. I woke up in the middle of the night and there was this cockroach on my pillow, it musta been three inches long. I wouldn't live in this country for anything."

"Not even all the rubies in Jaipur?"

"Forget it. If Bubbles wants to entertain little Miss Chloe, he can make a date to take her skiing in Gstaad. I hate heat. It's bad for my pores. Hey, Bubbles is cute, but he isn't serious, you know? All he wants is a good time. I got this boyfriend at Princeton who's an astrophysicist. That's more my style."

Soon after Bubbles appeared with Hideo, the Japanese photographer. They discussed cameras and lenses. Bubbles had planned to take us all the way to Amber by elephant, but the *Vogue* crew wanted to get on with it, so we set out by car and drove to where the fortress of Amber looked down from its mountainside, its golden-pink battlements glinting in the morning sun.

Bubbles jumped out of his car and the guard at the gate bowed to the ground and kissed his feet. Bubbles looked embarrassed and began giving rapid orders. A group of servants began to set up lights, unroll carpets and arrange draperies. Twenty elephants looked on quizzically at this fresh evidence of human folly. Bubbles suggested we might like to see a temple service in honour of Kali, the goddess of destruction.

In the darkness of the tiny palace temple, a group of devotees chanted and banged a gong to attract the attention of the evil-looking deity with her necklace of skulls, grim black face, and protruding scarlet tongue. Her dark, sparkling eyes reminded me of Miss Singh's and suggested an aspect of femininity that I didn't think I wanted to deal with. I offered her a few propitiatory coins and went back outside.

In the mirror hall of the palace the models posed, moving constantly while Hideo snapped shot after shot. Bubbles snapped his own camera for a while, then lost interest. He went out into the courtyard and greeted a party of tourists in the manner of a superior hotelier, genial but a bit perfunctory, then got into his car and drove off.

Sarah came over to me. "Geoffrey's asked me to go and look at palaces with him."

"Geoffrey?"

'The English movie guy. You want to come too?'

"Sure." We clambered into the waiting Mercedes and set off for Bundi. On the way Geoffrey told us about his plans to film *Heat and Dust*, a novel by Ruth Prawer Jhabvala. He had already approached Glenda Jackson and Julie Christie to be in it and planned to engage the Indian film star Shashi Kapoor to play the male lead. He was going on to Jodhpur the next day to talk to

Kapoor, who was shooting with the American director James Ivory. Would we like to go with him?

In Bundi we stopped in front of a delicately wrought façade. The iron gate was locked. Our driver knocked repeatedly and finally a turbaned face decorated with ferocious moustaches was thrust out of an upper window. The driver salaamed and said His Highness the Maharaja of Jaipur presented his compliments and begged permission for his guests to view the palace.

"His Highness has no jurisdiction here," shouted the man, his moustaches working furiously. He banged the upper casement shut and refused to respond to the driver's continued knocking.

We drove on to another town. Here we were received with elaborate courtesy and shown through some dusty, empty rooms decorated with charming paintings of hunting scenes. Geoffrey viewed the main courtyard from every possible angle and made notes. "It's almost too pretty," he said. "One doesn't want the setting to overpower the actors. I've seen too many films that made that mistake."

We went on to see two more palaces but none of them satisfied Geoffrey. One was too grand, the other too "tasteful." Finally we headed home, arriving back at the Raj Mahal Palace after dark. The *Vogue* contingent had left and we learned that Bubbles was not expected at dinner. The three of us ate a pleasant meal on the terrace by candlelight. "Must turn in," said Geoffrey. "Up with the birds tomorrow. You coming to Jodhpur?"

I looked at Sarah, who gave no signal. "We'll see you at breakfast if we're coming. Is that all right?"

"Of course, but I want to be on the road by seven." He headed indoors. Sarah and I sat together, listening to the bulbul. After a bit, Bubbles and his cousin appeared and suggested we all go for a walk in the garden.

We moved about slowly and I was aware that Bubbles tried to steer Sarah off alone while Miss Singh exerted her charms to distract my attention. After about twenty minutes of subtle but persistent manoeuvring, I lost track of Sarah and Bubbles. Miss Singh rested her fingers on my bare arm and I was aware of her fingernails digging lightly into my skin, sending a slight shiver down my spine. Worried about Sarah, I resisted temptation and steered our path back to the terrace, where Bubbles was waiting for us. He offered me a nightcap. "Your young wife is charming. You must be a happy man. I envy you." Then he abruptly excused himself.

Miss Singh smiled across at me. She was returning to Delhi in the morning. She gave me her address and offered to take me to the races if I wanted to call her. Then she drifted indoors, wafting a scent of musk. When I got to my room I found a note from Sarah. "I think we'd better go with Geoffrey. I asked the servants to wake us at six."

When we got to Jodhpur we found James Ivory and his Indian partner Ismail Merchant had almost run out of money and were trying to finish the shoot holed up with their technical crew in three rooms of a second-class hotel. We watched as they shot endless retakes of a street scene: either some donkey-driver crossed in front of the camera or else a beggar appeared from nowhere grinning toothlessly and did a little dance.

This brought guffaws from the onlookers. Nobody laughed louder than the star, Shashi Kapoor. Self-assured with a charming grin, the big, handsome actor waved and cracked jokes with the crowd between takes. A little girl came up giggling shyly and presented him with a garland of orange flowers, which he put around his neck and forgot to take off when the cameras rolled. Ivory blew up; Kapoor shrugged, "Ocha, what am I to do, James? Tell them to go away and forget about me? That would not sell many tickets, would it, now?"

Geoffrey learned that Ruth Jhabvala was in Jodhpur. He phoned and she suggested we go to her house for tea. I was looking forward to meeting this Indian novelist who seemed to have such a shrewd understanding of the foibles of both her Indian and British characters. Was she a Eurasian, I wondered. Her strong dark features suggested this, but in fact she turned out to be a Polish Jew who had spent her girlhood in London during the Second World War and had subsequently married an Indian architect.

She took an immediate liking to Sarah and wanted to know how she dealt with the unwanted advances of Indian men. Sarah said she'd learned to avoid eye contact. If a man persisted in harassing her she would challenge him openly at the top of her voice, hoping to embarrass him publicly. She was also studying silat, an Indian version of karate. Mrs. Jhabvala grinned approval. "My daughter is no longer afraid to go out alone in Delhi since she has been to school in New York. She carries a knife in her purse." She chuckled when Sarah told her how she had staved off the maharaja by telling him she was my wife.

"Perfect. Many Indian men have young wives, fourteen or fifteen, even. So of course he would think it perfectly natural. It wouldn't stop him for long, though. You were right to get away from him. He would have renewed his attack the following evening. Sex is in the air in India. The men think of little else. And yet everything is covered up. They are still in the Edwardian age here. Lust seething beneath corsets and starched shirtfronts. No wonder the English and the Indians got on. They are both fixated on social hierarchy and hidden passion. Would you agree, Geoffrey?"

Geoffrey reddened. "Up to a point."

"You must get yourself a little Indian wife."

"Actually I have been thinking I might be ready to tie the knot." He coughed and changed the subject. "You know I'm meeting with Kapoor this evening. I hope you've put in a good word for me."

"All you have to do is offer him a five-figure salary, with a decent advance. He's dying to be seen in North America, so you can get him relatively cheap. You could get Ivory cheap too. He's very broke right now."

"I don't want Ivory. He's too damned arty. Sorry, Ruth, I know he's an old friend of yours, but that's the way I see it." He coughed again. "I was thinking we might do a canter around the walls of the fortress. What do you say, Sarah?"

When we were alone, Ruth Jhabvala offered me some whisky and said, "He'll never make the film of *Heat and Dust*. He's not tough enough. He's paid a nice little sum for a two-year option, but when it lapses I'll come to terms with Ivory. He'll find some more money. Ismail's a financial wizard. And James may be arty, but he's tough as nails." (And indeed it turned out as Jhabvala predicted. The film of *Heat and Dust* was eventually made by Merchant and Ivory.)

We had dinner that night with Shashi Kapoor, who was expansive and jolly and anxious to know what we thought of India. He suggested we should go to Jaisalmer, the ancient trading city on the edge of the Pakistan border. "It is magical. Like the Arabian Nights. You must go now, before too many tourists discover it. I will arrange it. I know a wonderful camel-driver. Ranjit is a true Rajput. You know the Rajputs never surrendered no matter how badly they were beaten. They slaughtered their women and rode into the spears of the enemies shouting war cries." Kapoor washed down a mouthful of tandoori chicken with a generous swig of Chivas Regal.

The next day was spent on the backs of two camels crossing the desert. I didn't feel much like a Rajput warrior. I rode behind Ranjit on one camel, Sarah rode behind Geoffrey on another. The camels either ambled along, which was bumpy and boring, or ran, which was very hard on the behind. The sun was blistering. I got bitten by fleas. Geoffrey proved to be allergic to camel dander. We camped overnight in the desert. The food Ranjit made was inedible. Fortunately, Shashi had given us a bottle of Chivas Regal. We emptied it around the campfire so at least we slept soundly.

When we saw the walls of Jaisalmer looming up before us on the afternoon of the second day, it was like a mirage. We stayed in an ancient caravanserai that had hosted traders for four hundred years. The evening meal was wonderfully succulent and spicy, the most subtly flavoured food I had tasted in India. The next day I walked alone through the golden-toned streets of the old city as if in a dream. There seemed to be no other tourists, no motor traffic in the narrow winding streets. The city went about its business as it had for centuries, and I felt finally I was in the legendary Orient of my youthful imagination.

In the evening, Sarah and I walked along the walls of the ancient fortress and looked at purple sky stretching out over the desert. In a cool, level voice she said, "Geoffrey's asked me to marry him." I didn't know what to say. She paused for a moment before she said, "He's nice. It's too bad he's such a wimp." So I didn't have to say anything. "I think I should get back to school. Geoffrey said he'd hire a land-rover to get us back to Jodhpur and then I can take a train."

"What about the Taj Mahal?"

"It'll be there. You can go with Miss Singh."

We had a farewell lunch in Jodhpur with Geoffrey and Shashi Kapoor, who laughed with delight when we told him about our problems with the camels. "Shabash. Now you have seen the real India."

I walked Sarah to the railway station. She was humming a tune, which I recognized as Bunyan's hymn "To Be a Pilgrim." "It's something they sing at school," she said. "You know it?" We sang it together. To my surprise, I remembered all the words.

"So you're all right?"

"Sure, Dad, I'm fine. I'm learning all the time. I'm going to become a vegetarian. And get into yoga a bit more. I've found a guru, a woman I really like. Anyway, I should be home by August. I'd like to go to Kashmir for a week or two before I come home. I'll sell some clothes I don't need. And some of my tapes. It'll work out okay. You don't have to worry. I know where I'm going. Thanks for coming to see me. Have fun in Delhi."

She took my hand, then gave me a hug. It felt very different from the shy, tentative greeting that she'd offered me in Bombay ten days earlier. We stood together for a minute in the warm darkness. Then she turned and walked away without looking back.

REACHING OUT

On my return from India, Ann Saddlemyer offered me a contract at an increased salary with the title of artistic director of Hart House Theatre. She also informed me that she was going to try to get me tenure. This involved getting letters of recommendation from various people and then applying to the dean of the graduate school. The letters were forthcoming but when Ann took them to the dean, he said, "We don't have to do anything for this guy. He could be replaced any time, probably at a lower salary." I appreciated her efforts. Although Ann and I had our differences, there was mutual respect between us. I admired her determination, unfailing good humour, her seemingly boundless energy and her generosity. She had a house in Ireland and offered to let me use it for a month or two. I'm sorry I didn't take her up on it, but another young protégé of hers did. His name was Seamus Heaney. Although Ann saw theatre more or less as a hobby, she was always supportive of my efforts, particularly on a personal level.

I was by now confident of my abilities as a director. I had long ago realized the importance of casting in creating a successful show. An actor cannot hide behind an instrument as musicians do; he is the instrument. He brings on stage a physical appearance, limited by his height, his build, his age, and a voice, but also a certain personality. He may be able to modify this, but only to a certain extent. The use of make-up, wigs, costume, accent, and posture will alter him, but he is still who he is. Alec Guinness with a humped back, a false nose, glasses, and a reedy voice is still recognizably Alec Guinness. Meryl Streep with dyed hair, a mid-European accent, and platform shoes would never be mistaken for anyone else. Their essential qualities somehow shine through. Casting is an intuitive process. I look at an actor and see what I see. I used to do an exercise with my students whereby I would talk to them about myself for two minutes and then ask them what they had learned about me. Their answers were usually tentative. Then I would get them to talk about themselves for two minutes and tell them what I saw. Without being hurtful, I would be very frank. The point was to show them that they were not neutral but colourful personalities. I have occasionally directed a show in which I realized I did not have the key actor or actors I needed. It was always a disheartening experience.

It is essential when directing a play to have a firm knowledge of the text. In many cases I have cut or retranslated the text, which is one way of getting on familiar terms with it. I am fortunate in having a good memory and often by the second week of rehearsal I can prompt the actors without referring to the book. Although I carry a script into rehearsal, I rarely refer to it. I devote all my attention to watching and listening to the actors. For the same reason, I make very few notes. I make changes in the course of rehearsal until we get to a point where the actors know their lines and blocking and need to run scenes without interruption.

Blocking a show is very important. A director needs to have a clear idea of what he wants before he begins to rehearse. This involves close consultation and planning with the designer, but also a sense of three-dimensional space. A director who begins to execute a plan that is clear immediately gains the confidence of the actors. At the same time, he must be open to their suggestions and be ready to change if they come up with a better idea. A director is foolish to think that only he will have illuminating perceptions. Once the process is started, actors will often block themselves, especially in scenes involving only two or three characters. The director will then only modify what they come up with in the interest of maintaining balance and clear sightlines.

The director must also have a feel for the language of the play. In the case of Shakespeare or Sheridan he must understand the meaning of the words, which often involves a good deal of research. He must also have a sensitivity to the rhythms and textures of the words. He must be able to communicate this to the actors. I do not believe in giving actors line readings but I do suggest emphasis, pace, and inflection. In guiding actors, a director should bring out and help shape the characterization of the actor but not insist on the performance that he himself might give. If that is what he wants he might as well play the part himself.

The director also needs to have an understanding of the historical and social milieu of the play, even if it is set in the present. Partly this involves a feeling for the tone of the work. There are certain plays that I am not comfortable with, for whatever reason, and when occasionally I have attempted to direct them, the result has not been very successful. Aristophanes' *Frogs* comes to mind, but in that case I totally remade the play in my own image, with only a partial measure of success. Another somewhat different example is Ezra Pound's translation of *Women of Trachis*, which takes the story and characters of Sophocles' tragedy and marries them to robust contemporary American speech with a distinctly comic slant. I was aware of the complexity of this text but couldn't completely manage to realize it in production.

Part of the difficulty of presenting plays from another time and country is the difficulty of understanding what it actually meant to be an Elizabethan or a nineteenth-century Russian or a revolutionary Frenchman. Although I have always been willing to discuss this with the actors, I never find that it helps much. Later when I worked in radio and did several plays, which involved Quebecois characters, I solved the problem by casting actors who were French-Canadian and didn't need to worry about how to portray that aspect of their roles.

I have also found that it is good to involve all the actors in some kind of physical activity which will bring them together and make them focus on the acquisition of specific skills. Thus with *The Caucasian Chalk Circle* we all learned to do Ukrainian folk dances, with *Serjeant Musgrave's Dance* the actors learned British military drill, for *Troilus and Cressida* the actors worked at how to fight with broadswords, and for *The Kildeer* we practiced country dancing.

What does it take to be an effective stage director? A good eye, a good ear, a certain amount of intelligence, a lot of sensitivity and flexibility. How does one train for the job? I believe it is important to have acted, if only so that one understands the process. Work alongside one or more good directors, as an assistant or a stage manager or a designer. In my early years at the Drama Centre, I attempted to teach a course in directing. It was not very successful. Later when I was teaching classes in theatre, graduate students would some-times ask if they could sit in and observe, to which I would reply, "I have no objection to you watching, but if you want to learn anything, join the class and do the exercises along with us."

Early on in my time at the university my friend John Beckwith, who was then dean of the Music School, suggested that I might like to try my hand at directing opera. I was interviewed by Ezra Schabas, who asked me two questions: "Do you read music? Do you have some knowledge of German and Italian?" As the answer to both questions was yes, I was immediately assigned (at no extra pay) the task of staging scenes from the operas that the students were learning. I would get a call on Sunday night to say I was to stage the card scene from *Carmen* on Monday afternoon or the sweeping scene from *Hansel and Gretel* on Tuesday morning. This I could do by playing the scene several times over on my record player and improvising a staging. I would then be confronted by a group of students who had studied and learned the music. The pianist would ask me if I was going to use the Met or the La Scala staging and I would confess that I wanted to try something original. This was greeted with skepticism though the singers were willing to try to follow my ideas. But when I was asked to stage scenes from *Der Freischütz* or *The Merry Wives of Windsor* on short notice, I had to admit I was not up to the task.

I enjoyed working with the young singers, mostly women. Some of them, such as Janet Stubbs, Diane Loeb, and Rosemarie Landry were genuinely talented. However, in order to fulfill the quota of students needed to get their grants, the Music Faculty took on some considerably less promising individuals. These willing but wobbly and often ungainly women were treated by the coaches and pianists with more or less open contempt and I felt for them. Although I would use every opportunity to introduce music into my own productions, I did not find the rigidity and rigour of the world of opera congenial and have never tried to re-enter it. In any case, only star directors are respected in that rarefied firmament and I knew I was not a star.

One day, I was visited by two women wearing hats and gloves and carrying formidable purses. They stated their names: Evelyn Brownell and Peggy Snell. I knew two of their children and after a few minutes of amiable chit-chat, they came to the point. "We think you should be doing a Youtheatre production at Hart House Theatre during the summer. Of course you would need the approval of our board to get funding. But do not worry, because we are the board." I liked the idea, but would need to get permission from Ann. As she usually did, Ann gave the plan her immediate approval. It would not cost her anything and as she would be away in the summer, it would not involve her time. The staff of the theatre were less happy; they were used to sitting around shooting the breeze during the summers, but at least one person had to be on duty every week. I suggested that they just give me the keys and they could come and go as they pleased. They somewhat grudgingly accepted this arrangement.

I held open auditions for kids between the ages of fifteen and eighteen and chose about twenty, approximately equal numbers of boys and girls. I had a notion that I wanted to do a cut-down and modernized version of *Timon of Athens*, but when I looked at my fresh-faced young actors, I quickly changed my mind and reverted to *The Caucasian Chalk Circle*. I wanted the experience to be upbeat and successful. I knew the play well and the kids attacked the roles with enthusiasm. I was lucky enough to have Sheila Russell to play Grusha and Hal Eisen to play Azdak. Several of the kids played multiple roles, and I made a cameo appearance as the half-witted stable boy. I had a budget of five thousand dollars, which allowed me to hire several Drama Centre students as assistants: Barbara Stewart as administrator, Bie Engelen as movement instructor, David Moe as technical and musical director, and his wife Tulla to do props and costumes. It was a very happy company. We played the show three nights in the theatre and had good houses. Mrs. Brownell and Mrs. Snell announced that they were pleased with the whole enterprise and hoped it would become an annual event.

For the next three summers I presided over a summer Youtheatre program. With increased funding, I was able to take on up to sixty students and produce four plays, guaranteeing each student a part in at least two productions. Although the age range was supposed to be fifteen to eighteen, in fact we had students as young as twelve and as old as twenty-three. I took on a number of assistants besides Bie and Barbara, including Bradley Bernstein, Scot Denton, Reed Needles, David Rotenberg, Juliana Saxton, and Garry Schallenberg. My brother-in-law Jamie Cunningham came up from New York for a week of special classes. We did plays in the theatre, the Studio on Glen Morris Street, the Hart House quad, and the University College quad. We attracted sizeable and appreciative audiences, partly because many of our performances were free and partly because the shows were energetic and fun.

Borrowing a leaf from Robin Phillips' book of tricks, I co-directed a number of shows with my young teachers, including *Romeo and Juliet* and Brecht's *The Good Woman of Setzuan*. I played small parts in several of these plays: a tottering Lord Mulligan in Tennessee Williams' *Camino Real*, and a sympathetic priest in *Much Ado About Nothing*. I cut most of the classical texts, believing it was good for the students to have the experience of playing Shakespeare but realizing they should not be expected to handle full three-hour productions. We also did a few modern plays; Sam Shepard's *La Turista* and a new play written by a very talented Drama Centre student, Angus Braid, titled *Daughters of the King*, set on a ship bringing young brides to the habitants of New France. Angus had written a leading role for me, which I rather wish I had played, but I had enough to do keeping all the balls in the air.

During those four summers, we attracted many talented students, some of whom would go on to have theatrical careers; among others, Laurie Brown, Marina Endicott, Maurice Godin, and Stephen Yorke. Others would become writers: Jim Bradley, David Wilkinson, and a very shy little girl with dark, curly hair, Anne Michaels. We partied together, went dancing, and, with the older students, drinking. More than once, students both male and female let me know they were sexually available. Many of them were very attractive. It was after the introduction of the pill and before the advent of AIDS, when sexual mores were rapidly changing. I knew that a number of my colleagues had affairs with their students, but I resolved on a hands-off policy that included my students, my co-workers, the children of my friends, and the friends of my children.

The closest I came to breaking my rule occurred one night when a very handsome boy invited me after closing time at the Blue Cellar to go back to the apartment he was house-sitting for a family friend. After a couple more beers, he told me that his philosophy professor had offered to give him an A grade if he could have sex with him. The boy had had sex with girls, but thought I might be willing to coach him about sex with a man. I gave him a long look, downed the rest of my beer and left. During the '70s, people picked each other up in bars, on airplanes, and in the streets. Casual sex was readily available. Following my experience with Dan, I realized I had nothing much to offer in a relationship other than friendship though I did allow myself an occasional one-night stand, or more accurately, in most cases, a one-hour stand.

I encouraged my students to see as much and as many different kinds of theatre as possible. We took in the Bread and Puppet Theatre, visiting Japanese acrobats, and a Russian dance company. One of our most memorable encounters occurred on the first morning of our second year. Bradley Bernstein announced at the beginning of movement class that the British mime Lindsay Kemp, who was playing in Toronto, had invited all the clowns of Toronto to meet him at noon at City Hall. We all put on whiteface and trooped down University Avenue attracting a fair amount of attention. There were few other participants, and Lindsay looked a bit at a loss. Suddenly he leaped into one of the fountains and said, "We're going to create a water ballet." The kids gamely followed his lead and happily splashed about for fifteen minutes. I then told my gang that we would meet back at the theatre in an hour, when they had dried out. Juliana and I went to a small Chinese restaurant for lunch. We attracted astonished looks from the Chinese kids eating with their parents and were unable to understand why until we suddenly realized we were still wearing whiteface.

At the end of the fourth year, I was informed by the board of Youtheatre that they had decided to set up a small company of young actors who would receive modest salaries. They would be drawing on some of the actors I had trained. They had hired a promising young director who had been recommended to them by someone at the Canada Council. I would, of course, understand that they would have to cut back on my funding. I was annoyed by this high-handed treatment, but fortunately held my tongue.

In my second year working for Ann Saddlemyer, I decided I would like to initiate undergraduate studies in drama at the university. My friend Peter Russell was the newly appointed principal of Innis College and when I told him of my ambition he said, "It is part of my mandate to encourage new and experimental courses. I cannot give you any space or money, but I can give your students credit." Ann gave me permission to use the Glen Morris Studio two mornings a week, and I gathered together a few students and began giving classes. I did not attempt to give them professional training, but rather to provide an introduction to the world of theatre: improvisational exercises, a bit of voice work, some highly anecdotal theatre history. There was no syllabus and, in the first year, no written work. All that was required was regular attendance and a willingness to participate. Six months later I ran into Peter, who asked, "Did you do anything about your theatre class idea?"

"Yes, we meet every Tuesday and Thursday morning for two hours."

"How many students do you have?"

"Eight."

"And they've stayed with you? I wonder what would happen if we put your course in the calendar?"

The next year, twenty-seven students turned up to take the class. I interviewed them and selected twenty-two. I elaborated the course somewhat. I required each student to do a monologue and write an essay. I divided the class into three groups, each of which was to improvise and present a short play. I introduced some exercises borrowed from the British teacher Dorothy Heathcote, whose ideas I had learned about working with my friends John and Juliana Saxton, who were developing a training program for high school drama teachers at the College of Education. I also developed a rather experimental series of vocal exercises based on the work of the composer R. Murray Schafer. Reed Needles visited to give a class in stage combat, Bie Engelen did some stage movement. At the end of the year I handed in the marks. Peter summoned me to his office and informed me I would have to resubmit my marks. According to university guidelines, I could not award more than two first-class marks, I could not fail anyone, and I should be wary of too many third-class marks. This meant that most of my students had to be graded within a range between 68 and 74. I duly acquiesced.

The next year, sixty-three people applied to take my course. I told Peter that for one year only, I would teach two streams. As I was also teaching a practical graduate course, this meant I was carrying a full teaching load as well as running Hart House Theatre and the Studio. My salary had risen to eighteen thousand dollars a year. One of my classes this year was pleasant enough; the other was something of a nightmare, the sort of class that if I had never taught before would have persuaded me to look for some other kind of work. It contained several boys who were lazy smart alecks. It also contained two women who fought continuously: one was a curvy and outspoken strawberry blonde named Gingerina, who announced early on that she had worked as a stripper. The other was a plain prude who told me she thought the theatre was sinful. I asked her why she wanted to take the course and she replied, "I feel it is my duty to see for myself what goes on." These two had a number of verbal sparring matches in which they traded remarks like: "You're nothing but a brazen harlot" and "I'm not ashamed of my body but I can understand why you would be."

Just as I was about to expel both of them, the prudish one stopped coming to class. As the term went on, the boys kept razzing Gingerina about her monologue. "You gonna take it all off?" they asked rolling their eyes and smirking. Gingerina kept putting off the date until the very end of the course. On the final day she went down to the basement, returned in a Judy Garland outfit, and sang "Somewhere Over the Rainbow." To their credit, the boys cheered. A week or two after the end of classes, the prude appeared in my office and asked if she had passed the course.

"I made it quite clear at the beginning of the course that you could not miss more than three classes. By my reckoning, you've missed seven."

Her eyes filled with tears. "I really need this credit. I want to become a deaconess and if I fail this course they won't let me into the program."

After a long pause I said, "Very well, I'll give you a pass. But I want you to understand that this is an act of Christian charity." She reddened and scuttled out of my office. I never saw her again. Gingerina, on the other hand, I ran into a few years later in a fashionable restaurant. She was happily married with a large diamond ring on her finger and a cute three-year-old daughter by her side. Our paths would continue to cross occasionally in the years ahead.

In my fourth year of undergraduate classes, ninety-two students signed up for the course. Peter Russell came up with a small stipend for an assistant and I chose my longtime friend David Gardner, who had recently entered the Drama Centre as a student. David had worked as an actor, television producer, artistic director, and arts council civil servant and was highly qualified. We agreed to teach two streams, not taking classes together but alternating blocks of classes. David is eminently agreeable but also strong-minded and we had some differences of opinion, but we completed the year without quarrelling, the only time I have successfully worked in a team-teaching situation.

At the end of the year, Peter announced that the university had decided to set up an undergraduate drama program, but that they didn't think I was qualified to run it. I replied, "I should be insulted and I am. But my aim was to get an undergraduate program started and I have achieved that. Anyway, I have many other irons in the fire." The leader of the new program immediately announced that he had no wish to discuss my program with me and that he would forbid his students to audition for Hart House Theatre productions. Eventually the program would be taken over by Pia Kleber, a strong-minded former Drama Centre student. A tiny woman with flaming red hair and oversize glasses, she would use her formidable ability to connect with some of the most influential and talented theatre people in Canada and beyond to develop a unique program with a high intellectual content as well as meaningful practical experience that would produce a number of very interesting theatre practitioners.

With my reduced Youtheatre budget, I decided to mount a one-month summer season of two Shakespeare plays at the Glen Morris Studio using some of my most accomplished actors. *Twelfth Night* is probably my favourite play. The exploration of the unexpected twists and turns of the romantic heart, the rueful songs of Feste the clown, the one clear-eyed observer in a world of misguided fools and deluded lovers and the spontaneity of the language present a director with a challenge that is at once teasing and stimulating: an ever-shifting balance between light and dark, comedy and bittersweet romance. Bie Engelen as Viola and Barbara Stewart as Olivia brought both playful charm and the sharp edge of a bitter wit to their duel of courtship. Hal Eisen was a moping, moony Orsino, Gary Schallenburg a foolish, prancing Malvolio, and David Wilkinson a hilariously silly Sir Andrew. Again I was assisted by David Moe who designed and lit a set of simple platforms and his wife, Tulla, who clothed all the actors in white cotton overalls with cleverly chosen accessories.

Our second play was a heavily cut version of *Timon of Athens*. Hal Eisen was a self-involved Timon, more pathetic than tragic, and Bie Engelen employed her physical dexterity and androgynous appearance to create a wonderfully sour, mocking Apemantus. Peter Robertson made Alcibiades an arrogant bully. Again I wrote some lyrics which were set to music by the sweet-voiced actor-singer Laurie Brown, who played the whore Timandra.

"Night is blocking out
Bright colours of the day,
Sharp edges melt away.
I'm through with knocking out
Smart remarks, bright replies,
Glimmering images, shimmering lies.
I'm walking out
Into a shadowy oasis
Full of half-seen faces.
In the darkness I'm aware
Of them floating in the air,
Then a sudden breaking
Of the fragile rind
Around my mind.
No, there's no mistaking:
They'll go with me where I go.
What it means I do not know."

The cast wore the same white overalls as in *Twelfth Night*, and the set featured a sportscar. We received a rare rave from the acerbic critic Gina Mallet and played to full houses. I was as proud of these two shows as of anything I did in my whole time at the university.

Although the cast included Drama Centre stalwarts, many of the other actors in these plays had come to me through the Youtheatre program. Some of them had taken my undergraduate class and appeared in productions I had directed at Hart House or the studio. They formed the nexus of a large sprawling family that I had gathered around me. After every show I gave a cast party at my house. Judy cooked wonderful food and I supplied beer and wine. We had learned early on to save some provisions for the crew who would come later after the strike. One student who was caught dishing up a third helping confessed that he had not eaten for two days in anticipation of this feast. Ann and some of the other staff members would occasionally come to these parties. One night Ann took me aside and said, "You're a fine teacher, Martin, and I really appreciate what you have done. You have restored Hart House to what it was in its earliest days, a true community theatre."

I'LL TAKE MANHATTAN

One day in late May of my second year working for Ann Saddlemyer, she called me into her office to tell me she had just discovered that she had four thousand dollars left in her budget and if she didn't spend it immediately, she would lose it. She proposed I take the money and use it to finance a study of practical teaching methods in American drama schools. I realized this was a way of compensating me for doing what was essentially two full-time jobs for half the salary of an associate professor. She suggested I should write a brief report of no more than four or five pages and made it clear I didn't need to submit expense receipts. I thanked her and pocketed the cheque. Two day later, I was heading down the Thruway to New York.

I intended to stay with my brother-in-law Jamie, who was at this point running his own modern dance company. He invented freewheeling satirical pieces, which his troupe performed in Manhattan and then took on tour, spending a week or so on a university campus doing two or three performances and teaching a number of master classes. Soon after he split with Richard Silverman, he moved in with his new lover Bill Florio, a twenty-eight-year-old decorator at Bloomingdale's. Bill was in love with antiquity but most of all the '30s: Art Deco, Rodgers and Hart, Fred Astaire, Jeanette MacDonald. He had an apartment on Second Avenue four floors up, which looked like the set for a Visconti film: huge chandeliers with crystal drops the size of apples and pears, gilded Empire chairs sporting animal claws and sphinx's heads. There were yellow silk moiré draperies dripping with tassels, tall peacock-coloured art nouveau vases, ormulu candelabras supported by winged telamons, flawed portraits of countesses fondling their lapdogs that just might have been painted by Gainsborough or Vigée Le Brun. In the centre of all this was Bill with his mop of dirty gold curls wearing jeans and lovebeads, leafing through *Vogue* and listening to a recording of "The Carioca." He informed me Jamie was away on tour. He put down his magazine and asked me to dance. I tried gamely to follow his nimble bare feet, but my size eleven desert boots couldn't keep up. I sat down and watched as he spun around the apartment with one of the Empire chairs in his arms. He grinned at me and said, "We're going to have tea with Mrs. Astor." In a flash, he was outfitted in a neat blue suit and paisley tie, and we were heading up Madison Avenue in a bright yellow taxicab.

Mrs. Astor was a vigorous middle-aged woman in a severely cut grey flannel suit and tiny Italian loafers. She had just rescued a wounded bird from the balcony of her Fifth Avenue apartment and was busy trying to identify it in her copy of *Peterson*. The bird was large with a funny topknot and it eyed Mrs. Astor suspiciously. It seemed unlikely it was a native New Yorker. "Bird," said its hostess, "do not be alarmed. Brooke Astor will look after you." An aging manservant appeared with a tea tray and was ordered to take the bird to the kitchen and give it something to eat. He managed to get hold of one of its legs and carried it away flapping and squawking. I read later in the week that Mrs. Astor had given the Central Park Zoo, which was directly across the avenue, a million dollars.

Mrs. Astor poured us some tea and turned her attention to the redecoration of the apartment. It was not, apparently, where she lived, but rather a four-bedroom pad she kept for visiting friends. Sometimes they brought children, and she thought one room should be decorated with them in mind. "I bought some Miro lithographs when I was in Barcelona this winter that I thought they might fine amusing." She showed them to us and as I looked at the surreal shapes that suggested more than anything else floating vaginas and penises, I wondered about Mrs. Astor's theories of child-rearing. "It's important to stimulate them, don't you know?"

Bill showed Mrs. Astor some Italian fabrics.

"Simply stunning. I must have that one with the toucans." She set aside her Spode teacup and turned to me.

"We must plan your activities here in New York. There is an exciting new exhibit at the Museum of Natural History. It's all about the Near East. They're doing over the whole building and this is an excellent beginning. I myself am working with the Met on a new series of Chinese rooms. I am quite smitten with things Oriental just now. I was utterly ravished by those wonderful gardens at Suzhou. Have you seen them? You must go. But first there is an excellent new Chinese restaurant on Third Avenue. You must go this very night. I would take you there myself had I not promised to have dinner with the new Belgian ambassador to the UN. A darling little man. Rather like Hercule Poirot. So positive about the European Union, which I think can contribute so much to world peace."

"I'm afraid I don't know much about Chinese food."

"I will call the maitre d' and tell him what to serve you. And then you must go to see *Pacific Overtures*. The most exciting theatrical event in Manhattan just now. I will book tickets for you. And now you must let me go."

Neither Bill nor I were keen on Chinese food, but we did as we were bid and were pleasantly surprised. We were not expected to make five selections and mix them all together but were brought a succession of dishes, each one of which modified or complemented the one before, until the final offering, huge succulent red plums in syrup, crowned the whole experience. We set out for the theatre purring with satisfaction.

Stephen Sondheim's *Pacific Overtures* for me was everything Mrs. Astor had promised. At once slick and subtle, superficially witty, and sharply telling. I realized Sondheim's vision of Japan was probably no more accurate that Gilbert and Sullivan's *The Mikado* but somehow behind the screens and fans emerged a world of delight and violence, amorous pleasure and suppressed pain. I looked over at Bill, whose eyes were shut. Afterwards he said, "That was certainly boring. Pretentious crap. If you weren't Jamie's brother-in-law, I'd take you to see some real entertainment."

"I'm game."

We got in a cab and went across town to the East Side and entered a large forbidding-looking building. Bill negotiated our admittance to what turned out to be the Continental Baths. We were shown to our lockers by a Puerto Rican kid who appraised us we started to strip. "Nice buns," he commented.

"Take a hike." Bill handed him a dollar and he disappeared. We headed for the pool where some thirty or forty young men disported themselves, some wearing towels, some totally naked. They eyed our bodies with undisguised interest. One guy, lean as an alleycat, slinked over and said hello. He had been a dancer in Jamie's company. He also cut Bill's hair. He and Bill exchanged banalities and then he offered to give me a free trim. I said I'd drop by if I happened to be in his part of town.

A chubby elf began to play a white grand piano and a tiny red-headed woman sang a song I remembered from my high school days: "Come On-A My House." She had a deep, throaty chuckle and a singing style that owed something to both Ethel Merman and Barbra Streisand, but was more down-and-dirty than either of them. She was greeted with enthusiastic hoots and hollers and proceeded to tell dirty jokes, quoting Sophie Tucker and Mae West.

She sang "Life is Just a Bowl of Cherries," "I Got it Bad," and "The Man That Got Away." The crowd whooped like Indians as she sashayed out swinging her sequined bum in a parody of all the great Hollywood sex cats.

"Who is she?"

"She calls herself the Divine Miss M. Let's go. I've gotta work tomorrow. Brooke Astor expects her boys to hustle their bustles." Back at Bill's I realized there was only one bed, elegantly draped with a fringed canopy. Bill pulled off the spread and hopped in. "You're a very attractive man and I'd love to fuck you, but I don't think it would be a very smart thing for us to do." He rolled over and faced the wall. When I woke up the next morning, he'd already gone to work.

I began my theatrical survey at the Juilliard, where I had made an appointment with Sonia St. Denis, the widow of Michel, whom I had met when she came to Toronto to collect an honorary degree a few years earlier. I was permitted to watch her class in mask work, which I was given to understand was a unique privilege. It was conducted with all the solemnity of a religious rite. I have always found the stylization and exaggeration of mime tiresome except when conducted by masters such as Jean-Louis Barrault and Marcel Marceau. The ponderous posturing of this class of earnest young acolytes did nothing to change my mind. None of the freshness and invention of last night's show coloured their work, which seemed to me stilted, affected, and moribund.

"The point is to strip away idiosyncrasy and find a neutral position." Sonia's rich tenor resonated across the green tablecloth that separated us at the Russian Tea Room. "Most actors have little or no technique. For a singer or a pianist it is different; they must hit the notes. For an actor, there are no fixed notes."

"There are words."

"Not necessarily. Think of Chaplin. Actors rely on their personality. They exploit it to the full. This is egotism, not art."

"Chaplin's personality was what people paid to see. All the great actors, the great masters of disguise, Olivier, Guinness, they're always unmistakably themselves."

"But they must work to extend themselves. That is the point of the technique. You concentrate on something outside yourself, which leads you to discover something inside yourself. Something you didn't know was there." I thought of myself sitting long ago in the darkened chapel of St. Thomas

Aquinas before going onstage as Cuthman and conceded that Sonia had a point.

That afternoon I went to a matinee of *Equus.* It was raining and the audience was damp and restless. They shuffled in their seats and coughed. About a minute and a half into his first speech, Anthony Hopkins stopped and addressed them directly, "I'm going to give you one minute to settle down and if you don't, we're not going to do this." We were totally silent and concentrated for the next hour. On one level, I found Peter Shaffer's play irritating. The whine of a man of limited abilities complaining because he's not a genius. Get used to it. But it also presented an intriguing paradox: self-exploration needs something to bounce off, the spontaneous outpouring of a simple spirit is not enough.

After the show, I met Bill who took me to meet his friend Peter von Blanckenhagen. Peter was a Russian baron, born in St. Petersburg at the turn of the century. A hunchback, he had been taken by his mother to Switzerland at the age of twelve to see if his spine could be straightened and thus escaped the revolution. Peter's body could not be mended, but his mind was expanded as he and his mother travelled in Italy. Eventually he became an art historian whose specialty was Caravaggio. He owned a number of minor Renaissance paintings, one of which contained a shepherd boy, which he asserted was almost certainly the work of the Roman master.

Some years earlier Peter had seen Bill staring wistfully into one of the rococo rooms at the Metropolitan Museum and asked him home for tea. They became lovers for a few months and remained good friends. They shared a passion for late eighteenth-century porcelain and Peter had introduced Bill to dealers and experts. Over Meissen teacups they discussed Bill's latest acquisition, a French clock. Peter told me he had recently made a will leaving Bill his apartment with all his treasures, except the family silver which would go to his twin brother, a giant of a man who ran a publishing house in Munich and who had gone though four wives and sired nine children. Peter corresponded with him but had not seen him since 1921. To see his own features echoed in those of this prolific heterosexual extravert was something he simply could not face.

Peter took me around his apartment, commenting on his treasures, their provenance and history. Pale, delicate, and diminutive, he had something of the air of Miss Havisham or la Folle de Chaillot, a figure whose world he had reshaped to correspond to his own fantasies. He never allowed women to visit his apartment and rarely received heterosexuals. He only went out with Bill and one or two other close friends. I understood that I was highly privileged to be allowed into his sanctuary. He had prepared a simple supper for us, lamb chops and a salad. He hopped nimbly around the kitchen while I sat on a tall stool and Bill handed him various implements. Then we sat in his dining room, dwarfed by two enormous candelabras and drank from heavy crystal goblets a claret that we couldn't have found on the open market, even if we could have afforded to buy it. The meal ended with a pungent cheese and Tokay in amber-tinted glasses rimmed with gold, while Peter expounded his critique of Visconti's *Death in Venice*, the only film he had seen in the last five years.

"Apart from pornos," interjected Bill.

"I hear there's rather good new French film at that little theatre on Fifty-fourth Street."

"You want to see it?"

"It is rather late . . ."

"Never to late to kick up your heels." Bill executed a few tango steps.

"But your friend here . . ."

"I'm studying the art of performance."

We piled into a cab and headed downtown. Peter insisted we get out a block away from the theatre and walk the rest of the way, even though Bill ridiculed this show of discretion. We stumbled down the aisle and found seats near the front. The film showed a bunch of young French soldiers being trained by a rather brutal sergeant. They were taken on a route march through rough terrain until finally they turned on the sergeant, stripped off his uniform, and forced him to service them in a variety of humiliating ways. I found myself bored with the repetition of a few variations of what was an essentially simple physical function. It seemed rather like watching a training film for dentists or plumbers. I looked over at Peter sitting on the edge of his seat, tense with attention. Beyond him, Bill had gone to sleep.

The next day I took the train from Grand Central Station to New Haven. David Rotenberg, one of my former students, was at the Yale Drama School and he had set up an interview for me with Robert Brustein and tickets for a production of *The Brothers Karamazov* that evening. I was surprised how rundown the town seemed with its scruffy bars and black hookers who propositioned me at eleven o'clock in the morning. Brustein kept me waiting for nearly forty minutes and made it clear I should consider myself lucky that he was prepared to see me at all. He pointed out that Yale turned down twenty applicants for every one they took and if a student made trouble or wasn't prepared to work his ass off, they kicked him out. "There's a lineup waiting at the door and believe me, they know it."

"Don't your students complain about being overworked?'

"What I say to them is — sleep less."

"Do they all find work when they graduate?"

"They do if they know how to sell themselves."

"What about your playwrights?"

"The smart ones figure it out. Some of them get grants. Some of them find a rich woman to support them. Some of them become advertising executives." Maybe it should have been called the Yale Drama and Business School.

I watched a movement class in which some of the participants actually groaned with pain and an acting class in which the instructor reduced most of his students to tears. At the end of the afternoon, I met David for a half-hour supper between his afternoon rehearsal of a Pinter play and his evening rehearsal of a sketch he'd written for an upcoming revue. Was he happy? Was he learning a lot?

"Happy, I don't have time to think about. I'm learning how to work, how to live on one meal a day, how to override twelve egos even bigger than my own, and how to direct someone I just broke up with two weeks ago. If this doesn't prepare me to work in the theatre, what will?"

"What about Brustein?"

"He's a maniac. I wish I had time to tell you about him, but I gotta get back to rehearsal."

Later I sat through a murky, surreal version of Dostoevsky's masterpiece. I had read the novel, but I found it hard to follow a good deal of what was going on. At the centre of it was an incandescent young actress who was by turns funny, wild, perverse and tantalizing, enigmatic one moment, transparently vulnerable the next. At the end of the show I checked out her name in the program: Meryl Streep.

The next day I was back in Manhattan in time for lunch at the Plaza with Bill and his friend Audrey, a plump, hearty Englishwoman with the air of an aging St. Trinian's schoolgirl. Audrey had been in the WREN during the war and worked down the hall from Churchill, whom she claimed to have serviced on her knees on one occasion, while he held a cigar in one hand, a brandy snifter in the other and dictated instructions to the First Lord of the Admiralty. "He didn't know the first thing about strategy, but he was a consummate performer," she chortled.

It turned out Jamie was back in town and would be performing that evening at a little theatre in the village. Audrey agreed to go with me, but when I phoned her later in the afternoon, she begged off. "I'm like the Irishwoman who was asked by a friend to go for a walk and replied, 'Sure and I'd love to, but you see, me husband's fuckin' me, the baby's suckin' me, and I'm after havin' a smoke.'" After I hung up I remembered Bill had told me Audrey was having an affair with her best friend's husband, who often dropped in on her for a quickie on the way home from work.

Jamie's dance piece was the first item on the program. He appeared as an addled professor stumbling out onto the stage in shabby tweeds and proceeding to lecture the audience on the use of the thyrsis in ancient Dionysian ritual. As he talked, a faun appeared and tweaked him from behind. The professor finally sees the faun and is completely enchanted by him. They play a game of hide-and-seek and finally danced together in a rapturous pas de deux: E.M. Forster meets Nijinsky. The audience was small but wildly enthusiastic. Then piece that followed involved a woman who did a variety of movements with hula hoops. I found it less than riveting. I made my way backstage and Jamie suggested I skip the rest of the performance. He gave me the address of a friend who was hosting a party after the show and suggested I turn up around midnight.

I went across the village and found a little bistro called The Cookery where the black singer Alberta Hunter was performing. She had begun singing as a teenager in the '30s in a brothel in Chicago and made a number of recordings. Then she retired and became a nurse. When the hospital she was working for forced her to retire at age sixty-five (she was actually seventy-three), she went back to singing. She had a distinctive voice and a repertoire of songs, many of which she had written herself. She came out and sat at the piano, a diminutive and somewhat wizened black woman with a wide, winning smile. She beamed at the audience and said, "It's so good to see all you good people here. God bless you. I want all you good people to know that I am a believer in God, a good God who loves and cares for all of you. And now I'm goin' to sing for you a song I used to sing in Chicago. It's called 'My Man Put in the Bacon and It Overflowed the Pot.'"

After her second set, I managed to find Jamie's party. I was handed a glass of red wine and introduced to Ted, the dancer who had played the faun; it turned out he really was Greek and in real life he was a lawyer. Tonight was his last performance; he had just been offered a job with the New York Council of the Arts, the result of an encounter with Kitty Carlisle Hart, who apparently called the shots in that organization. She had been very receptive to his ideas about audience development and also, I gathered, to his Mediterranean good looks. She had insisted he start working for her immediately.

The loft we were in was owned by Jamie's lighting designer who came over and talked to me about how successful Jamie had been and how concerned he was that Jamie was ready to throw it all away. I listened inattentively and watched as people danced, rolled around on cushions or sat intensely rapping. Wine was drunk, joints were smoked, people came and went. I eventually fell asleep on a couch and woke in the middle of the night to discover the hairdresser from the Continental Baths lying beside me. He looked at me with his cat's eyes and whispered, "Don't worry I just want to hold you . . ." Fine, I thought, why not, and went back to sleep.

When I got back to the apartment Jamie was already up, sitting on the fire escape drinking lapsang souchong tea and writing in his journal. We went around the corner to the Elephant and Castle for breakfast and a good gab before he went to his therapy session. He had been in analysis for six years, and I wondered what he and his therapist found to talk about. He replied that at his last session they had discussed who in his company should room with whom on their tour. This morning he would talk about replacing Ted, as none of his other dancers had the requisite sex appeal.

"I thought you told me Ted is straight."

"Oh, he is. I don't actually have to sleep with whoever dances the faun, but I have to want to."

We agreed to meet for dinner later and Jamie took off. He is one of a number of people who have been in therapy for years and who seem to believe it has changed them out of all recognition, but it is hard for me to see any difference. I think the important thing is it makes them feel better about themselves. Someone in the trade described it as "paid friendship."

I set out for NYU to investigate their theatre program. Deborah, another former student, agreed to meet me in a grotty lounge near Washington Square. Her morning class had been cancelled because the instructor had challenged two of the boys in it to face up to the true nature of their sexuality and they had complained to the dean. "He's quite brilliant but I don't think we're ready for him. This has been a horrible term. My best friend quit and went to stay with her grandmother in Portugal after she broke up with one of the voice coaches. Our last production was cancelled because the director had a nervous breakdown. I've learned a lot about myself though. I realize I have a highly developed super-ego and that's what's saved me. That and Tai Chi. I've found a dynamite new instructor. I won't be coming back here next year. I'm going to take a course in massage therapy and then go to China."

I took Deborah to lunch at a vegetarian restaurant in Union Square, where she claimed she had once seen Danny Kaye. He was not in evidence, but we did see Geraldine Page alone in a booth, mumbling to herself. As we munched on beet and walnut salad, Deborah told me I absolutely had to see a new musical called *A Chorus Line.* I walked up to Times Square and got a half-price ticket for the matinee. It knocked me out with its sheer energy and verve. It seemed to encapsulate my whole experience of New York: the tension between the striving to master technique and the force of individual personality, the need for stamina and the power of endurance, a blend of ruthless and unashamed narcissism, the element of absurdity that made all of this effort both ridiculous and fresh.

After the show, I dropped into the Chelsea Hotel for a margarita and decided to check in for my last night in New York. I figured Bill's bed could hardly accommodate the three of us. And I could breathe in the atmosphere of earlier legends: Patti Smith, Leonard Cohen, and Dylan Thomas.

At dinner, Jamie announced he was at a crossroads. He and Bill would always be friends but had ceased to be lovers. He had achieved his ambition of having his own company and gaining recognition for his work, but at a cost of having virtually no private life. Now he wanted to reassess and redefine his goals. "My therapist feels I owe this to myself."

"What do you feel you owe to Bill? He's provided you with a place to live for five years and designed a lot of your shows. You have a lot of interests and friends in common."

"I'm thinking of teaching."

"I haven't been overly impressed by any of the schools I've visited here.

My only conclusion is that the best schools are the ones that work their students the hardest."

"It doesn't have to be like that. You don't operate on that principle. I'm off to a seance. Do you want to tag along?"

"I'm a skeptic. Won't that hinder the proceedings?"

"Not in the slightest. You'll enjoy it. And you might even be convinced."

About twenty of us gathered in a rather frowsty living room where we were offered tea and bought cookies by a plumpish man in a colourful dressing gown and tasselled slippers. He introduced himself as Alex and collected twenty dollars from each of us in a chipped Amari bowl which he put on the mantelpiece. He waited for a few late arrivals, including Peter von Blanckenhagen, who winked at me in a confidential way from the other side of the room. Alex dimmed the lights and sat in a battered wing chair in the middle of the room. He explained he had a nasty cold and this would prevent one of his favourite mediums from speaking with him, as she was a hypochondriac. He would try to make contact with a Siberian shaman to see if she would tell him what herbs she used to treat bronchial conditions, but so far she had been unwilling to reveal her secrets. Suddenly his voice cracked and he began to speak in some tongue which was unintelligible. A dialogue ensued between Alex in his own voice and the high-pitched croak of the Siberian ancient who seemed to work herself up into a fury and started to shriek like a banshee. Alex's face was convulsed and distorted until finally he fell back in his chair, eyes closed as if he had fainted. Nobody moved to help him and after two or three minutes, he began to sing very slowly and sweetly a Southern lullaby:

"Hush little baby, don't say a word,
Momma's going to buy you a mockin' bird."

A middle-aged black woman began to sob and Alex, without opening his eyes, addressed her in a soft drawl. "Don't cry, Clarice, honey, Aunt Dodie has forgiven you everything. She knows why you done stole her earrings and run away and she wants you to know she's happy where she is now and she still love you, honey." There followed a dialogue between the black woman who leaned forward in her chair, her cheeks wet, as she questioned Alex about long-dead relatives and friends from her home in Georgia. Finally, she said a tearful farewell to her auntie and Alex again sat in silence.

When Alex's voice surfaced again, it was the thin, prim tone of a spinster with a New England accent. It began with some lines from a hymn in a quavery soprano:

"Time like an ever-rolling stream
Bears all its sons away
They fly forgotten as a dream,
Dies at the opening day."

The delicately modulated voice asked if anyone recognized the lines. A brisk grey-haired woman replied they were the words worked into a sampler she had recently bought on a holiday in Maine. The sampler had been worked by the speaker whose voice was issuing from Alex's pursed lips.

"I did it in memory of my sweet brother Abel who was drowned when I was just sixteen. He was the only man I ever loved, so I didn't marry. I kept my maiden name. Hannah Amos.

"Why, that's the name on the sampler. I asked everyone in the town who she was but nobody seemed to know."

"Well, now you do, dearie. I'm so happy my little bit of needlework is in good hands."

Alex slumped in his chair. He looked worn out. He opened his eyes and looked around and suddenly began to sing "Ach, du lieber Augustin." He was now inhabited by the spirit of an eighteenth century Prussian cavalry officer who wished to speak to one of his descendants who was here in the room. My eye turned to Peter who was leaning forward in his chair, lips slightly parted, just the way he had looked at the porno screening.

The cavalry officer launched into a tale of how he had been picked by Friedrich der Grosse to carry a secret missive to the great Empress Catherine, Mother of all the Russias. He had ridden for thirteen days across the steppes and had finally delivered the secret document to Catherine while lying beside her in her canopied bed. His reward was a silver samovar, which even now stood on his descendant's sideboard. And in a secret compartment under the lid was a diamond worth a thousand rubles. Peter groaned audibly and fell back in his chair.

Alex got up and announced brightly, "Time for tea." The lights were raised and people began to chatter while Alex padded off to the kitchen to put the kettle on. We went over to Peter who smiled at us enigmatically. Jamie asked if he would like to share a taxi and to my surprise, he agreed. We compared notes on the seance as we drove uptown. "Of course his German accent was Bavarian, not Prussian, and there are no steppes between Potsdam and St. Petersburg."

"It's interesting that every one of the characters started with a song."

"Alex is very musical. He plays the cello."

"Still, he seemed literally possessed by those characters. It's like going back to the source. Where theatre really comes from."

"Speaking of theatre," said Peter as we approached Times Square, "I don't suppose you'd like to catch the last show at the Gaiety?"

"Why not?" said Jamie. I paid off the driver and we threaded our way across the square. The Gaiety turned out to be a theatre devoted to the art of male strippers. We watched while six young men of different physical types came out one after another and danced to a popular tune. Each did one number clothed and one number naked.

The first was a tall, sulky blond dressed as a construction foreman in work boots and a hard hat which he kept on for his nude dance; then came a mischievous-looking black boy wearing overalls that ripped apart with a crackling of Velcro to reveal an impressive erection; a Mexican who lay down on the floor and masturbated; an extremely hairy Italian who moved like an orangutan; and a skinny white-skinned redhead who didn't dance at all but merely flip-flopped his long limp foreskinned organ in our faces. The standout was a lithe Brazilian boy who danced to a salsa beat with the adept footwork of Ray Bolger and the vivacity of Carmen Miranda.

Jamie was very taken with Marlon the Brazilian. "That kid can really dance. He'd be fabulous as my faun." After the show was over, we sauntered into the little lounge off the lobby and found Marlon working the levers of a pinball machine. Jamie engaged him in conversation and in no time the kid was rubbing up against Jamie's leg. They disappeared into the back room behind the stage. Meanwhile, Peter was negotiating with the construction worker. He came over and told me he had invited the boy to come home with him but was afraid of being roughed up. Would I be willing to go along to make sure there wasn't any trouble? He was so obviously excited at the prospect, I didn't have the heart to refuse.

I got in the front seat with the driver while in the back the boy gave Peter a handjob. He pocketed a cool one hundred dollars and asked if he could touch his hump for luck. Peter acquiesced, and the boy kissed him and got out just north of Columbus Circle. Peter sighed contentedly, thanked me, and invited me to come to his apartment for a nightcap. We sat in his elegant drawing room and drank brandy until I could contain my curiosity no longer.

"Aren't you going to look under the lid of the samovar?"

Peter chuckled and led me into the dining room. He had to stand on a chair to reach the lid. Sure enough, there was little sliding door that revealed a tiny hidden compartment. In it was a pawn ticket for twenty thousand rubles. The date on it was 1896.

The next morning I had breakfast with Jamie at the Elephant and Castle before hitting the road. He was keyed up. That afternoon, he was going to start rehearsing Marlon as the faun.

"Has he any experience as a dancer?"

"He's a natural. I'll teach him what he needs to know."

"You think performing can be taught?"

"We both know damn well it can't. But technique can be taught. Anyway Marlon's the real thing. You could see that the minute he stepped out on stage last night."

"At a strip joint."

"Stripping is what it's all about. Showing what you've got. Revealing yourself. In another way, that's what Alex does. Reveals the secret lives bottled up inside him. He's like someone with multiple personality disorder, only he's found a legitimate outlet for it, that's all."

"Maybe I'm wasting my time trying to teach kids about theatre."

"Not at all. If the kids who come to you are ready to learn."

"I often think the main thing I can do for them is provide them with an opportunity to try things."

"What's the matter with that?"

"It doesn't seem like much."

"At the same time you're developing. Working on yourself."

"Manipulating myself. Manipulating them. A bit like mutual masturbation."

"I don't think of myself as manipulating my dancers."

"Oh, come on. That's what directing is. You use what they've got."

"Maybe. The important thing for any artist is to keep working at his art.

You need a context. Every artist needs a certain amount of stability. Continuity. You've got that. Much more than I have. My dancers come and go. So do my grants. I kind of envy you the support you get from your ongoing emotional and professional ties."

"You don't think you are idealizing my situation?"

"You'll know when the context you're working in no longer serves your needs."

"But if you've nowhere else to go . . ."

"There's always somewhere else to go. The whole thing's a kind of balancing act, isn't it?"

"Okay for you. You're an accomplished high wire artist."

"But you've got your feet on the ground."

"Okay, you take the high road and I'll take the low road. Maybe with a little bit of luck I'll be in Hollywood afore ye."

"Right. Only who wants to be in Hollywood?"

"Good question," I thought as I headed up the thruway and back home.

PLAYS AND PLOYS

Sometime in 1975, Ann Saddlemyer asked me to invite British critic Robert Cushman to lunch, to inform him that she would not be hiring him as a special professor at the Drama Centre as she had decided to hire Ronald Bryden instead. This was not exactly the most auspicious way to meet the man who would eventually become Toronto's most informed and respected drama critic, but by the time he was writing regular columns for the *National Post*, I was no longer producing or directing on a regular basis.

Shortly thereafter, Ronald Bryden came to visit me at Hart House Theatre. I had never met him; he had left Trinity College for Cambridge before I arrived but I knew him by reputation and had attended a production of *Saints Alive*, a lively and amusing musical in the manner of *Salad Days*, for which he had written the book and some clever lyrics. The most memorable song began "Does an oyster have a love life?" Ron was by now a rather orotund fellow with the Colonel Blimp–ish accent then favoured by British university dons. He was, in fact, a Trinidadian and like many of the sons of the white traders and planters of the Caribbean had been sent to school in Canada instead of England during the war years of the early '40s. He had then proceeded to Cambridge where he took an active interest in theatre.

Eventually he became drama critic for the *Observer* and the only serious rival of Kenneth Tynan. Laurence Olivier co-opted Tynan as literary advisor to the National Theatre, reportedly to silence his critical voice. Tynan had championed the new English writers, especially Osborne, but Bryden had discovered Tom Stoppard and brought him to national attention. He then followed Tynan's example by becoming literary advisor to the Royal Shakespeare Company. He provided useful advice and background to the various star directors at the RSC, including Peter Brook, John Barton, and Trevor Nunn, and hoped to be able to direct there himself, but this did not pan out. When he was offered a professorship at the University of Toronto at a considerably higher salary than he could earn in Britain, he accepted with alacrity.

I found Ron gracious and friendly. I quickly realized he knew a great deal more theatre history than I and had certainly seen a lot more theatre, especially in England. He had read widely in the European repertoire and could quote with seeming ease from Webster or Schiller or Wedekind. He had amusing stories to relate about British actors and directors and a ready wit. He presented himself as a colleague whom I could turn to for knowledgeable assistance and support. Nevertheless, there was something slightly predatory in his gaze as he looked around the theatre; this guy is probably going to try to get me out of here, so he can take over himself, I thought. I intimated as much to Ann, who dismissed the idea as paranoia on my part.

In my attempts to involve the Drama Centre students more directly in our Hart House program, I decided to cast the first play of the season with as many incoming students as possible. I chose for this enterprise a little-known eighteenth-century play by Gay, Pope, and Arbuthnot, *Three Hours After Marriage.* I had already had minor success with a short play by David Garrick, *Miss in Her Teens,* in which I was lucky enough to have Rita Davies and Maarten van Dijk playing the major roles, as well as a handsome American lad Richard Ludgin. This time luck was again with me. The central figure of the Gay/Pope/Arbuthnot piece is an old bachelor who takes on a young wife. In my incoming class was Russ Waller, a mature actor/professor from Queen's who played this role with relish and enthusiasm. A pretty young woman, Dorothy Kelleher, was the stylish bride and there were other good roles, a bluestocking poetess, two randy young suitors of the heroine and a preposterously pompous critic, Sir Tremendous.

The play presented some problems of tone: the first act is satire and the two following acts are farce. However, this worked somewhat to our advantage by providing variety and the whole piece was short, spirited, and quite hilarious. Martha Mann provided a very clever set and some ravishing clothes. John Fraser, who had just been appointed drama critic at the *Globe and Mail,* gave us a very strong review and the show sold surprisingly well, considering that no one except a few English scholars had ever heard of it. The incoming students complained to Ann about the workload, but the rehearsals were fun, they met with a strong audience response, and they discovered they had discharged their practical obligations in the first five weeks of term, leaving them free to study for the rest of the year. Ann commended my experiment but said she was doubtful whether I should try it again. Ron did not know the play and my success in bringing it to life apparently impressed him.

Ann had attached several new people to the Drama Centre. Michael Sidnell was an English professor who shared her enthusiasm for Irish literature. He was a handsome fellow and well aware of it, and a would-be actor. He had already played Humphrey Cobbler in *Leaven of Malice*, a role that Robertson Davies confessed had been padded to assuage the vanity of Donald Cook, the American "star" who played it on Broadway. Michael announced halfway through rehearsal that he would leave the cast if I cut any more of his lines. Perhaps I should have taken him up on it, as his final scene in the first act was obviously five minutes too long. Although he did not act for me again, he continued to play roles in Hart House Theatre productions. In Denis Johnston's *The Moon in the Yellow River*, I took on the role of a young English officer, adopting a fake accent. Fortunately an older Englishwoman who was a graduate student coached me to attain some semblance of authenticity.

Another of Ann's protégés was the young lighting designer Michael Whitfield. I quickly understood how superior his work could prove when we first discussed a show he was preparing to light for me; he had read the text and had a distinct take on what it should look like. When it came time to do a hang-and-focus session, he painstakingly adjusted the first three cues over a four-hour session. I thought we would never finish but then to my surprise, everything fell into place. My few suggestions were easily incorporated and he would continue to refine his design throughout the next rehearsals without any need to consult with me. Michael loved puns and wordplay, the more outrageous the better, and he kept us entertained throughout the lengthy tech sessions. I had recently given up smoking and might easily have returned to it during these periods, when I was required to sit still for hours in a darkened theatre, if it weren't for Michael's whimsical interventions. He would work for several seasons at Hart House before he went on to become a celebrated designer at Stratford and in the United States.

The next show I tackled was *Macbeth*. My friend Richard Monette maintained that it was Shakespeare's funniest play and I have seen several productions that proved his point. But this play always sells well and we needed a crowd-pleaser to offset the rather obscure choices that made up the rest of the season. The play has a reputation for bringing ill luck to the people involved in it and so it would prove for me, although it took a while for that to become fully apparent. The problem began with casting. We had set up a scheme whereby Drama Centre actors could play a major role and then write about it as part of their thesis. I had two actors, a man and a woman, that I thought could play the thane and his wife. However Martha, who was designing the sets and costumes, let it be known that her husband Rex Southgate believed that I had promised the role to him. We had indeed talked about it, but I didn't believe I had made a commitment. When I spoke to Ann, she advised me to consult with Ron, who said he thought I would be foolish not to use Rex, who was after all an experienced actor. And also to cast Bie as the lady. I took his advice, and offered the student actress the role of one of the witches. "I am a witch," she replied haughtily and turned me down. I was, however, lucky with some of the minor casting. Two aging French professors, Robert Finch and Clarence Parsons, played Duncan and the old man and John Gilbert made a manly and imposing Banquo; Reed Needles was an engaging Malcolm; and Peter Robertson a suitably doughty MacDuff.

I had some interesting ideas about the staging. The witches were part of the court and appeared in various scenes. With Michael Whitfield's help, we managed a sort of hologram for the imaginary sword and Banquo's ghost, who appeared and disappeared seemingly from nowhere in an effect of "now you see it, now you don't." But the main problem was the major actors. Not only did Bie and Rex have very little chemistry, but Rex attacked the role in the fustian style of a latter-day Donald Woolfit. I worked very hard to wean him away from this high-blown rhetorical stance and thought I had succeeded, but on opening night he reverted to his old tricks and even though I went backstage at intermission to admonish him, he never completely abandoned his extravagant physical and vocal postures. We packed in the crowds but I considered the show a failure. I now realize that Macbeth should be played by a young actor who initially has the charm and authority that would recommend him to his peers as a possible king. If he is a neurotic wreck from the beginning, there is nowhere for him to go. He should initially resist his wife's ambition for him, and only gradually succumb. I am unlikely ever to attempt this play again, but I do think this is a major key to making it work.

I had met Robin Phillips when he first came to Canada and we had a mildly ribald exchange of pleasantries. I had very much admired his work at Stratford, particularly his productions of Measure for Measure, Hamlet, and As You Like It. I was conscious of a need to broaden my experience as a director and while it may have been presumptuous of me to consider myself ready to work at Stratford, I had in fact directed over a dozen large scale productions, six of them by Shakespeare, and worked in both proscenium and arena-style theatres. I therefore wrote to Robin expressing my interest in working for him and received a courteous reply suggesting I get in touch with Urjo Kareda, who was then his literary advisor and eminence grise. Urjo suggested I come to Stratford to meet with him. Our encounter was brief: I expressed my willingness to work as an assistant and learn what I could. Urjo told me flat out that he and Robin were not remotely interested in my work. He then asked me if I could drive him to Toronto. I agreed, but on the road my alternator gave out. I was able to pull over to the side. Urjo pulled himself out of the car and thumbed a ride into the city while I waited for the CAA truck to arrive.

I saw little of Urjo after that, although we spoke on the rare occasions when we met at some function. I would occasionally send him a script to read and he would return it reasonably promptly. (Something no other Canadian director seemed willing or able to do. I once had a conversation with Leon who informed me, "I was cleaning out my desk the other day and I found a script you sent me three years ago. I didn't read it. I threw it in the garbage.") Urjo always included an intelligent critique of the work, mainly negative but carefully thought out. In time, he became artistic director of the Tarragon Theatre, which he ran with taste and good judgment, especially after two or three attempts at directing himself, for which he had no gift, as he fairly quickly realized. I am not quite sure why he was so antagonistic to me; it didn't seem to be personal, although at one time he may have coveted my job. I think he genuinely believed I was utterly lacking in talent. He was certainly a good critic, boldly partisan, as all good critics are, articulate and witty. The enormous crowd of people at his funeral attested to how much he meant to the Toronto theatre scene.

It was also about this time that I decided to see if I could get the union out of the theatre. Jimmy Hozack had been succeeded by Jan Bessey, an attractive, smart-talking and competent woman in her forties, with whom I had a superficially amiable relationship but whom I did not see as an ally. She was not particularly interested in students, except for a few favourites, and seemed only too ready to tell me why I could not do whatever I was planning: either the fire marshall would object or the budget wouldn't permit it. As I did my own budgets I was sometimes able to argue my way around her. I remember when we were doing a Greek tragedy she said we couldn't possibly afford the costumes. The next day I went to Mark's Work Warehouse and arrived with ten pairs of white overalls and a dozen simple cotton dresses, which I dumped out on the office floor. "There are the costumes. Now let's talk about the next play on the program." This sort of tactic did not endear me to Jan.

The play was *The Women of Trachis* by Sophocles in a vivid translation by the American poet Ezra Pound. The play was set in a sort of mythical Southern setting. The music was provided live by a group of students playing rhythm and blues and the set was a series of louvred screens. It worked reasonably well, but I didn't completely understand that it should have been played as comedy rather than tragedy. And so Pound's language was somewhat blunted by the actors reaching for emotions they couldn't quite come to terms with. The reviews were mixed, but Marshall McLuhan wrote to the *Globe* in defence of the play and the production and consequently we played to a larger audience than we might otherwise have attracted.

Hart House Theatre employed two union members to run lights and sound and supervise the technical requirements. They were chosen by Jan in consultation with the head of the union. They varied in temperament but rarely took an interest in teaching the students. They liked to build the sets on the stage so that it could not be used for rehearsals. They were mostly older men who considered this an easy gig and realized that if they didn't antagonize Jan they had nothing much to worry about. I approached the president of the university, George Connell, a friend from Trinity days, and explained the situation to him. The union had been installed in the theatre in the '30s during the Depression when work was scarce, as an act of Christian charity, by then-president Canon Cody. George was sympathetic to my arguments and agreed to speak to the vice-president in charge of staff. A few days later, I was called into the vice-president's office. He didn't ask me to sit down but merely barked at me, "I have forty-one unions on this campus and yours is the smallest. Now get out of here. And if I hear another mention of this, you'll find yourself out of a job."

Herbert Whittaker had retired from his post as drama critic of the *Globe and Mail* but at the age of seventy-something was still full of piss and vinegar. He was constantly getting in touch to advise me about what to do, which I did not appreciate. I think he probably felt he should have been offered my job. He also had a curiously ambivalent relationship with Ron Bryden, whom he had chosen to be his successor at the *Globe*. Ron had turned the job down when Ann offered him a better salary and Herbert felt his trust had been betrayed. I suggested that maybe we should offer Herbert a spot as visiting director; he had after all directed more plays at Hart House Theatre than anyone else, including myself. Herbert agreed to tackle the play he was offered, Pirandello's *The Rules of the Game*. He wanted to produce it in a futurist style and Martha, after a few skirmishes, suggested he design it himself, both sets and costumes. Herbert was pleased by this challenge. He got busy with drawings and held auditions.

Herbert was insistent that I should be a member of the cast. I told him I was too busy to take on a large part, but I eventually agreed to appear as the cook in the last act. Ron opined that Herbert really only wanted to prove he could still exercise his authority over me and he may well have been right. In a fairly brief scene in the third act I had to cook an omelet on stage and serve it to two of the principal characters, talking all the while. Herbert told me after a week of rehearsal that he was highly disappointed with my work. He had expected me to show much more panache. I told him I would go away and work on it for a week and if he didn't like what I was doing when I came back, he should replace me. I then proceeded to develop a grotesque persona with a humped back, a limp, and a scratchy voice using only my lower vocal register. Herbert was delighted with this creation and, I must admit, so was the audience. Perhaps Herbert was determined to prove to me that I could have been an actor after all. However, he succeeded in antagonizing the entire theatre staff and Jan Bessey decreed, "That man will never work in this theatre again, at least as long as I am here." And he didn't, although David Gardner and I did stage a mammoth event there to celebrate Herbert's eightieth birthday.

John Gielgud came to visit us at the Drama Centre when he was in town playing in *No Man's Land* at the Royal Alex. Ann organized a stand-up lunch in the Upper Library at Massey College. Sir John chatted amicably with the students for half an hour and then gave an impromptu talk for another half-hour regaling us with amusing stories of his famous colleagues. The students were so delighted with his performance they invited him to dinner at a house several of them shared in Chinatown. I was delegated to pick him up at his hotel, which I did. As we headed down a dark, narrow alley behind a noodle shop, he suddenly clutched my arm. "How exciting. Are we going to an opium den? You won't leave me, will you, dear boy?" He was reassured when we got to the student co-op and told stories for another two hours, never once repeating himself. A true performer, anxious and willing to give an audience what they wanted.

In my last year working for Ann my final production was *All's Well that Ends Well*, which had not been seen locally since the first season of the Stratford Festival. I had a very strong cast including David Gardner as the King of France, Brenda Davies as the Countess, Sandy Leggatt as Lafeu, Barbara Stewart as Helena, and Rod Beattie as Parolles. These last two were by now members of the Stratford company but were still working on degrees at the Drama Centre. Actors' Equity decreed that they could not appear unless they were paid. However, I argued that they were only fulfilling their technical requirements as students. "Couldn't they do that by being ushers?" the union officials asked. "Yes," I replied, "but they are actors and of course they would rather extend their experience by playing major roles in a great play." Equity conceded the point and they were allowed to go on "by special permission" of the union.

I had obtained the services of Brenda Davies by asking Robertson if he would approach her. He was happy to do so. At about our third rehearsal, she began engaging in some rather peculiar movements. When I asked what she was doing, she said she was employing her fan and adjusting her train. Apparently Rob had been coaching her at home. I said, "Brenda, I cast you in this role because of your own natural dignity and warmth. You do no have to add a lot of fancy business. You're not playing Lady Bracknell." She gave an immense sigh of relief and said, "Well, you can imagine . . ." That was all, but indeed I could. She gave a beautifully restrained performance. I also had some qualms about directing David Gardner. He agreed to play the role but told me he could only rehearse two nights a week. This was perfect. I would be able to rehearse his scenes but not have him hanging around during the other rehearsals. When we came to final run-throughs, his wife, Dorothy, sat in the audience. David turned up the next day with a sheaf of notes that Dorothy had given him.

"Too late," I responded. "We only have time to tech before we open." David also gave a splendid performance, by turns imperious and petulant, gracious and short-tempered. Rod was an excellent Parolles, vain, extravagant, and witty, a charming rogue, and Barbara was lovely as Helena, strong-willed yet fragile. All in all, I think this was the most successful of all my productions at Hart House Theatre.

Ann Saddlemyer served a five-year term as director of the Drama Centre but let it be known that she was not interested in extending her stay. I had been signing a yearly contract for her, which was a matter of pride with me, not to say vanity; if my work was not satisfactory, then I could easily be dismissed. In her last year she urged me to sign a two-year contract, which she felt would give me some protection if I didn't get on with her successor. I had hoped that Annibale Noce, the head of the Italian department, would be willing to take on her role, but after giving it some consideration, he declined. One day, Robertson Davies phoned me to say that the relevant committee had met and the only person willing to take over was Michael Sidnell. Did I think I could live with Michael? I should probably have said no, but I didn't.

Ann's last year as director, coincided with the sesquicentennial of the university. To celebrate this occasion, I proposed that we mount a season of four Canadian plays to be performed by a company of former Hart House Theatre graduates and senior students, all of whom would be paid. Ann got behind this plan and we applied for arts council funding, which was duly approved by the Ontario government. Ann was already preparing for her next academic adventure and told me that I should work out the details of the season with Ron Bryden. We agreed that we should commission new plays by Robertson Davies and James Reaney. I had written a play called *Family Compact* that I hoped David Gardner would be willing to direct, and I proposed to revive Mazo de la Roche's 1930s success *Whiteoaks*. Her estate graciously gave us permission, but Ron said the play was "old hat" and unworthy of revival. He also nixed my play, which he said the press would condemn as a vanity production. David Gardner told me that he was sorry to say he didn't "get it" and readily acceded to Ron's suggestion that he direct a Tennessee Williams script, *Sweet Bird of Youth*. I was to be assigned a production of Chekhov's *The Cherry Orchard* in a new translation to be crafted by Ron working with Barbara Stewart. Like everyone else in twentieth-century theatre, I idolized Chekhov. But I felt Ron had pushed the season into a very different shape than I had intended.

Not surprisingly, the theatre staff was less than enthusiastic about the prospect of us staging two extra plays in the summer. This meant that Martha and I had to overcome their passive resistance. I realized we would need a publicist to work on the season and suggested my old friend Molly Thom, who was knowledgeable about theatre and design and looking for something to do as she had just separated from her husband, the distinguished architect Ron Thom. Ann said she could not find funding for a publicist but she could hire Molly as a producer with the understanding that she would be responsible for publicity and public relations. Molly commissioned Theo Dimson to do two wonderful posters and managed to get a very positive promotional article in the *Globe and Mail* written by John Fraser.

David's production of *Sweet Bird* starred Charmion King, who had played Saint Joan in Bob Gill's initial season. She gave a suitably flamboyant performance and was surrounded by a cast of actors chosen by David, many of whom had no Hart House connection. He also chose to use a version of the play that we later realized was sanitized for high schools. The cast included a very young Geordie Johnson and Dennis Simpson. The staging was inventive and the production was colourful and vigorous, if not exactly edgy (one reviewer said the actress playing Boss Finley's mistress was "about as sexy as Queen Victoria"). The play is not one of Williams' best; the first act is a tour de force, but the political shenanigans of the middle act have always seemed to me rather contrived and reflect the political views of Elia Kazan, who directed the original Broadway production rather than Williams' own intuitive perceptions. The notices were respectable but the audiences were thin.

There was some overlap in casting but I got most of the actors I wanted. I had hoped that Jackie Burroughs would play Ranevskaya and she initially agreed, but then she backed out at the last moment, which affected the balance of the ensemble. Meg Hogarth, who took her place, was beautiful, willful and elegant, but Ranevskaya is essentially a silly woman and this was not part of Meg's conception. Interesting performances were contributed by Bie Engelen as the eccentric governess; David Gardner as a sentimental, pompous Lopakhin; Eric House as a vain, sad-eyed Gaev; Robert Joy as the accident-prone misfit Yepikhodov; Dorothy Kelleher as a sweet-natured Anya; Rex Southgate as the dignified old valet Firs; R.H. Thomson as a stubborn, awkwardly idealistic Trofimov; Terry Tweed as a sour, downtrodden Varya; and Mary Vingoe as the pushy maid Dunyasha. I have listed their names alphabetically deliberately. Molly's poster featured the principal actors as Meg Hogarth, David Gardner, and Eric House, thus opening up ongoing hostility between Meg and David which culminated in a long, confidential session in my office when Meg let off steam about David, every word of which he heard sitting outside my door.

The company assembled to read the script and approved it. Ron had gone back to an earlier draft, which contained some scenes that Stanislavsky had persuaded Chekhov to cut. This was of course interesting to a few Russian scholars, but I came to the conclusion that Stanislavsky knew what he was doing, too late, alas, to cut them out of the script. The entire cast spent the first hour of every rehearsal learning how to waltz, something that had the effect of bringing the company together. But there were problems. Eric House seemed to ignore any direction I gave him; it was ten days into rehearsal before I learned that he was really quite deaf. Rex felt that he should have been playing Gaev and was often less than cooperative. It was hard to schedule rehearsals because the play has characters constantly coming in and out, so that I had most of the actors in the theatre all the time. While I was working on stage with two or three of them, the others would be in the wings dreaming up various kinds of mischief.

Occasionally, an actor would surprise me with an interesting bit of business and then tell me David or Ron had suggested it. I was unfazed and usually accepted it; I didn't imagine I was going to have all the good ideas. Ron and Molly both sat in on many rehearsals. As producer and translator they both felt it their prerogative to give me notes. I got further notes from David, some of them suggested by his wife, Dorothy, who often came to rehearsals. I frequently felt as though I had lost control of the whole process, but I soldiered on.

Martha produced beautiful costumes and cleverly organized the many changes. The show had been wearing to direct; many people in the cast were personal friends but by the dress rehearsal I was thoroughly fed up with the lot of them. Chekhov called his play a comedy and I had worked hard to elicit comic performances from the actors, not with sight gags and farcical business but with performances rooted in the foolishness of the characters. I told Bie I thought I had succeeded at least in this. "Not with Meg," she said, and she was right. The show opened. I had expected a sympathetic review from John Fraser, but the *Globe* had sent him off to Beijing. The new reviewer, Brian Johnston, was not about to hand out bouquets in his first week on the job. He praised much of the acting but attacked the set. It was not a pan, but was the sort of notice that made the reader think, "I don't have to go and see that." The audiences were meagre and lukewarm.

On the Saturday afternoon of the first week, I came home at five o'clock to learn that David Gardner had cut off his big toe with an electric lawnmower. We had no understudies. I went on in his place that night, carrying a book in the first act, and then abandoning it. I knew the blocking and most of the lines. The cast rallied around me and, in fact, the performance had a new energy. I should have played the remaining performances but Meg said she wanted a real actor. So mid-week we brought in Kenneth Pogue as David's replacement. He never learned his lines and gave a rather sullen performance. The show closed and Judy insisted we go to the cottage to get a rest in spite of the fact that the Youtheatre was remounting my production of *Timon*. I thought, "If this is what being a professional director is like, I don't want any part of it." Years later, I told R.H. Thomson about this and he said, "That's too bad. I had a thoroughly good time in that show."

The next show was the new play by Robertson Davies. Actually, it was not a new script, but a composite built around parts of the first play ever written in North America, supposedly by Major Robert Rogers, a British officer who more or less invented guerilla warfare when he sent his soldiers into action wearing green uniforms in the woods instead of the traditional scarlet. Ron had discovered the play and persuaded Rob to write a courtroom drama in which Rogers was tried for insubordination and a group of strolling British players performed parts of his play as part of his defence. The original play was called *Ponteach* (as in Pontiac, the aboriginal warrior chief). Rob called his play *The Green Man*, but I wanted to retain Pontiac in the title in order to see if we could get some sponsorship money from General Motors. The fundraising department of the university quickly put the kybosh on that notion, but the awkward title remained.

This was by no means the only awkward thing about the production. The script was long and unwieldy. Rob had added to the fustian of the original text a good many long-winded diatribes. I succeeded in getting his permission to cut large chunks out of both his text and Rogers' blank verse. Rob had also written the lyrics for a couple of songs. We approached Harry Somers to compose tunes but he declined. We then turned to Derek Holman, who accepted the commission. He came up with some tuneless ditties, which Rob disliked intensely. The composer riposted by saying the whole play was rubbish anyway. It was decided the play should be mounted as a collaboration between the Drama Centre and the Faculty of Music and presented in the MacMillan Theatre. There was to be an orchestra backstage and a soprano soloist. The musicians resented being stuck backstage and said the music should have been recorded. The soprano, to her credit, did the best she could under the circumstances.

I assembled the cast for a first reading and they had the good grace to wait until Rob had departed before grumbling about the text, which they thought (with some justification) to be overwritten and unfunny. As Brenda was playing the leading lady of the acting company, they needed to be tactful. Rob had written for specific actors: David Gardner as the self-justifying Rogers; Judy as his nagging wife (one of the many tiresome women to be found in Rob's plays); Michael Tait, Ron Bryden, and Kevin Sullivan as the trio of officers who had put Rogers on trial; Brenda as the leader of the acting troop; Rex Southgate and Rod Beattie as two of her actors, who would play noble savages and a host of extras. Among these were my nephew Ben Stein and his friend Nick de Pencier, aged about thirteen. As the men's dressing room was full, the two young boys were put in the women's dressing room. Nick would later tell me how grateful they were for this. As they sat about watching the women squeeze into their bustiers, they felt they were getting a real education.

To add some colour to the rather dreary courtroom proceedings, I talked Rob into writing a part for a French-Canadian lawyer. (The trial was set in Montreal.) I persuaded my friend Laurier LaPierre to play this role. He could only attend three rehearsals, but he stole the show with his mischievous wit and Gallic elegance. Of the others: Brenda, when coached in eighteenth-century gesture, was formidable as the actress, Rex was grandly dramatic as Pontiac, Rod had a few comic moments, and Michael Tait had presence as the presiding officer (in spite of the fact that he drank continuously during the performance). Judy looked very pretty in a blue satin dress that Martha had made for her and Ron looked very much of the period in his white wig and regimental scarlet. In her review, Gina Mallet said the casting must have been done over brandy at Massey College, which was more or less accurate. The whole enterprise was more like a Sunday school pageant than a play. However, it attracted a sizeable audience, largely because of Rob's reputation. They apparently felt they were being entertained, or so they told me. I was just happy to have the whole thing over with.

James Reaney had stipulated that his play *The Dismissal* was to be produced by actors familiar with his work under the direction of Keith Turnbull who had staged the Donnelly trilogy for him, originally at Tarragon and then on tour. The group included some good professional actors who were welcome to our audiences both because of their novelty and their skills. The show sold reasonably well and brought the sesquicentennial adventure to a close. It was not what I had intended either in terms of its beneficial experience for young actors or its acceptance by Toronto audiences as a welcome addition to Toronto's theatrical fare. It was impossible for me to take pride in any of my productions, nor had it been a happy experience for me personally. We had lost a good deal of the government's money and done little, if anything, to enhance the reputation of Hart House Theatre.

At the beginning of his first term as director of the Drama Centre, Michael Sidnell summoned me to his office. He had not been impressed by the special season. He had just been visited by someone from the Ontario Arts Council who pointed out that the money allotted was for the production of four Canadian plays and obviously the Chekhov and Williams plays did not fill the bill. Ron had assured me that Ann had cleared the revised lineup with the Council, but Ann was now away on sabbatical and could not be reached. And there were other horror stories. The two students who had wanted to play Macbeth and his lady had complained that I had cast my friends instead of them. Various other students felt they had been overlooked as directors. The theatre staff felt I was insensitive to their needs. They felt that mounting four plays a year was beyond their capacity.

Michael suggested that I should go away for a month and think about all this. I replied that I didn't need time to think about it. I had already decided that I should move on, both for my own sake and the good of the theatre. "Excellent," said Michael, "I've been worrying about how to get rid of you." Under the circumstances, I thought he might have spared me this exhibition of his obvious relish. "As of now, Ron will have supervision of the theatres. As you are contracted for another year, you will direct two productions: *Antony and Cleopatra* at the studio in conjunction with a study of the play in a course Ron will be teaching and at Hart House you will direct Wedekind's *The Marquis of Keith*. Ron tells me it is a very good play. As of next week, Jan Bessey will take over your office at the theatre. Good day."

I was certain Ron had been involved in these decisions. I knew he loved intrigue. When I confronted him he did not deny it but merely smiled an avuncular smile. "It's been clear to me for some time, dear boy, that you are not happy here." He asked me to participate in his class on *Antony and Cleopatra*. I did attend the first three or four of his lectures, but I could tell he found my presence and comments mildly irritating and I decided to stay away after that. None of the students in his class were interested in performing in my production. I told them they were welcome to attend my rehearsals and a few of them dropped in occasionally, but I guess they found it boring, because they rarely returned. I hadn't quite understood how much more academic the students of the Drama Centre were becoming. It was apparently no longer attracting people who were interested in the practice of theatre.

I prepared a very stripped-down version of the text. I was lucky to find a Cleopatra. A striking young woman named Rosalind Goldsmith appeared out of nowhere and gave a sharp, sexy, and vibrant performance. Peter Robertson played Antony. He was tall, handsome, and manly but had become a rather mannered actor. I worked with him to try to get rid of some of these tricks and thought I had succeeded, but in performance he reverted to them. I have had this experience with a number of actors. I suppose they feel safer doing something that worked for them the last time. Ron's class came and saw a performance and there was a discussion that seemed to me rather perfunctory. Herbert Whittaker came and was so taken with Rosalind's performance that he recommended her to a leading drama school in London. And a visiting American Shakespeare scholar invited me out for a drink to say how splendid he thought my production was. "The Drama Centre is lucky to have you on their staff." I didn't suggest he relay this information to Michael Sidnell.

The Marquis of Keith by Frank Wedekind who created the *Lulu* plays is an intricate drama of deceit and imposture, which may be one reason Ron was so fond of it. The central character is a charming poseur who pretends to have an English title and is ambitious to become a cultural entrepreneur. I did not find an actor who was right for the role but cast Nic Labriola, a smallish Italian-Canadian who brought theatricality and a certain little-boy-out-of-his-depth quality that was appealing but diminished the sharp edge of the work. His mistress wants to be an opera singer and I cast Laurie Brown who was beautiful and had a splendid voice and gave her two arias to sing. Martha made her a ravishing dress and she stole the show, though she had little sense of period style or the ambiguity that the character is meant to possess. I also had another pretty girl with a good voice in the cast, Jackie Gelineau, and I arranged for her to sing accompanied by my twelve-year-old nephew Ben Stein on guitar. I also took the characters of the bourgeois businessmen and turned them into a sort of Gilbert and Sullivan chorus centred around Gregory Sinclair in a splendid Austrian cavalry officer's uniform. Once again

I had turned the play into a semi-musical. Actually, it would make rather a good musical. My lyrics included the following bit of drivel, which probably represents my real talents as a versifier.

"Mean, mean Emmeline
Couldn't keep her knickers clean
All her sisters and her aunties
Begged her not to soil her panties
All the boys spread nasty rumours
About Emmy's dirty bloomers
To get even Emmeline
Drank a quart of gasoline
Then with all her skill and art
Blew a most enormous fart
Sent them all to smithereens.
Mean, mean Emmeline."

Ron Bryden persuaded me to cut it.

In many ways, the most entertaining person in the show was Jack the Chickenman. Jack delivered fresh chickens to our house every Friday, as well as to many other clients in Rosedale and Forest Hill. He was a theatre nut and would often say to me, "Martin, I was reading Stanislavsky last night and he says you got to use some past experience in creating a role. What do you think?" He also asked me repeatedly when I was going to cast him in a show.

So one day I said, "Okay, Jack, it's now, baby, or never, because this is my last show at Hart House." Jack was delighted and always arrived for rehearsal half an hour early.

After about an hour he would excuse himself, saying, "Them chickens get up awful early, you know, Martin." He couldn't really act or sing, but it didn't matter because he was full of energy, a colourful character, and a natural comic.

About a week before the show opened, the box office manager said to me, "We're really selling tickets for this show. I don't understand it." It turned out that Jack was selling tickets to all his customers as he made his rounds delivering chickens. We played to full houses, including some very distinguished people. Ron's reaction was ambiguous; he didn't feel I had realized the play, which was true, and the *Varsity* critic called it a travesty. But the audiences seemed to enjoy it.

Towards the end of term Michael and Ron told me they wanted to throw a goodbye party for me. My initial response was to refuse to attend but that seemed overly churlish. A good many students turned up, past and present. I was presented with a four-volume set of Restoration plays, two of which were duplicates. I pointed this out to Ron, though I didn't much care, as I didn't imagine I would wade through all four volumes. I was expected to speak and did. I thanked Robertson Davies, who was present, and Ann Saddlemyer, who was not, for their support and encouragement. I was grateful for the chance to direct many extraordinary plays and to work with some highly talented and interesting students. I then said I hoped they were going to find some young and energetic director to replace me. Michael said that he and Ron felt that they didn't really need anyone to do what I had been doing. I replied, "Theatres don't operate without direction. It's not that I'm so remarkable, but if you don't replace me with a capable director, you won't be running this theatre in another two or three years." Which was exactly what happened.

It was about eleven o'clock when we arrived at the airport in Cairo. Although it was winter, the night air was balmy as we crossed from the plane to the custom shed. We had been told that it would be easier to buy visas for fifty Egyptian pounds on arrival than to go through the red tape of obtaining visas in Toronto. There was indeed a crowd of men hawking visas, but the prices demanded ranged from one hundred to one hundred and fifty pounds. I ended up paying one hundred and ten apiece. We managed to reclaim our luggage by paying another twenty pounds and Judy and I got into a taxi. Although it was after midnight, the streets were jammed with every kind of vehicle and our progress was slow and noisy. People shouted, honked, and cursed. It took us an hour and a half to reach our destination in Zamalek, a fashionable part of the city. The taxi driver demanded a hundred and forty pounds.

Andrew Watson, our host, came down to meet us. He haggled with the driver and the price was settled for thirty pounds. "You must realize that bargaining is the national pastime," he informed us. "People not only expect it but are deeply disappointed if you give in too easily." He led us upstairs to his apartment, which was spacious and furnished with an assembly of Oriental treasures: carpets, pottery, and brassware, as well as several comfortable divans. "Are you hungry?" He produced some delicious sweet pastries made with honey and walnuts. "Not my own creation. I have a woman who comes in every other day to cook and sweep the sand out of the flat."

I had known Andrew as an undergraduate at Trinity, where he was editor of the literary magazine; he had taken an interest in me as a burgeoning writer before he set off for Oxford as a Rhodes scholar, proceeding then to the École Pol in Paris and then back for a graduate degree at St. Anthony's College. Following this extended academic stint, he had taken up a post as an economic historian at the University of Toronto. He had been a naval cadet, a good tennis player and skier, an accomplished piano player, but most of all a linguist, fluent not only in six European languages but also in Arabic. He worked early in his career for the Ford Foundation in the Middle East and this had given him credibility as an economic consultant. He was currently working on a two-year contract for the International Relief and Development Council, a non-governmental organization for whom he vetted projects.

Headquartered in Cairo, Andrew covered a territory that extended from Morocco right across to Pakistan. He spent half his time travelling and the other half writing reports. "A month ago I was in Beirut and caught the last plane out just before the American marines arrived. I love Cairo, but it does have drawbacks. The telephones only work about a third of the time, and the traffic is horrendous. Egypt has its own supply of oil, so it is very cheap and everyone who has any kind of vehicle is out riding around most of the time. If I am asked to a function that I can't walk to in twenty minutes or so, I simply don't go. Tomorrow I must get up and go to the office, but you should sleep in."

And sleep in we did. We had been in the air over twelve hours, as well as a five-hour layover at Heathrow. But we were seasoned travellers by this time and knew enough to travel light and catch sleep whenever we could. After leaving the university, I thought it would be a good idea to get out of Toronto for an extended period. Judy was able to get a year of unpaid leave from the board of education. We had been invited by both Andrew and the Fulfords to visit them in the Middle East. I had managed to get a very good deal on our airfare, and we had set out to discover the part of the world where our civilization had begun.

That night Andrew took us to dinner on a restaurant floating on the Nile. He also invited a young American scholar, Will, who was studying post-pharonic Egyptian art and architecture. Will would make himself available for a modest fee to show us around Cairo and guide us wherever we wanted to go. "His Arabic is not as good as mine, but quite serviceable." He was thin and blond with the accent and look of an Ivy League college kid in his white button-down shirt and chinos. He had a wry smile and chain-smoked. "Andrew believes that learning Arabic is a lifelong commitment. I've just started."

The food at the restaurant was good, tingling with subtle spices and unusual textures, but the main feature of the evening was to be the belly dancers. "Belly dancing is a very great art. It can be comic, ethereal, sensuous, spiritual, even tragic." Andrew pronounced. "Tonight we shall see a very famous belly dancer as well as some lesser practitioners." The first dancer was a young Moroccan woman, very lithe and almost snake-like who flirted openly with Will, who played along with her gamely. Then came the head-liner, a rather heavy-set woman, obviously middle-aged. She was unsmiling, given to very theatrical poses, and had a soulful air, as though she were motiv-ated by some inner sorrow. She moved slowly and had no overt contact with the audience, who nevertheless applauded her enthusiastically.

There was a pause while we drank thick Turkish coffee and ate a sweet sticky dessert. Then another dancer appeared, who was obviously Caucasian. "She may have been taught as a child. Many girls were kidnapped in the old days. They were valued for their white skin," Andrew told us. This new dancer was not quite as heavy as her predecessor and she danced more quickly with a curious, rolling motion. She came towards our table and seemed to be coaxing one of us to get up and dance with her.

"Is that allowed?" I asked.

Andrew shrugged. "This is a tourist restaurant. They wouldn't want you to get in trouble." I stood up. The dancer circled me, never touching me but stooping and swaying until she ended on the floor. I extended a hand to help her up.

"Where are you from?" she asked.

"Canada."

"So am I. Halifax."

"You came here to study dancing?"

"I've been dancing since I was a teenager. I'm studying Middle Eastern history."

"You're a Muslim?"

"Actually, I'm a Buddhist. My name is Bonnie."

I led her to our table. "This is Bonnie, the Buddhist belly dancer. From Halifax." Andrew rolled his eyes in disbelief, but suggested she join us for more coffee. They were soon involved in a discussion about how the Mamelukes were recruited by the Ottoman sultans in central Russia. Before we left Andrew had promised to introduce her to some of his contacts. "I see what you mean about the universality of belly dancing," I ventured on the way home. Andrew shot me one of his looks.

The next day, Will arrived early. Andrew had instructed him to take me somewhere I could change money. He thought it would be better for Judy not to come. We set out on foot and found ourselves going down ever nar-rower and darker streets. Finally we came to what seemed like a carpet shop.

Will and the proprietor exchanged pleasantries in Arabic and we were served coffee. Eventually, we were shown into a back room where a shrewd-looking old man in pyjamas sat cross-legged, reading what I assumed was the Qur'an. There was silence for probably five minutes before more coffee was brought in, at which point the man acknowledged our presence. He and Will conversed in Arabic. There were several extended pauses. At one point, Will got up to go, but the old man asked him to sit down again. Another long pause ensued, then a quick exchange. Will turned to me and asked me to give him my money, perhaps a thousand dollars. The exchange was quickly transacted and I found that I had been charged about eighty percent of the official rate. Another cordial bit of conversation and we left.

As we walked back towards the centre of town, Will was accosted by two young men sitting at a café. He apparently knew them and we joined them for yet another coffee. One of them offered me a cigarette, which I refused. We talked in somewhat stilted English about American politics. I tried to lead the conversation to a discussion of local politics, but without success. We were interrupted by a sudden minor explosion, followed by a gush of water up into the air. Half a dozen workmen who had been plying picks and shovels stood and stared as the gushing continued. Will explained that Cairo was finally installing a subway system, but no one had ever mapped the water pipes or electrical lines under the ground and so this kind of sudden eruption was a frequent occurrence. After his friends left, Will said, "It's a pity you don't smoke. The offer of a cigarette by a stranger is a courtesy that indicates he would like to be on more intimate terms."

"I gave up smoking some years ago. I didn't mean to offend him."

"It's all right. I just thought you should know."

Will took us out to see the great pyramids and the Sphinx, rising above the sands of the desert. We had already experienced and marveled at the complexity and grandeur of the Mayans who built Uzmal and Chichen Itza and the Hindus who constructed Angkor and Borobudur. And now these colossal Egyptian monuments towered above us. The paws of the Sphinx were several times my height. Will also took us to see a vast archeological dig on the outskirts of the city, acres of dirt and fragments that dated back beyond the time of the pharaohs, where young people of many lands came together in an atmosphere that seemed to be one part scholarly fellowship to two parts summer camp. Will knew some of them, and we were greeted in a friendly fashion by deeply tanned young men in shorts and work boots and equally tanned young women in halter tops and floppy canvas hats. There was even a Canadian couple working under the auspices of the Royal Ontario Museum.

Will took a day off while Judy and I visited the museum to view the King Tut treasures. We had already seen many of them in London and Toronto, as well as the extensive collection of Egyptian antiquities at the Met in New York but here in this dusty and somewhat shabby setting, they seemed even more mysterious and eternal. We had both been in a play that Dorf Goulding wrote for the Toronto Children Players when we were teenagers. It was set in a museum where the statue of Horus came to life at night, and somehow this seemed a real possibility. As often happened, we separated to spend time looking at something that interested one of us more than the other and agreed to meet up at the entrance at lunchtime. Judy informed me that no fewer than three of the guards had beckoned her to come into a shadowy alcove for a bit of a sexual dalliance. I wondered whether they were the same guards who had tried to lure me with a similar intent.

The next evening, Andrew hosted a dinner party for us. His guests included an Egyptian feminist who had spent several years in jail for her radical views and activities, a rather handsome middle-aged man who had some familial connection with the late King Farouk and whom everybody called the Prince, and a charming woman named Claudia Roden, an Egyptian Jewess now living in London, who was the author of several popular cookbooks featuring Mediterranean dishes. Andrew was rather nervous about the food he had provided, but Claudia was most complimentary and indeed it was delicious. Will was also a guest. He was apparently accustomed to helping Andrew by pouring drinks and generally seeing that things went smoothly. He flirted a bit with both Claudia and the Prince but not the feminist, who lamented the fact that Egyptian women seemed to be regressing. More and more of the young wore headscarves and long-sleeved dresses, which their mothers had never done. She was concerned and not optimistic about the political future of her country and tried to draw the Prince into discussion, but he countered that he was too frivolous to take any interest in politics. The dinner, which had begun at nine o'clock and consisted of several courses, went on till well after midnight, at which point the ladies departed and Will offered to drive the Prince, who was more than a little bit tiddly, back to his lodgings.

Andrew announced that he was flying to Damascus for a few days. We were of course welcome to stay as long as we liked, but he knew we wanted to go to Luxor and see the tombs and monuments and he had asked Will to go with me to a travel agent and help me book a cruise. My friend Bill Toye had told me that there was a great deal to see in Luxor and advised me to spend at least three days there before joining a cruise. With Will's help, I managed to get bookings at about a third off the usual price. Because of the recent troubles in Beirut, tourism was down and the agencies were offering deals. We also got a booking at a hotel in Luxor for four days and tickets to fly there, which would take about an hour rather than the six-hour train journey.

On our last day in Cairo, Will took us to see several splendid mosques. Judy went back to the flat to pack and left me with Will at a café. He told me that Andrew had instructed him to make sure I experienced Cairo to the full. Was there anything more I wanted to do? Visit a hammam and have a massage, for instance? He could take me to a place where there was a masseur who was very accommodating. He also told me that the Prince had taken a fancy to me and invited us for coffee. Would I like to go this afternoon? He could take me there and then leave us discreetly alone together. I decided I would try a massage. Will led me to the bathhouse. On the way, we passed some men who were doing a strange circular dance. They seemed drugged. I asked Will about them. "Dervishes."

"I thought they only had dervishes in Persia."

"These are African dervishes. You can see the influence of tribal dancing. Today is the feast day of a Muslim saint. They will continue far into the night."

At the hammam he set me up with Abu, who turned out to be a giant man weighing about three hundred and fifty pounds. I lay facedown on the table and he proved to be an expert at his trade. For half an hour he worked over the muscles of my neck, my back, my legs. Finally he asked me to turn over and worked his way down my chest and stomach to my genitals. I started to protest but he firmly but gently brought me to orgasm. Will was waiting for me at a nearby café. "Good?" I smiled and shrugged. We walked along past the dervishes who were still wrapt in their trancelike whirling. "Now what about the Prince?"

"I think I've had enough stimulation for one day."

"He will be disappointed, but as you like." I gave Will a handsome tip and thanked him for all his attention. "Perhaps we will see you again. When we get back from the cruise."

"One never knows, does one?"

Our hotel in Luxor was small and a bit shabby, but the staff was pleasant and accommodating. We set out in the afternoon to visit several of the tombs and were besieged by would-be guides who came up with colourful details about the lives of the pharaohs and their families, largely, we suspected, of their own invention. We discovered it was possible to pay them off after listening to a fairly brief spiel and continue examining the wall paintings and carvings on our own. We were more interested in their artistic quality than their historical significance, and the guides had no knowledge of the various styles, but instead concentrated on lurid details mainly of a sexual nature. After our experience at the Cairo museum, we agreed to stick together.

That night, we went to the great temple at Karnak to see the *Son et lumière* performance, which was truly spectacular. I had seen several similar spectacles in Rome, Delhi, and Mont St. Michel, but this surpassed them all in its evocation of another age. Karnak, for me, was more impressive than the Sphinx or the great pyramids. I could understand how the ordinary people would be in awe of the gods and the priests who served them. Afterwards, we went back to the hotel and became involved in a conversation with a French couple, whom we had seen at the show. It turned out that the man had designed the performance and was visiting to ensure that it was up to his specifications. He had been asked to come up with something special for the projected visit of the French president a year later. I suggested that they stage Verdi's *Aida*, which after all had premiered in Egypt. Our French friends thought this was a brilliant idea, and indeed it took place, with I believe Plácido Domingo. Much to our surprise, we received invitations, but by that time we were back home and involved in other things.

We continued to explore the temples for the next two days until our tour boat arrived. Judy had a tendency to suffer from seasickness, but the Nile is perfectly flat so this was not a problem. We would spend four days aboard, stopping at intervals to view monuments. The first two and a half days we spent in Luxor, and although we reviewed several tombs we had already seen, our guide was more knowledgeable than the locals and gave us much more valid information. He told me off more than once when I rushed ahead to take in one more tomb than was on the official tour.

The boat was designed to accommodate one hundred and fifty people, but there were only about sixty of us. For the most part the passengers were friendly and intelligent. They included an American clergyman and his wife and their daughter, who was studying in Cairo but had become homesick, so that her parents had decided to visit her and cheer her up. She was obviously very shy but not unattractive. There was also an English harridan named Mrs. Wortley, who was travelling with her grandson, a pleasant-looking young man of about seventeen. One morning at breakfast, when Judy was sleeping late, she beckoned me to her table. "Have you ever ridden a camel?"

"Yes, have you?"

"Gran's ridden everything, including an ostrich."

"Don't be facetious, Jeremy. In fact I am rather an accomplished horse-woman. I still hunt, though I don't ride sidesaddle anymore. His mother does eventing. Had a nasty fall a month ago. Broke her collarbone and her arm and bashed in the side of her head." She laughed at the thought of it. "I brought young Jeremy on this cruise with me to give her a break. Though why he chose Egypt when we could have gone to Portugal, I can't imagine."

"I'm interested in ancient history, Gran."

"He's going to Cambridge next year. To King's, I believe. I don't approve. It's full of the most dreadful queers."

"Some of the finest scholars of our day have been homosexuals, Gran."

"Oh, belt up, Jeremy. Go and read a book." Jeremy turned bright pink and left the table. As soon as he was out of earshot, Mrs. Wortley continued. "I'm very concerned about that boy. He shows every sign of becoming an utterly weedy little prig. I believe he's still a virgin. At seventeen. Ridiculous. I lost my virginity at fifteen during a hunt ball. And went downstairs and danced the polka directly afterwards."

"You were obviously precocious."

"Not a bit of it. I was considered a late bloomer." She chortled. "Do you think you could have a word with Jeremy? Shake him out of his cocoon? I can see you're a man of the world."

"I don't mind talking to him, but I make no promises."

The next day I came back from our morning tour and was hailed by Nigel, an Englishman who was honeymooning with his third wife, who had brought along her sister as a companion. He could be found at the bar any time after ten thirty in the morning and by noon was a bit spiffy.

"Come and join me for a pick-me-up, old chap."

"It's a bit early."

"Nonsense. Get the day off on the right foot, what?"

"You didn't go on the tour?"

"Well, no. The girls wanted to shop. Damn good thing too. Keeps them out of my hair till dinnertime. Anyway, I know this territory. Served in North Africa during the war. Spent several months in Cairo doing intelligence. Interesting chaps, these Egyptians. A damn sight more pliable than the Wogs. Pretty much anything goes. Of course it was more fun when old Farouk was still around. Knew how to have a good time. Wasn't all hung up on religion. The Egyptians aren't Arabs, you know. Don't know why they bought all that stuff about Allah being the one god, when they had a perfectly good religion of their own. Of course I understand why they resent the Jews getting all that American money. No wonder they've cozied up to the Russians. Hello, there's that nice-looking lad who's travelling with that ferocious old battle-axe. You know him?"

"We've met."

"Signal him to come over here." I waved at Jeremy and he approached somewhat tentatively. "You look as though you could use a drink."

"Well, I . . ."

"You don't drink?"

"I suppose I could handle a lager."

"Good man. You'll have one too?"

I acquiesced, seeing my chance. "Perhaps you could join us for dinner tonight, Jeremy. We're at a table with a very nice American family. Their daughter is studying ancient history in Cairo."

"Well, thanks awfully but I'm supposed to be looking after Gran."

"Frankly, I think she can look after herself."

"Leave the old bat to me. I'll invite her to our table," chimed in Nigel, picking up the scent. And so it was arranged. Jeremy did indeed hit it off with Jennifer, who quite blossomed under his attentions. This shipboard romance was noted by many of the passengers with a certain amount of sentimental indulgence. Whether it was consummated, I have no idea, but old Mrs. Wortley winked at me broadly whenever we met.

I went on the final morning tour and managed to sneak in visits to two extra tombs at the end. I knew we were to leave just after noon. When I got back to the jetty I saw that the ship was already heading up the Nile. After a moment of panic I hired two Nubian boys to go after it in a felucca, telling them I would double their pay if they could catch up with our boat. They rowed like demons and within about fifteen minutes we were alongside the boat. A rope ladder was lowered and I clambered up on the deck, which was filled with all the passengers who cheered me roundly. Thus I became a bit of a celebrity. Nigel propelled me to the bar and stood me a double whisky.

Our last night on the boat was a costume ball. I wore a caftan Judy had bought and tied a towel round my head like a turban. A woman from San Francisco had got herself up as Cleopatra and the minister and his wife both wore shorts and solar topees. Nigel appeared in a kilt. I asked him what this had to do with Egypt and he replied, "Those chaps all wore skirts, don't you see? Kilts, same thing." But the hit of the evening was the young Jeremy, who appeared as a mummy. "Splendid chap. Completely covered in loo paper. He gets the prize. Waiter, bring us a big bottle of bubbly." And he presented the young couple with a magnum of Taittinger.

The next morning we landed at Aswan and flew to see the gigantic statues at Abu Simbel and then back to Cairo for a final dinner with Andrew. He was in good form, and talked about his recent visit to Syria and Turkey. He had written up reports on various projects there, which he asked me to proofread. I complimented him on his ability to lay out complex issues with admirable clarity. I told him I envied him this ability because I was already beginning to think about what I should do next, and writing was uppermost in my mind. He smiled and said, "Why not? The important thing with writing, as with most other things, is to keep doing it. Get started and keep going until you finish a draft. Then you start to revise. It's very difficult to revise a blank page." I have scrupulously followed this excellent advice.

The airport at Tel Aviv was in sharp contrast to the chaos of the one in Cairo. Uniformed soldiers examined our passports and stamped them on special removable sheets, which could be discarded if we were traveling to any of the surrounding states, which denied Israel's existence. We stood in lines while we and our baggage were searched. The Israeli officials were not exactly rude but came across as curt and rather surly. I had been told by Jewish friends at home that "Israelis have to be like that. They live in a hostile world."

I had decided to rent a car and we set out immediately for Jerusalem, where we were to stay in a hotel recommended by Andrew Watson. After driving around the city for an hour and a half without locating it, I stopped a taxi driver and paid him to lead us to it. The American Colony was a hotel set in an old Palestinian palace. It had apparently been founded by Peter Ustinov's grandfather and was well known to many distinguished foreigners who had business in the area. Diplomats, writers, publishers and journalists passed through. Every night the hotel offered its guests a free pre-dinner drink in the bar, which was relatively small and cozy. The guests readily talked to each other, as they often used to do in upscale European hotels, where a common level of intelligence and behaviour was assumed.

On our first night in the hotel we fell into conversation with a rather rattled American woman who had just returned from a trip to the Sinai. She had been assigned a car and a driver, who stopped the car in a deserted spot, put his hand on her knee, and said, "Are you like *Dallas*?" He apparently thought all American women behaved like characters in the television series, which was then current. She had some difficulty persuading him that she was a married woman and was not looking for sexual adventures. She paid him a substantial bribe to keep his hands off her and when she complained to his employers they shrugged, but said that of course he would have expected to be paid a similar sum if she had accepted his proffered services.

The next day we were visited by a friend of Annette Cohen, a female filmmaker named Zippi Trope. She was an attractive woman of about our age who insisted on driving us around Jerusalem so we could get our bearings. She pointed out the Dome of the Rock, the Wailing Wall, the Church of the Holy Sepulchre, and a few other landmarks. She strongly suggested we walk everywhere in the city as it was relatively small and parking was almost impossible. She insisted that she would like to have us to dinner on the following Friday when her family gathered at her house for Shabbat, a ceremony we were familiar with from Judy's sister who was married to a Jew. I was a bit wary of this invitation because I had learned from Jewish friends at home to tread carefully if the conversation turned political. However, Zippi turned out to be a thoroughgoing liberal. "We should get out of the West Bank immediately. We should give back all the occupied territories except Jerusalem. It is terrible living like this. Our closest friends lost a son only three weeks ago. Terrible. And it will only get worse, believe it."

Zippi insisted on taking us to lunch at a very good little restaurant hidden away in a cellar. She talked about the difficulty of making films in her country. Like many Israelis, she was jealous of some of the American Jews, particularly academics, many of whom spent several months of the year in Israel and then returned to highly paid jobs in the United States. After lunch she had meetings to go to, but gave us very specific and detailed instructions about how to get back to our hotel. "If you need anything, if you get sick, God forbid, you are to call me, no matter what hour of the day or night." She insisted. She also offered to drive us a few days later to the country to visit the kibbutz where she had grown up.

We spent the next several days wandering about the walled city. We experienced the stark churches built by the crusaders, the intricate patterns of tiles and arabesques in the Dome of the Rock, the dim cathedral of the Armenians where priests chanted century-old anthems while a block away a group of black Americans gathered to sing gospel hymns. On Friday, we saw the monks who follow the Via Dolorosa, the path Christ reportedly tread carrying his cross. We visited the Mount of Olives, where in the nineteenth century the Romanovs had built a splendid domed church. It was inspiring to visit all the places we had heard about since we were children going to Sunday school, to see all the different sects of Christianity jumbled together in this one place, the crossroads of the three great monotheistic religions. We were shown two tombs and three rooms of the Last Supper, but it didn't matter. For me this was not a religious experience, but a cultural one. And looking out from our hotel at the walled city bathed in the last light of a sunny afternoon, I understood why it was called Jerusalem the Golden.

Zippi had to cancel our invitation to dinner but she did drive us to her kibbutz, which was still operating as a collective of several families, where the children from three on up spent their days in classes while their parents worked. The kids in the same year were treated as siblings and intermarriage between them was rare when they grew up. They were very well cared for and fed by their teachers, so much so that they were often referred to as "the sour cream kids" because their diet was superior to that available to their parents. The kids seemed bright and involved and Judy, as a teacher, was impressed by the quality of their instruction. We also visited an orphanage that was being funded by a brother and sister we had met in a restaurant. They were American Jews from Washington and they were shocked to discover there were no Palestinian kids in the orphanage. "We gave our money to support all the children in Israel, not just the Jewish kids," they protested to the supervisor, but we never learned whether their protests had any effect.

I discovered that one of my acquaintances from my time in External

Affairs was First Secretary at the Canadian Embassy and he joined us one night for drinks and dinner at the American Colony. He was enjoying his posting. "For one thing, I only work a four-day week. Friday is a Muslim holy day, Saturday is the Jewish Sabbath, and Sunday is the Christians' turn to pray, so we get a three-day weekend. Lots of interesting people come through here and they all have opinions about how to solve the country's problems, but whatever your 'Dove' friends may say, the Israelis are not going to cave into the Palestinians' demands. They're tough as nails and getting tougher all the time. They've learned that politically they can get almost anything they want from the Americans and that's all they care about. And, of course, now they've got the bomb. And don't imagine they wouldn't use it."

We usually ate breakfast and dinner at the hotel. There was a very good-looking waiter called Hassan, who I quickly realized was giving me the eye. One day he followed me into the washroom and proudly displayed his impressive member. "I want fuck you. Fifty dollar, I make you holler." I was somewhat flattered but not used to paying for sex. I turned him down, but he continued to ogle me at breakfast. Some of the other waiters picked up on this. One of them even said to me, "Hassan very good boy. He make you happy."

One night when Judy had a headache and retired to bed early, who should turn up in the bar but Will from Cairo. I invited him to dinner but he already had a dinner invitation from an English banker who lived in the centre of Jerusalem. Why didn't I come along, as Judy was indisposed? I did and was greeted by a handsome and charming man of about forty, who instantly presented me with a formidable martini. Mordecai and Will were friends from the time Will was studying in London. After two more martinis, some food was brought in from the kitchen by a beautiful teenage boy wearing only a jockstrap. Mordecai fondled the boy's bare ass and the kid whispered in his ear. Mordecai laughed. "He wants to kiss you. He is a wonderful kisser." The boy came over and kissed me on the mouth. "You see?" The boy giggled. "Now go back to the kitchen, Ali."

"He's not an Israeli?"

"An Arab. I found him in Bethlehem. He will stay here with me until I go back to London in two months. Are you coming back to London, Will?"

"I don't know. Andrew keeps finding things for me to do."

"I am lucky to live in two worlds. I don't really belong in either of them but that in a way is the fun of it. As an outsider you are given a bit more leeway. Aha, here is my world-famous pilaf. I do my own cooking. Ali is my sous-chef. He will eat with us of course. *À table.*"

We sat at a splendidly appointed table lit only by candles, ate stuffed pigeons and other delicacies that Mordecai had prepared, and drank a good deal of wine. Mordecai continued to fondle the boy so that by dessert he was sitting on Mordecai's lap and eating sweetmeats that Mordecai poked into his mouth. What followed was an orgy. My somewhat blurry memory is that I had both Ali and Will. I awoke the next morning with a raging headache and returned to the hotel in a taxi. Judy informed me that she had been visited in her room by Hassan, who claimed I had paid him to service her sexually. The Arab's revenge. He leered at me during breakfast but I resolutely averted my gaze. We left the hotel that afternoon and set out for Eilat on the Red Sea.

It was an easy drive. There were no checkpoints and few cars, as the tourist trade was down because of the uncertain situation in Lebanon, although the intifada had not yet begun. We stopped at the Dead Sea, where I floated effortlessly on the water and Masada, where I climbed to the high plateau where the last Jewish dissidents had held out against the Romans. Eilat itself struck me as being a slightly updated version of Miami Beach, before its modern facelift. It had roughly the same complement of aging couples on walkers or riding tricycles. We met one couple from Manhattan who had decided to spend their golden years in Israel. They were already having doubts about the wisdom of their decision. "I miss the *New York Times*," the man said ruefully.

It was nice to take a break and spend a few days at the beach. Even in January the water was warm and great for snorkeling, offering a multitude of colourful little fish and coral. We ate at our hotel where we had gotten used to marinated fish, stuffed vine leaves, sour cream, hummus, and tabouleh for breakfast rather than Rice Krispies or Shredded Wheat. We got up late and sat watching our neighbours. Two French grandmothers were encouraging their four-year-old granddaughter to experiment with a lighted cigarette. "Elle fume, elle fume," they cackled with delight.

An Italian woman was complaining to her husband that there was nothing to buy. The elderly couple we had met on arrival joined our table on our last morning. "We've decided to go back to the States. We leave at the end of the month." I can't help thinking, knowing what has happened in Israel since, they had made the right decision.

The plane to Jeddah was not full, but the first-class section contained a number of pretty women in stylish dresses. They chattered to each other and drank champagne. Then about ten minutes before landing, they suddenly donned voluminous black *abayas* that covered them from head to foot, with *niqabs* that left only slits for their eyes. The Qu'ran commands women to "cover their charms" and they were going to one of the strictest Muslim countries in the world. Saudi Arabia does not have a tourist industry because they do not allow tourists to visit. They do give visas to workers, high-level professionals like doctors, engineers, nurses, and teachers from the western democracies, menial servants from poorer Muslim countries like Indonesia and Pakistan. And thousands of the faithful visit every year for the Haj, the pilgrimage to the holy city of Mecca. When the religious ceremonies are over, the Saudi police spend two months rounding up stragglers who want to stay on and deporting them.

There is nothing for the tourist in Saudi Arabia: no shows, no concerts, no bars, no restaurants, no impressive monuments, not even splendid mosques such as one finds in Istanbul, Cairo, or Agra. Jeddah is a city with little charm, no trees, no fountains, and the palaces of the princes are without architectural interest. The markets or souks are colourful, but without the variety of goods to be found in Alexandria or Fez. Women are not allowed to roam the streets even when totally covered, and indeed groups of more than four or five people are illegal unless they are all members of one family. There are no political meetings or rallies, even in private homes, and the religious police may invade even there to search for and confiscate forbidden alcohol. We would not have dreamed of visiting the country, except at the invitation of our friends the Fulfords.

Dwight had recently been appointed Canadian ambassador and arranged our visas. He picked us up at the airport in his chauffeur-driven official car and took us to the residence, a comfortable and roomy bungalow with a courtyard containing a swimming pool and a separate guest house. His wife Barbara greeted us and we sat down to lunch as we exchanged gossip. None of the six Fulford children were in residence: one was in Vancouver, one in Tokyo, one in London, one in Buenos Aires, one in Shanghai, and one in Montreal. Barbara spent part of the year visiting some of them. She had not taken to life in Jeddah and missed her work as a child psychologist.

In a year, the Saudis were moving their capital to Riyadh. A new Canadian residence was already under construction there and Barbara had informed Dwight that she had no intention of moving into it. She would return to Ottawa and only make a yearly visit for a month. There was little for a diplomat's wife to do in this closed society and Barbara was not about to sit around at home. She had already mastered a few useful phrases of Arabic, penetrated the kitchen to learn whatever she could from her male cook, as well as teaching him some of her favourite recipes. Upset by the arid and circumscribed lives of her four male servants, she had ordered a car for herself, which as a woman she was not allowed to drive, so that they could visit friends or go to coffee houses on their own. Always something of a rebel, Barbara was obviously enjoying bending the rules as much as possible, while Dwight looked on with amused approval.

The following day, Barbara invited a young woman she had befriended to visit with her two small children. Sultana was the wife of the deposed sultan of South Yemen. She was an Egyptian and used to a good deal more freedom but she could not persuade her husband to leave Saudi Arabia, because he hoped that one day he might regain his kingdom. They lived in a small apartment and Sultana found it hard to keep her sons amused. The day she visited we soon had the boys in the swimming pool and were teaching them to swim. They were initially shocked to see Barbara and Judy in bathing suits, but took to the water like little ducks. For the next week, they would come by almost every day and soon learned to dog paddle. Sultana was delighted but embarrassed to intrude on Barbara's hospitality, so Barbara suggested that we all go to the shore of the nearby Red Sea. The boys were delighted with this outing and Barbara offered Sultana the use of her car and driver whenever they wanted to repeat the experience.

The third day of our visit Barbara played host to a group of women, all of whom were wives of Saudi men. They came from Tunisia, Turkey, Pakistan, and Lebanon. Once inside the residence they shed their *abayas* and revealed their smart Western dresses. They were surprised that I was present but accepted it gracefully. They turned out to be intelligent and knowledgeable about world affairs. Most of them had been to universities in Britain or the United States. One had been a journalist, another a teacher in a girls' school, still another a hospital administrator. When I asked them how they could submit to the stifling regime they now found themselves in, they replied that it was restful and they had their children, but also almost all of them spent several months a year in London or New York or Paris or Los Angeles. Their husbands were affluent and tolerant; they had good friends both in Jeddah and in the west. Didn't they miss having careers? Apparently not much.

A couple of days later Hamid, the cook, allowed me to go shopping with him in the souk. He bought vegetables and chickens. The merchants wrung their necks once the deal was made. He bargained for everything and the process took a considerable amount of time. No one was in a hurry. He also pointed out a veiled woman followed by a dark man. "That man is a slave," he said. "There is supposed to be no slavery in this country, but it still goes on." I asked Hamid if he would drive me to Mecca. "It is forbidden," he said. Dwight had already told me this. I offered him a substantial bribe. "There is nothing to see." I upped the ante. He hesitated and then agreed. It was about an hour's drive, and when we got there he was proven right. There was a big, black rectangular tent and that was all. But at least I'd satisfied my curiosity.

One night after dinner, I asked Dwight whether he had been satisfied with his career in External Affairs.

"On the whole, yes. I spent most of my working life in Latin America. I was able to do a few useful things."

"When we were in Buenos Aires during the junta, Dwight actually prevented a war between Argentina and Chile," said Barbara.

"They were prepared to fight over possession of a few tiny islands. When I suggested in an article in one of the papers they submit their dispute to the Pope for arbitration, they agreed. The church is very powerful in Argentina." Dwight grinned.

"The trouble is that External has never really known what to do with Dwight."

"I am fluent in Spanish, but I'm not much of a linguist. Unlike Barbara."

"Or our friend Andrew Watson."

"Andrew has a keen ear. I think that is crucial. You know he could play the piano by ear. He could play almost anything," Barbara volunteered.

"He has visited you here?"

"No, I couldn't get him a visa."

"Why not?"

"Because he is an agent for MI6."

"Really?"

"He went to St. Anthony's College, which is a prime recruiting ground.

And every time there is a crisis somewhere in the Middle East, he turns up in Beirut or Damascus or somewhere."

"Have you ever confronted him with this?'

"Once. He merely smiled and said, 'That's an interesting idea." But you know Andrew. He doesn't give much away."

Two days later, Dwight hosted a dinner party. He explained, "It's complicated. The Saudis don't respond to invitations so you don't know whether they will come or not. They may or may not bring their wives and most of them have several. They're allowed four each. And they bring friends or relatives with them. Sometimes as many as four or five." On this occasion there was a good turn-out. Most of the Saudis had been to Ivy League schools and they behaved like American college kids: jokey, prankish but friendly. One of them took a particular shine to Judy.

"I have been wondering. What can I buy, now that I have everything? I think a black hole in space." He laughed delightedly. "Unless I buy a nuclear missile."

As the other guests were leaving, Judy said, "Prince Ali Reza, why don't you stay on for a bit?" He did and they spent the next half hour talking about animals in Africa. The prince fancied himself as a game-hunter, "like Teddy Roosevelt." Dwight's father had also hunted in Africa and he joined the conversation with an amusing story about how his father had been charged by an elephant and only been saved when Dwight's brother diverted it by imitating its mating call. When the prince finally decided to leave, Judy said, "I would really like to see a Saudi Arabian household."

"My wife will call you in the morning."

The next morning a six-foot bouquet of flowers arrived: lilacs, roses, irises, and daffodils. "Where would the prince get this?"

"Twice every week, fresh flowers are flown in from Paris."

Half an hour later, the phone rang. It was the prince to say that his car would pick up Judy in half an hour to have coffee with his wife. She came back several hours later to report that the women of the household had served her Turkish coffee in solid gold cups and offered her a great variety of sweet pastries. They then watched an Egyptian soap opera, which the grandmother ridiculed. It is the one hour a day of dramatic television. The rest of the day consists of mullahs reading from the Qu'ran. "Don't you wish you were married to a Saudi Arabian prince?" I asked.

"You must be kidding."

On our way to the airport, Dwight asked, "You don't regret bailing out of External?"

"Honestly, no. It has been wonderful to be able to visit the countries of the Middle East. We have met some fascinating people. But sadly, most of them have been bent on killing each other for thousands of years. And as far as I can see, they still are. It can only get worse."

"I'm sorry to say it, but I'm afraid you're dead right."

THE VICAR'S WIFE

Every time I go to London, I experience the same mixed feelings of exhilaration at being in one of the world's great capitals and alienation from the British, whose devotion to "proper form" seems to triumph over everything else. After we left Jeddah, Judy and I were the guests of our long-time friend Powell Jones. We had all been child actors together. Powell had been a very beautiful boy, but he also had a sharp tongue, a ready laugh, and was a gifted comic. As a young man he had given brilliant performances as Lucky in *Waiting for Godot* and the Professor in *The Lesson*. He saved his money and headed for the London Academy of Music and Dramatic Art and after graduating played in various provincial repertory companies. At some point he met Peter Jamieson, an Anglican priest, and they became partners. They were then living in an old Victorian vicarage on the edge of Islington. The house was spacious and furnished with appropriate period furniture, some pieces redolent of fading grandeur, others comfortable and a bit shabby. In April the house was chilly and the church even colder. Perhaps for warmth, Peter almost always wore his cassock, even outdoors. He had somewhat the air of an amiable, perambulating tea cozy.

Powell had settled into the vicarage and taken on the responsibilities of a devoted wife. He shopped and did the cooking and ran the Sunday school. He also taught drama students at the City Lit, along with his good friend Rodney Archer. Rodney had also been a child actor in Toronto. He was also a good-looking boy, had gone to drama school in England and decided to stay there. He and his mother bought an eighteenth-century house in Spitalfields. It was a mere shell with no plumbing or heating but with the original panelling. The two were gradually restoring it. Rodney at this time did not have a partner and went out cruising several evenings a week. He would often relate his adventures to Powell when they met for "elevenses." Powell would cluck as he savoured the juicy details, rather like an old mother cat hearing the tales of a randy tom kitten.

Rodney and Powell had collaborated in the writing of two plays, *The Kitsch of Death* and *Foreplay and After*. Both were extremely verbal, full of puns and double entendres and displayed an unmistakably "queer" sensibility. They were already working on a highly imaginative play about Jack the Ripper, *The Harlot's Curse*, which would be performed by candlelight in an abandoned synagogue and won a prize in a competition sponsored by the *Evening Standard*. My brother-in-law Jamie Cunningham would later direct it in New York.

About two months before our arrival in London, Powell made an amazing discovery. He was teaching a class when he heard a laugh that sounded familiar. He looked at the girl who was laughing and realized that not only was the laugh familiar, but she looked very much like Judy's sister Alison. Powell had been in London and knew Alison at the time she had given up her first baby for adoption. This girl would be exactly the right age and the resemblance was unmistakable. Powell invited the girl, whose name was Annika Bluhm, out for coffee and questioned her. Yes, she had been adopted and she knew her birth mother was Canadian. In fact, she had come to Powell's class hoping he might have some clue about her identity. She was amazed to learn that Alison had married her natural father David and that they had two other children who were her full siblings. Powell asked if she wanted to reconnect with her Canadian family, and she and her foster mother Liz agreed that they would like Powell to go ahead and get in touch with Alison and David.

As it happened Jamie and his mother Jean were coming to London a few days after we arrived and Powell invited us all to the vicarage for tea to meet Annika and her mother. Annika arrived first and we all marveled that she sounded and looked like Alison, even down to her gestures and posture. Obviously these things were genetic, as she had never even met her mother. Powell had a picture of Alison at the time she was pregnant, which corroborated our observation. Jean was particularly thrilled. "Every time I have been in London I've thought to myself, 'There's a little girl somewhere here who is my granddaughter. And now I finally get to meet her," she said, smiling through her tears.

Liz arrived a bit late, probably by design. She was tall and statuesque and had obviously been something of a beauty. She spoke with one of those slightly incomprehensible upper-class accents that are the result of never moving the lips as she informed us that she and her husband had separated some years ago and eventually he was found dead in a ditch in France. Whether as a result of foul play had never been resolved. She currently had a boyfriend, a retired military man with three children of his own, whom Annika referred to as Gloomy, Grumpy, and Dopey. It was clear that she didn't much care for

Liz's current consort and that Liz didn't really care. They sparred amicably over the tea and biscuits until Peter suggested it might be time for a drink. Liz brightened noticeably.

The next day I had lunch with my old friend Robert Troop at the Café Royale on Regent Street, which Robert explained had been a favourite haunt of Oscar Wilde. Robert was now working as an editor at a small publishing firm in nearby Golden Square, where he was a partner with another man. They published a number of trade magazines and he also had a column in the *Times*. "I've become the foremost property writer in England, which is not what I intended. But it's a living. And I do get to go on junkets to Florida and the south of France."

"Are you still writing novels?"

"Yes, but nobody seems to want my stuff."

"What about the screenplay you were working on with Peter Hall?"

"Nothing came of it."

"Perhaps we should collaborate on a film script."

"I've always wanted to do a film set in Rio, ever since I went there with George when I was seventeen." George was Robert's father and had been a senior executive in the Canadian company Brazilian Traction.

"How about the visit of a Canadian minister trying to sell a CANDU reactor to the Brazilians."

"And meanwhile his son is an anarchist who decides to blow up the statue of Christ on Corcovado as a protest."

"Brilliant. We should start working on it right away."

And we did. I went home that afternoon and typed out six pages on my portable Olivetti and Robert and I met regularly for lunch during the rest of my stay in London. We also went to hear his son's fiancée, Patricia Rozema, sing at the Guildhall.

We were invited to dinner at Liz's house in Stoke Newington. Judy had come down with a cold and begged off, so I went alone. The house was small but very tastefully renovated in what was still a rather rundown neighbourhood with a sizeable population of Hassidic Jews. "Silly twits," said Liz, eyeing two young men passing her front window.

"I thought your husband was a Jew."

"He was, but he didn't go around with ringlets and a black hat mumbling in Hebrew. How about a whisky?"

"What a good idea."

We were fairly smashed by the time we sat down to an Indian curry dish that Liz had prepared. She poured us fresh glasses of whisky. "I forgot to buy wine."

"It's what the Indians drink. I like what you've done with the house, Liz."

"You obviously have good taste. I'm convinced this neighbourhood is going to go up in value fairly soon and I shall sell it and buy a little house in the French countryside. Why don't you come in with me? We could each use it part of the time and rent it the rest. How's your French?"

"Passable. Interesting idea. But who'd look after it when we aren't there?"

"We'll get some local froggy to keep an eye on it for us. Lots of Brits do that."

We were interrupted by the arrival of Annika. "Sorry I'm late. I was having an idle bonk with Joseph."

"Who's Joseph?"

"One of my classmates. A real poppet. Anyway I thought you two might like some time alone together. You haven't got up to anything yet?"

"Don't be silly, dear. I do rather fancy him but he's your uncle. Really, the poor girl is sex-crazed."

"I wonder where that comes from. Would you like to hear the speech I've got to do in class tomorrow? I'm Rosaline in *Love's Labours Lost*. We're going to perform next month at Arundel Castle."

"That's a bit of a coup."

"I'm blindly ambitious."

She launched into a convoluted speech with great gusto. I closed my eyes and realized I was starting to nod off. I got to my feet as soon as she was finished. "Excellent. Powell tells me you're one of his most gifted students."

"Darling Powell. He treats me like the daughter he never had."

"I think I should toddle along. Your Tube shuts down so early." I stumbled to the door and out into the bracing night air.

The next day, I went to see Dick in a green-painted Georgian house in Soho Square, which he rented from Lord Rothschild. He greeted me with a grin and a cackle that took me back thirty years. "You're just in time for our weekly screening," he said, as he led me to a miniature theatre in the basement. "We've just done five straight weeks on *The Thief*. Now we have to do commercials for a couple of months to pay the bills." The lights were turned

off and we saw about ten minutes of inventive and complex animation featuring two principal characters: a sad little runt whose head was surrounded
by a halo of flies but who somehow continued to outsmart the diabolically
wicked Grand Vizier. "A lot of the initial impetus came from Idries Shah when
I illustrated his book about Nasruddin."

"Do you remember your mom taking us to see *The Thief of Bagdad* when we
were maybe about six or seven?"

"I've seen it again several times. I also spent about a month in the city of
Fez sketching. It's amazing. The centre of the city is exactly the same as it was
five hundred years ago. And I learned enough Arabic to talk my way into the
forbidden mosques. You know Margaret wrote the initial script." (Margaret
was his third wife.)

"Is she here?"

"No, she's in California. Margaret's been great. She's a terrific organizer
and she certainly helped me get things straightened out financially. But by
the time she's dealt with the kids and her parents . . . They're typical mind-
less Californians. They sit around the pool all day smiling and saying, 'Have a
happy.' I'm afraid that's over. I've closed my studio there. The trouble is when
I'm here, the people there rob me blind and when I'm there everything falls
apart here."

"Margaret doesn't like England?"

"She doesn't like the fact that I work twelve hours a day at the drawing
board and then play my trumpet for three hours every night. 'Do you have to
do that seven days a week?' she asked and I said, 'That's my life.' I'm getting
really good. I'm playing with some really good guys right now. It's just around
the corner from here. You should come and hear us. If you come here around
nine, we could grab a bite and then you could catch our first set."

The next day Judy went shopping with her mother. Powell informed me
that the bishop was coming to lunch and invited me to join them. Powell
had set the table in the dining room with the best china and glassware. The
bishop arrived, wearing a grey tweed jacket with leather patches on the
elbows. He seemed a bit surprised to see Peter in his cassock but didn't comment on it. He was led into the drawing room and offered a glass of sherry,
which he accepted as he looked around the room. "What a splendid piano,"
he observed. "Do you play?"

"He's a very accomplished pianist. Play us a tune, Peter."

"But not a hymn, please." The bishop gave a jocular chuckle.

Peter played a movement from a Mozart sonata, which the bishop promptly identified. "Do you mind if I try it?" He sat at the piano and knocked off two or three pieces from Schumann's *Kinderszenen.* "Excellent tone. How old do you suppose it is?"

"Probably sixty years or so. It came from my grandfather's house in Kent."

The bishop accepted a second glass of sherry and Powell headed for the kitchen. We moved into the dining room where Peter ladled out some soup I had made that morning. "This is excellent," said the bishop. "What's in it? Spinach and peas and . . . No, don't tell me. Let me guess. Mint."

"Yes. The mint has to be fresh."

"Well of course once mint gets going, there's no getting rid of it." The talk turned to gardening, which it turned out was one of the bishop's enthusiasms. He spoke knowledgably about what kind of soil was ideal for delphiniums and peonies and irises. His wife had a passion for irises and they had some thirty-seven varieties. I realized this was going to be one of those conversations where nobody ever says anything revealing. There was no discussion of things religious or political or even topical, but only the smallest of small talk. Powell brought in a fish loaf on a platter and set it in front of Peter who served it to us. "Well done, Powell."

Powell blushed slightly. "Thank you, dear heart." It was then, I think, that the penny dropped. The bishop looked around the table with a slightly sharper eye than before. There was a slight pause. "And what do you do, Mr. Jones?"

"I'm an actor."

"Ah, the theatre. I love the theatre. I am old enough to have seen Richardson and Olivier at the Old Vic when I was home on leave as a young chaplain. And they're still at it. Astonishing." And the conversation turned to theatrical reminiscences until Powell brought in the pudding. We then retired to the drawing room for coffee. The bishop declined the offer of a glass of port and stood up to go. At the door he turned to Peter. "How long have you two been together, may I ask?"

"About sixteen years."

"I see. Well, thank you for lunch. Keep up the good work." And he was gone. I went to the kitchen to help Powell with the dishes and Peter went upstairs for his afternoon nap.

The next day I hired a car and we drove to Sissinghurst with Liz to see the gardens that Vita Sackville-West had laid out. We arrived at eleven in the morning to discover that the gardens didn't open till one. We repaired to a nearby pub for lunch. "Why are the English so crazy about gardening?" I asked. "Gardening and dogs."

"I suppose to cover up their inability to deal with their fellow humans."

"If they were only prepared to be a little more open with each other."

"Ah, but you see they're schooled not to be. I'm speaking of the upper middle classes. It's the effect of spending half a dozen years in a boarding school. You learn not to trust anyone. Not to be vulnerable. I was lucky. I escaped all that. I had TB. Then when I was seventeen I had two boyfriends, one in the country and one in the city. The city boy was a cockney and bold as brass; the country boy rarely said a word, but he was a fabulous lover. Of course I wouldn't have dreamed of marrying either of them."

"Because they weren't your class?"

"I suppose partly. But mainly because they didn't have much above the neck."

"So you're an intellectual snob."

"I suppose I am. Annika is more of a social snob."

"You think so?"

"I know so. Just wait and see. She may be having it off with the pretty boys in her class but she'll try to snare someone from the landed gentry." (Which soon after she succeeded in doing.)

The gardens at Sissinghurst were in full bloom and we were able to wander through them on our own for about an hour before the motorbuses arrived crammed with eager tourists. We retreated to the tower and stood looking out over the parterres and pergolas from the window where Vita had her study. "You know before the war she employed fifty gardeners," Liz informed us. "I expect now they have to make do with about twenty. One of the sons still lives here."

"I didn't realize she had children."

"Two boys. Although both she and her husband had lovers of their own sex, I believe they had a very happy marriage." Ah, the English. Carry on regardless.

That night, we took ten people to see *Follies*. Liz loved it, the Troops were mildly amused but Peter, Powell, and Annika all hated it. Before they had

Andrew Lloyd Webber to look down on, it was fashionable to sneer at Stephen Sondheim as a tuneless wordsmith who should have stuck to doing acrostics.

The next day I called on Peggy Ramsay with a letter from Ronald Bryden. I was shown into an untidy office where the top agent in Britain sat in a swivel chair, which she swung around hiking up her skirts so I could see her knickers and jangling an armload of silver bracelets. "How is dear Ronnie? Does he like the colonies?"

"I think he likes the money."

She gave a delighted cackle. "He started out as a colonial, of course. Not many people here knew that. He certainly perfected the Oxbridge accent. But now it's gone out of style. Ever since John Osborne and Joe Orton. You know I discovered Joe Orton."

"I do indeed."

"Are you a writer?"

"Mmm."

"Well, send me something and I'll read it. But if you want my advice, don't bother with the stage. Write something for television. That's where the money is. Goodbye." And she swung her chair back to her desk.

Somehow or other, Mordecai managed to get my telephone number. I must have given it to him in Jerusalem. "Hello, darling."

"Hello?"

"It's Mordecai. Only in England I'm called Mark. How about supper tonight at my flat in the West End?"

"I'm afraid I can't."

"Lunch then."

"All right."

"There's a rather good fish restaurant on Jermyn Street. Or better still the Ivy. Noel Coward's favourite haunt. One o'clock tomorrow?"

Mordecai/Mark was already sipping champagne when I turned up. He asked the waiter to pour me a glass. I had forgotten that upper-class Englishmen always ordered the food when they invited a girl out to supper and from the look in his eye, I suspected he was thinking of me as a potential bedmate. "You're looking rather predatory."

"Am I? I'm just remembering our little encounter in Jerusalem."

"I have to admit I don't remember much about it."

"That's a load of old codswallop. You thoroughly enjoyed it. Don't try to tell me you didn't."

"I was drunk."

"You were randy as hell. Have some more champagne. You know you shouldn't suppress your sexual appetites. It's bad for you."

"I'm a married man."

"I'm not suggesting you leave your wife."

"What are you suggesting?"

"Just that you let yourself go a little."

"Thanks for the advice. Let's talk about something else."

"The Elgin marbles?"

"If you like."

The rest of the conversation was playful but not personal. And the Dover sole was excellent.

On Saturday, Rodney came round for coffee. We had just settled down for an amiable gossip when the doorbell rang. I answered and was confronted by a middle-aged man with green hair. "We can't stand it no more," he said.

"Can't stand what?"

"Them witches. Where's the father?"

"He's upstairs."

"That's what they get for puttin' up public housing on a witches' graveyard. They ain't got no right."

Powell had gone upstairs to fetch Peter, who appeared in his cassock.

"You better get that cross, Father. We're goin' to need it." And he trailed after Peter into the church.

"What will Peter do?'

"He'll say some prayers and tell them not to watch so many late-night shows on the telly."

I told them about my interview with Peggy Ramsay. "Maybe we should collaborate on a TV series."

"What about?"

"A family. One that spans the Atlantic with members in both Canada and Britain. It could be a co-production."

"Like Whiteoaks?"

"A bit more up-to-date and urban. No horses."

"People love horses."

"I don't. I'm allergic to them."

"So is Powell."

"All right. No horses."

We spent the next hour roughing out a plotline and came up with a title: *Cousins.* After Rodney left I said to Powell, "Do you really think we can do this?"

"I've always believed in your talent."

"And I in yours."

"I was in love with you. I'm sure you must have known that."

I had known it.

"After you decided to marry Judy, I wanted to get away. It's partly why I came to England. Lucky for me I found Peter."

"You don't feel that you've buried yourself here."

"No. I chose this. Peter's a good man. He loves me. You know the other day when the bishop came to lunch he figured out our situation. You must have been aware of that. Afterwards when we were in bed together and Peter was doing his needlework I said, 'This will probably mean you won't get a better church. Does that bother you?' And he said, 'I'd rather have your love than a bishopric.'"

"As you say, he's a good man. You're lucky."

"I think so."

That night, I had dinner with Dick. He told me he had a new girlfriend, Mo. Short for Imogen. She was an aspiring filmmaker. The only problem was she wanted a large family. Dick already had four children: two by Cathy in England and two by Margaret in California.

"You're ready to start a third family?"

"I don't know. At least Tep and I didn't have children. She came to see me a few months ago. She needed to have her teeth capped, so I paid for it."

"That was generous."

"Yes, well . . . We were happy when we were young and had nothing. And I could never have made *The Little Island* without her help."

Afterwards I went to hear him play. He had become a very accomplished trumpeter and could reproduce almost all of Bix Beiderbecke's solos. He obviously loved playing and I envied him his facility. He stood there on the tiny stage totally absorbed by the music, linked by sound to the musicians but isolated, blowing bright arabesques and curlicues, working his way through improvisations as distinctive as his drawings. Dick was irreverent, incorrigible. His need to perform superseded everything else; he took whatever caught his fancy and used it any way he pleased, totally unconscious he might owe anything to the people whose work he plundered. As Ron Bryden had once said, "Dick is the Picasso of animation."

On our last night in London, Judy and I went to Covent Garden to hear Strauss's *Arabella*, an opera we didn't know. Then to the Savoy for supper. It was a sort of celebration of our twenty-fifth wedding anniversary, which was some three weeks away. We danced for the first time in some years and managed to career around the floor without falling down.

Judy said, "I'm glad we did this. While we still can."

"We've spent too much money. But we'll manage somehow. I've talked with Dick and Powell and Troop. They all think I should settle here."

"Is that what you want?"

"I don't know. I'd like to see if I can have a career as a writer."

"You'll have to decide, darling. I'm keen to get back home."

"Of course I'm coming with you. I can always come back here on my own."

"You're free, you know. I've always said I wouldn't stand in your way."

"I know. Thank you for that. I guess we'll just have to see how things work out."